Welcome!

This is a complete handbook for reaching breakthrough collaborative decisions using the process of Convergent Facilitation.

Convergent Facilitation has been used successfully in a variety of contexts around the world, including:

- between longtime enemies with polarized perspectives;
- to create breakthrough legislation with bipartisan support;
- to resolve problems in half the time at a multibillion dollar corporation;
- to create a collaborative leadership structure at nonprofit organizations with a geographically diverse staff.

Through vivid case studies and practical examples, Miki explains

- how to guide people towards solutions that integrate everyone's needs and concerns and don't require compromise;
- how to keep people on track with the task at hand;
- how to invite dissent and engage with it productively;
- how to attend to the power differences that so often interfere with collaboration.

How? By upending conventional ways of making decisions such as majority rule; top down decision-making, which can result in coercion; or consensus, which can drain a group's energy. Instead, Convergent Facilitation efficiently moves through three phases of a process that can bring groups to outcomes that are profoundly collaborative and genuinely supported by all.

Praise for The Highest Common Denominator

Endorsements appear in full at https://thefearlessheart.org/store/the-highest-common-denominator/endorsements/

Part instruction manual, part philosophy book, *The Highest Common Denominator* is an incredible contribution to the world of facilitation, decision making and group dynamics. Convergent Facilitation is a paradigm shift in how we work in groups. By creating space for all needs to be heard, inviting dissent without fear or animosity, and attending to the power dynamics that are in the room, Miki guides us through this revolutionary new way of collaboration. A must read for any leader or facilitator.

KAZU HAGA
Founder, East Point Peace Academy;
author, *Healing Resistance*

In these times of uncertainty and crisis, this book is a simple, straightforward, and deep introduction for those who want to master Convergent Facilitation. This process, born of Miki's brilliance and vast experience, will steer us away from wasting time and accelerate our work for the Great Turning.

JOANNA MACY, PH.D.
Root teacher of the Work That
Reconnects, author, and activist

This book represents a major breakthrough for human collaboration. Whether at home, in the workplace, or amidst social movements struggling for change, the tools in this book could be revolutionary. I long for all of us to have access to them.

DR. NEIL HOWARD
Prize Fellow in International
Development, University of Bath

I was one of the participating stakeholder representatives in the custody dialogue group featured in Chapter 7 of this book. At first I was skeptical as to whether consensus could ever be achieved given the level of distrust and profound disagreement between participants. Miki Kashtan's Convergent Facilitation process was a transformative experience and helped bring us together to develop and enact bold and far-reaching legislation. This model should be followed by Congress and state legislatures, and this book now makes it accessible to everyone to learn and use.

MICHAEL DITTBERNER
Family law attorney

I've been part of many activist movements and anarchist groups that aim to actively live out our principles. As we try to do that, so many of us have found decision-making to be fraught with tension between individual autonomy and collective needs, between including everyone and actually getting things done. We may think the only options are consensus and majority voting, each with major drawbacks that can drain group energy or leave out key perspectives.

Convergent Facilitation offers us another path. *The Highest Common Denominator* contains clear and accessible wisdom for making collaborative decisions, even when people seem totally stuck on opposite sides of an issue.

MARIAM Z GAFFORIO
Facilitator, community organizer,
musician, and mom

If you only add one book to your library on facilitating meetings, on collaborative decision-making, or on conflict integration, please let this be that book. The ability to achieve high-quality decision-making under high-stakes conditions *is one of the most important skills for the human family to* develop on a broad scale. The vitality, the freshness, and practicality that Miki Kashtan's Convergent Facilitation model embodies are based on both deep scholarly rigor and poetic artfulness. This book is a gift to and a prayer for the future.

VICTOR LEE LEWIS, MA,
Director of the Institute for Healing Justice Education
and co-facilitator of the "Hard Conversations,"
online learning communities for racial justice

Humankind's "winner takes all" model is an unmitigated disaster that is quickly taking us towards extinction. This detailed guide provides clear steps to another option. If you make decisions you need to read it.

PETER MACFADYEN
Past Mayor and Leader of Frome Town
Council and author of *Flatpack Democracy*,
a DIY guide to independent politics

Appearing at a time when conventional politics operates by the lowest common denominators, Miki Kashtan's book is a loving guide for those wanting to replace it with something more like government by the people. That means each of us, starting locally, where we live but dreaming big.

PATRICK CHALMERS
Author and filmmaker, *All Hands On*,
a documentary series on radical
democracy in action

Miki Kashtan generously shares her innovation, experience and knowledge in a practical yet heart-based book which uses a tried and tested facilitation method to transform group decision-making. Essential reading for our times.

MARIA ARPA
Founder of the Centre for Peaceful
Solutions and Executive Director of
the Center for Nonviolent Communication

The lessons Kashtan imparts in this work push beyond mere inclusion, showing us how effective collaboration requires at core an ethos of belonging in taking on everything from everyday cooperation to the largest systemic challenges of our day.

JOHN POWELL
Director, Othering and
Belonging Institute, UC Berkeley

Convergent Facilitation is without any doubt one of the most powerful and transformative processes I have worked with. I've directly experienced its ability to support people to come together fully and effectively, creating conditions for something very beautiful to emerge even when it looks impossible. I believe this book is immensely valuable, offering an in-depth guide that people will find clear and practical, enabling them to put these principles into action. I would go a long, long way to learn what Miki has articulated in these pages.

PAUL KAHAWATTE
Facilitator, mediator, and trainer
supporting groups and projects working
for social and environmental justice

I have found the tools of Convergent Facilitation to be effective, accessible, and even miraculous. Whether one is already committed to nonviolence or just looking for practical ways to break through decision-making gridlocks, this book can change the world.

ANNE SYMENS-BUCHER
Co-founder, Canticle Farm, Oakland

I want to celebrate Miki's nuanced exploration of the gifts and challenges of facilitator transparency, as well as her powerful framing of self-awareness and self-connection as essential for developing our intuition as facilitators.

ROSA ZUBIZARRETA
Author, *From Conflict to Creative Collaboration:
A User's Guide to Dynamic Facilitation*

The Highest Common Denominator suggests that it's possible to bring a diverse range of stakeholders impacted by a seemingly intractable challenge together, take them through a skillfully facilitated process of collective discernment, tap into the group's creativity to come up with solutions no one thought existed, and finally reach a unanimous decision on a plan that will work for everyone. If, from the most local to global level, we were equipped to make decisions in this way, humanity would have a future. *The Highest Common Denominator* is for anyone who wants to increase their leadership capacity to help groups resolve their differences, move fast, and achieve lots.

VÉRÈNE NICOLAS
Facilitator, educator, and member of
the Nonviolent Global Liberation collective

Miki Kashtan's journey to discover the fundamental nature of the society in which we all live, and a path that leads to a vision for a nonviolent, compassionate, and loving society, has been a blessing for us all. This book is a milestone on this journey.

SHARIFF ABDULLAH
Author, *Creating a World
that Works for All*

In this book, we accompany Miki Kashtan, Convergent Facilitation's remarkably self-aware innovator as she tracks subtle, unfolding dynamics and choice points in both herself and the groups she works with, offering us a vivid vicarious experience of navigating those shifting waters through the mind, heart and eyes of a master facilitator who is constantly learning -- as she invites us to learn -- what it means to truly help.

TOM ATLEE
Founder of the Co-Intelligence
Institute and Wise Democracy Project

THE HIGHEST
COMMON
DENOMINATOR

*Using Convergent Facilitation to Reach
Breakthrough Collaborative Decisions*

Published by

FEARLESS HEART PUBLICATIONS

P.O. Box 22872

Oakland, California 94609

U.S.A.

www.thefearlessheart.org

ISBN: 978-0-9900073-5-7 Paperback

ISBN subject categories: Social Sciences
Cover design and editorial design by Nicias Sejas García

*For all the people who've never experienced
what a solution that works for all feels like*

Contents

Foreword

by Skeena Rathor and Gail Bradbrook

AS ORGANIZERS AND ACTIVISTS WITH EXTINCTION REBELLION, a global environmental movement dedicated to preventing ecological collapse, we have struggled, as so many others have, while working in groups trying to make change. What we want is to feel unified, to make good decisions, ones that help us to build the world we are longing for. Instead we have experienced endless meetings where decisions don't get made, or decisions get made that are compromises that deflate everyone, or power moves are made that force decisions on others without their buy-in.

The Highest Common Denominator, Miki Kashtan's book on the group decision-making process called Convergent Facilitation, is a gift to the world. It explains in great and deeply practical detail how to support groups in a way that attends to the needs and concerns of all their members, including honoring and listening to marginalized voices and to "outliers." This isn't done because it is the moral thing to do (though of course it is), but because better solutions are achieved that way: A decision can be reached that everyone can truly accept as their own and thus be energized about implementing or championing.

So often we feel the pull to rush things in XR – we are in a climate and ecological emergency, after all. And by rushing we can be so inefficient; the tensions and conflicts created as a result take up more time and energy, as we repeat the mistakes of the current culture we live in.

As we try to bootstrap our way out of a system and culture that is destroying life on earth, we find ourselves trapped by the traumatic wounds that our bodies hold, created by the patriarchy we have been steeped in. Convergent Facilitation works because it brings a depth of wisdom and understanding of humanity, as has been held in Indigenous traditions. First Nations Canadian Jeannette Armstrong (Okanagan), executive director of the En'owkin Centre in British Columbia, describes the Okanagan process of *En'owkin* used to sort through difficult decisions.

> ... The point of the process is not to persuade the community that you are right, as in a debate; rather, the point is to bring you, as an individual, to understand as much as possible the reasons for opposite opinions. Your responsibility is to see the views of others, their concerns and their reasons, which will help you to choose willingly and intelligently the steps that will create a solution – because it is in your own best interest that all needs are addressed in the community.

The emphasis in this book, then, on our internal storymaking and the dance of these stories with those of others, feels of vital significance. It reminds us that internal collaboration comes before we collaborate with others. This is how we become our own most empathic friend, refresh our perceptions through our intuition, and model daring transparency. We strive for the "Know thyself" that ancient traditions and religions the world over emphasize as the work of a human life.

The work of Convergent Facilitation deeply challenges our cultural norms and calls for a shift in behaviors on a fundamental level. If, as Miki asks us, we are to invite dissent, welcome failures, and deeply listen to outliers, then where does that take our collective culture? We imagine a stage of relentless challenge and discomfort; Convergent Facilitation finds a way of making that discomfort manageable, generative, and even fun. Extinction Rebellion is all about inviting dissent as a crucible for creating regenerative cultures. There is much to embrace that challenges our unconscious conditioning. This is also vital work for XR in the context of our principles and values that ask us to be welcoming of everyone and every part of everyone.

There is something beautifully simple in becoming the kind of facilitator that Miki is suggesting we can be. It reminds us of the mothering instinct that we all have – that capacity in us for attending to as many needs as we can see in the best way we know how. It's what mothers and grandmothers practice day in and day out as a spontaneous way of being, which over centuries has become invalidated and sacrificed by choices we have made together in pursuit of material and abstract "prosperity." Extinction Rebellion's vision is that we might be able to reconnect to life's call and life's nurturing imperative to become aware of more and more needs, including the needs of the earth that holds us – and that we have shared needs that align us into one human family. Martin Luther King described it as our single garment of destiny. This book gives us a way to try on this garment of oneness.

What we love about the work of Convergent Facilitation is its capacity to surface and mobilize the needs of the human heart – and, indeed, of our whole bodily intelligence – in a way that is accessible and safe for our rational mind to enter into the proceedings. In this way the work of finding our highest common denominator, which emerges from focusing on what Miki calls "the noncontroversial essence" behind each divergence, extends way past simply being a facilitation technique or collaboration formula. This offering is more personal and profound than can be expressed because, like all revolutionary work, it needs to be experienced. How blessed and exciting for XR to be working with such visionary practices.

Convergent Facilitation has been taught to a number of activists within XR, and its principles and insights have been incorporated into twice-monthly coaching calls that Miki gives for XR activists. We are seeing the ripple effect of Convergent Facilitation across different activities in XR as a result. It is clear to us that the Convergent Facilitation process is made for these times – for our deep reckoning with the mindsets that have divided us, and for our aspiration for reconciliation to become possible.

When you believe, as activists often do, that you are speaking for the highest good on behalf of the most disadvantaged, your attachment to being right can be overwhelming. Added to this, there aren't many subjects in social change movements as sensitive as racism. Being involved in a Convergent Facilitation process about anti-racism work, where Miki was able to hold these attachments and then steward us in the work of discovering criteria that we could all align with, changed relationships, removed stuckness, and restored flow. Every single person involved reported greater well-being as a result. Here's what one of our members experienced:

> When we reacted to the fact that, at grassroots level, the movement was creating demands related to racism in haste as everyone was responding to the murder of George Floyd, I knew that whatever we did to bring everyone together as a group would need facilitation that could hold a space fraught with hurt, distrust, suspicion, and anger. We then asked Miki to take us through a Convergent Facilitation process. It was a gift to all those who participated. In fact, after our process

I had one individual call me in tears as the feelings that had been conjured up in her were alien to her and she couldn't understand why she was feeling the way she was. This has also brought us closer as we embark upon this journey – the destination of which we are uncertain, even while knowing that the process we are following is solid and that we can do so without fear.

Reading Miki's wisdom, born of much experience and shared with clarity, is like having a trusted big sister tell you all her best insights into how to develop your skills in both leadership and in group work. After working with Miki directly, we said we would love to have a "Miki App" which would give us advice about what to do for the best. This book is the operating system for such an app! Miki's humility and her dedication to service with integrity, to continually learning and improving, are deeply inspiring. So much of this world and its wounds and divisions would encourage us to close down to narrow our lives, to stay in "comfortable numbness." It is inspiring and heartening to read of a life lived and expressed with the aim of staying truly alive, aiming to be less affected by personal "stories" and more lived with love in the heart. Our gift back to Miki is our commitment to sharing and undertaking our own experiments with the tools and insights of her work, so that we might collectively, in her words, "get to where the tide turns and collaboration in decision-making becomes the norm."

Stroud, England, July 2020
GAIL BRADROCK, Co-founder, and SKEENA RATHOR,
Guardianship and Visioning, Extinction Rebellion UK

Author's Preface

I WROTE THIS BOOK TO MAKE AVAILABLE TO ALL who seek it a method I developed for reaching group decisions that is both collaborative and efficient.

I began experimenting with decision-making in groups in the late 1990s. My quest arose from seeing the unhappy tradeoff between collaboration and efficiency that continues to be so prevalent just about everywhere I go. It results in opposite kinds of dysfunction:

- Many efficiency-oriented organizations merely give lip service to collaboration because the only ways they know to collaborate are unsustainably inefficient. As a result they lose the energy and talents unleashed by true collaboration.
- By contrast, many alternative groups and organizations are so committed to collaboration they are willing to sacrifice efficiency, to the point of driving away innumerable people who resonate with their ideals and vision and cannot stand the endless process.

I didn't want to believe this was all we could do.

I started by noting where collaboration would break down. I then began to experiment with ways of overcoming the obstacles that would utilize resources better – the very definition of what efficiency means rather than the narrow equation of efficiency with simply linear time that we have become accustomed to.

My first experiments were about small decisions that involved many people. By 2004, I could reliably apply principles of efficient collaboration in many instances. The key breakthrough at that time was the insight that focusing on inviting dissent is key to efficient collaboration.[1] It sidesteps the pressure to agree that so often bogs down consensus process. It also brings forth, with amazing speed and focus, the core issues that need to be addressed before a decision can truly be acceptable to all. When I was able to lead a group of 300 tired people, within 10 minutes, to a decision about how we would structure the remaining hours of a conference we all participated in, I knew I was on to something with potential.

It took a few more years of experimenting to realize that for bigger decisions, it would be far more efficient to begin by collecting all the needs in the room *before* coming up with a proposal for how to move forward. That's how Convergent Facilitation's typical three-phase process that I describe in this book finally solidified.

I have no illusion that Convergent Facilitation is the only method that can achieve this feat. I only know that it is one key that opens this door, and that the results are often truly astounding. So much so, that one of those results was edited out of my *New York Times* article (see Chapter 6), because the editor considered it "over the top" and thought readers would not believe it.

At some point, I began teaching Convergent Facilitation around the world. Seeing that people who have studied with me are also able, even in initial experiments, to create breakthrough results, I resolved to write this book. My aim here is to share as much of the methodology – its breakthrough insights, principles, and practices – as can be done in writing, to accelerate the pace at which individuals can learn this method and put it to use. It's important to me because I believe we either have a collaborative future, or no future.

---

1 Just how much dissent to invite is one of the core intuitions developed over time when using Convergent Facilitation. I delve deeply into this question in Chapter 5.

Why Convergent Facilitation?

INTRODUCTION

WE LIVE IN EXTREME TIMES. With every passing year, the pressing issues of climate change, environmental degradation, and resource depletion; war and violence; poverty and social inequality; and individual malaise, loom larger and become more urgent. In 2020, the year this book is finally moving to production, the Covid-19 pandemic has created unprecedented changes in human life, the outcome of which is impossible to anticipate, and is clearly beset with additional crises. No one alone would be able to solve any of these issues, because even the most powerful people on the planet do not, individually, possess enough wisdom and knowledge to identify solutions without massive input from others, nor is there anyone who has sufficient power to enact solutions unilaterally – our systems are just too intricately interwoven. We need to come together.

At the same time, for the last several thousand years most people have lived in societies and institutions organized first around outright coercion and then around the subtle coercion of competition and incentives. Our collaboration muscles have all but atrophied. Not equally or across the board: There are definitely pockets of individuals, groups, communities, and even regions in the world where collaboration is still known and practiced. There is also a growing commitment to collaboration, and an increasing number of small and large scale experiments, perhaps the largest of which is Wikipedia. Nonetheless, I have noticed a pervasive inability to collaborate effectively in every country I've taught at (and the list is large), and in every organization I have worked with.

> I don't want to be identified with a side. We are no longer doing that. We are a group of people working together to solve problems."
>
> —Minnesota legislator

A Different Path

Convergent Facilitation is part of my response to this state of affairs. Over the years, my experience has been unequivocal that it brings about dramatic and breakthrough results in groups, even groups that have been stuck for a long time. The last chapter of the book is an extended case study of the most dramatic example of such a breakthrough that I have facilitated, which I did in person and on the phone for over two years. This group was comprised of Minnesota legislators, lobbyists, lawyers, advocacy groups, judges, and child development experts. The issue they were facing was child custody legislation. They were about as divided on the issue as any group could be. So much so, that it took a major effort to get them all to agree to be in the same room together. Two years later, the group approved, unanimously, 16 different changes to their state's legal system that they all thought were an improvement on what previously existed. Along the way, one legislator said: "I don't want to be identified with a side. We are no longer doing that. We are a group of people working together to solve problems."

If this sounds like incredible magic, extraordinary luck, or exceptional talent, I see it differently. I have trained many people in this methodology, including people who didn't necessarily imagine they could achieve spectacular results, who then went on to have their own amazing successes. I have had a passion for making everything I do teachable, and Convergent Facilitation is no exception.

I myself came into this capacity without ever having

imagined it initially. If anyone had told me years ago that I would learn and then teach others how to facilitate groups, and that I would, in particular, develop a method specifically for supporting groups in reaching collaborative decisions, I would have emphatically and vigorously shaken my head. I was the girl that, at 11, was an outcast. In my twenties I worked as a computer programmer because I found it calming not to have to deal with people all the time.

Both of these experiences have been helpful to me in mastering the art and craft of facilitation, and, especially, in teaching it to others. Because of having been an outcast, I have a visceral understanding of the dynamics of individuals and groups, knowledge that I use when there is major polarity in a group to support convergence and movement without sacrificing individuals. Because I have very highly honed analytic capacities, I have used them to make the concepts, principles, and practices that are in this book as clear and simple as possible.

No one else who reads this book is likely to have exactly this set of experiences. The reason I am mentioning them is that I am confident that you have had your own experiences that you can mine for gold, whether easy, hard, or neither. Group facilitation, I have come to believe, requires a level of clarity and ongoing attention that are unusually high. Anything that can make your experience of facilitating easier is a total bonus. I would love to believe that you will be able to learn things from your experiences that I couldn't possibly ever teach you.

On a number of occasions I have engaged groups of people in a simple activity that has always yielded profound results. I ask everyone in the circle to name a particular quality or strength that they bring with them to their leadership. What works so amazingly well about this activity is that at the end of it everyone has learned two important lessons. The first is that everyone has *something* that is a valuable leadership quality. The second is that the variability is staggering, and that, therefore, your strength is uniquely yours. I have rarely heard two people say the same thing.

My goal and hope with this book is that you will be able to gain enough knowledge and confidence to start experimenting. How far you can go on your own, just with this book, depends on many factors. If you are already an experienced facilitator, most likely reading the book alone will be enough for you. You have your own experiences, you know what works for you as a facilitator, and you will likely find a way to apply the principles and integrate them with what you already do. If you are reading this because, like many, you have been awakened to the need for more and more of us to step into leadership, and you are willing to take the plunge despite having no previous experience, your journey is likely to be more complex. This book is not a facilitation primer. You will need to gain experience in the field, as they say, to put things into practice even while knowing that facilitating without much experience can be overwhelming.

Collaboration and Leadership

When I first learned about the existence of a mode of thinking and communicating that enhances collaboration, I decided to join the ranks of those who have dedicated their lives to the living and teaching of this practice, known today as Nonviolent Communication, created by Marshall Rosenberg.[1]

1 Nonviolent Communication was created by Marshall Rosenberg starting in the 1960s and is taught today by many hundreds of trainers worldwide. Convergent Facilitation, the decision-making methodology I present in this book, is an

My assumption then was that the way to build a collaborative organization or world was by reaching and teaching enough individuals how to collaborate internally and with each other. I no longer think that. I neither think that we can reach enough people fast enough and well enough to turn around the destructive path I believe we are on, nor do I think that learning as individuals how to engage with individuals is comprehensive enough to change systems and structures.

Instead, I have gradually shifted my focus to the role of leadership and the methodology or structure that supports efficient collaboration. I have a broad view of what counts as leadership. I am referring in that to all the people who, whether by dint of role, function, or individual inclination, assume responsibility for the functioning of the whole. More and more of my work these days is focused on supporting everyone I come in contact with to step into that responsibility. In tandem with this invitation, I provide designated leaders with concrete and specific tools to support them in using their power for the benefit of the whole, in collaboration with everyone who is affected. This is not any simpler than my previous focus; it's only that any forward movement ripples faster. When a leader acts collaboratively, the system as a whole moves towards more collaboration without requiring every individual within the system to adopt a more collaborative attitude.

In this book I am focusing, in particular, on one specific aspect of leadership: The facilitation of groups, especially groups that are trying to make something concrete happen, such as organizations that offer products or services, groups that manage resources together, or multi-stakeholder groups

application of the *principles* of Nonviolent Communication to the field of group facilitation, without relying on the specific linguistic forms that constitute a core *practice* of Nonviolent Communication.

that aim to establish public policy, to name a few examples. The common thread: These are groups that face the necessity to make decisions together.

Overview: What Is Convergent Facilitation?

Convergent Facilitation is a three-phase process that makes it possible for groups to make decisions about matters of significance to the group. Its aim is a decision that everyone can wholeheartedly embrace even if it's not their preference. I sometimes refer to the resulting decision as the highest common denominator of the group, inviting people to notice that coming together doesn't imply loss of quality.

What does it look like in practice? Here's one story that illustrates the process.

> Lori Draper, the Vice President at a bank, attended an early version of a Convergent Facilitation workshop and put what she learned into practice immediately when her boss assigned her the project of reorganizing the layout at one of the bank's branches.
>
> On her first visit to the branch, she could see that the configuration of the desks, cubicles, and private offices wasn't working for the customers and most of the personnel. Business bankers and the staff who assisted them had large cubicles in the front of the branch. A new customer who wanted to open a personal checking account would wait in the line for the tellers only to be redirected to the back where the personnel who took care of this responsibility were crammed in small cubicles.

Lori made an initial plan for moving everybody around but realized that the people who had in some cases worked there for 20 years would probably have ideas that would be far more informed than hers. She was also energized by the prospect of having a change that would be met with resistance. She told her boss that she wanted to solicit their input. He said, "What a mess that meeting will be! Everyone will be complaining and talking over each other. They'll only come up with reasons why this move is a bad idea, not solutions for the task at hand. Just tell them how you want it done and have them live with it." Despite his strong doubts, he agreed to let her try the process she wanted.

She convened an initial meeting in which she told everybody at the branch that the floor plan would be changing and she wanted their participation in a meeting the following week to create a proposal. She presented to them the criteria they might want to consider in creating proposals: more customer convenience, smoother traffic flow, and privacy for confidential conversation.

Of the 17 people who worked at the branch, 13 attended the second meeting and eight people brought in detailed proposals that included measurements and plans for accessibility for people with disabilities.

Everybody enjoyed the pizza Lori brought and then they went to work. First they reviewed Lori's initial list of the needs that the final plan would need to meet to yield the best results for everyone, and added cost containment to it.

They then made a grid and evaluated each proposal by checking off the boxes for the needs each fulfilled. It became clear to everyone that one plan met the most needs. The winning plan was actually created by a business banker who moved HIMSELF to a smaller cubicle in the back of the branch. Even the people who weren't happy to move their offices weren't angry because they could see how their own inconvenience served the collective purpose.

If you are amazed by the generosity of that banker, I no longer am. I have seen such gestures regularly, because the process supports it. When people know that their needs matter, when they take in other people's needs, and when they are invited to care for the whole, the creativity and generosity that ensue are often deeply moving. This is the core insight that is at the heart of Convergent Facilitation.

From this example you can see that Convergent Facilitation breaks down into a process with three phases that, together, maximize willingness to stretch towards the shared purpose, generosity, and efficiency.

Breakthrough Insight: Cultivating willingness

Before giving you a breakdown of the different phases, here's one of the core insights that guide the entire process: Preferences rarely line up and yet people are very often willing to let go of their preference and adopt a different decision if certain conditions are met. Mostly, it's when they know they matter and their needs are included, and when they have successfully been invited to steward the whole, as discussed below. This understanding is one of the keys to the possibility of convergence. Here's why.

When a conversation is focused on finding something that everyone is *happy with* instead of what everyone is *truly willing to live with*, discussions often bog down as we try this or that strategy hoping that it will align with everybody's preferences. If, instead, the focus is on willingness, people can be invited to stretch towards each other to find something they can all willingly accept.

Here's a diagram of the process and the core question that guides each element.

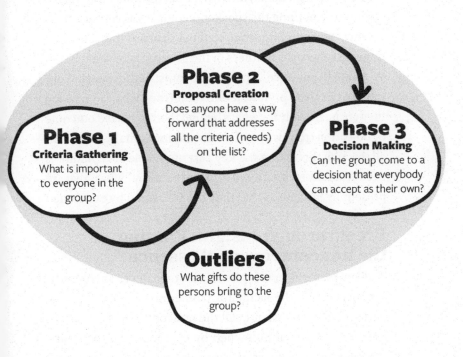

Here is a quick overview of the three phases which I describe in detail in Chapter 5.

Phase 1: Criteria Gathering. The purpose of this phase is to come up with the list of criteria that will guide the rest of the process by listening carefully to what matters to different individuals in the group. This phase is key to creating both goodwill in the group and sufficient healthy, creative constraints to enable a solution to emerge and be decided on later. It's when people are heard, when needs – the "why" underneath people's opinions and suggestions – are taken into consideration, and when shared ownership of all the needs is established. The key element in this phase is that whatever anyone says is converted by the facilitator (sometimes with the help of participants) into what I call the noncontroversial essence: something the speaker recognizes as capturing the essence of what's important to them that is at the same time noncontroversial for others in the group.

In my experience, most people, most of the time, are not invested in their preferred outcome (the "what") provided they are heard fully for what's behind their preferred outcome or objection (the "why"). This distinction is vitally important all through this process. A key part of the role of facilitator is to continually translate and capture the many "whys" that are present in such a way that they can be owned by everyone.

Breakthrough Insight: Finding the noncontroversial essence

The key element in this phase is that whatever anyone says is converted by the facilitator (sometimes with the help of participants) into what I call the noncontroversial essence: the "why" that can be owned by everyone. It's something the speaker recognizes as capturing the essence of what's important to them that is at the same time noncontroversial for others in the group.

Here's an example from the Minnesota child custody project described in detail in the last chapter of this book. A participant stated, in short, that there was an insurmountable philosophical disagreement, in that he and others thought a legal presumption of joint custody was just not wise. Clearly, on that level the conversation would stay stuck in endless debate and argument. It took an extra question to get an initial answer as to the "why." His answer was something like: "You can make too many mistakes this way, because you end up looking at all families in the same way." That, still, wasn't the noncontroversial essence, and yet it was enough for me to find it. It was wanting each family to be handled according to its specific circumstances. The man agreed, and so, immediately, did his fierce opponent.

Phase 2: Proposal Creation. The purpose of this phase is to come up with one or more proposals that attend to the list of noncontroversial criteria from Phase 1. This is the most undirected, emergent, and creative part of the Convergent Facilitation process. So long as people trust their concerns matter and have emerged from the first phase with goodwill and a commitment to solutions that attend to the entire list of criteria, at least as much of it as possible, they will find potential paths forward that very often are totally out of the box, new, daring, and clearly beyond either/or frames.

This may seem fantastical as so many groups do not operate on this plane and, instead, are rife with mistrust, divergent agendas and expectations, and damaging history. Still, my experience is unequivocal: When you bring faith as a facilitator, and invest sufficient attention early on in the process on surfacing all that is important, not just what's "allowed" to be said, the level of commitment is likely to surprise you.

Breakthrough Insight: Reaching a shared commitment to the whole

Participants are now shifting their intention to serving the common good rather than advocating for their own position or expressing their own needs. They are now stewards of the whole, not advocates for their position. What they are stewarding is both the concrete list of the needs that they all participated in generating earlier and the felt sense of the totality of the group, its dreams, its trust, however tentative it might be. It's from within this orientation that they develop proposals. This shift is pivotal to the success of the process, and the process doesn't move forward until the shift is truly wholehearted.

Phase 3: Decision making. The purpose of this phase is to convert one of the proposals to a decision, or find some other combination of strategies that will amount to a decision. By now, groups usually have unleashed stores of energy through the trust and goodwill that emerge from the earlier phases. They *want* to find a solution, and they are generally committed to making it work for everyone.

The process is complete when everyone in the group is wholeheartedly willing to accept the decision as their own. The "requirement" to find a solution that attends to all the needs, without giving up on anyone, unleashes co-creativity that transcends either/or options.

Note: In many situations where the decisions are simple, very small and local, or particularly time-crunched, this phase may be the only one that the group goes through, with needs being named only as dissent is expressed.

Breakthrough Insight: Inviting just enough dissent

The key element in this phase for the facilitator is to know how much dissent to invite by asking questions that open more or less discussion depending on how far down the process the group is, how significant the ramifications of the decision are, how much energy the group has, and various other factors. Once dissent is invited, working with the underlying needs that give rise to dissent and incorporating them into the solution that the group will adopt in the end is the art within this phase. Although I elaborate and offer examples in later chapters, this skill can only be mastered *through experimentation.*

Focusing on inviting dissent, and just enough of it, is key to efficient collaboration. It sidesteps the pressure to agree that so often bogs down consensus process. Although in Convergent Facilitation there clearly is an intention to reach agreement, the path there deliberately goes through inviting disagreement. This path brings forth, with amazing speed, the core issues that need to be addressed before a decision can truly be acceptable to all.

Outliers. In any of the phases of Convergent Facilitation, the presence of outliers – those who have dissenting views, who stand apart from the group, or in any other way are outside of a potential emerging agreement about anything – serves as a powerful invitation to transcending either/or stances and incorporating even more creativity. There is no assumption of majority vote that will determine things. Outliers give the group the gift of the opportunity to benefit from the full range of wisdom and perspectives that exist within it, and are often the catalysts for breakthrough moments.

Breakthrough Insight: Engaging with dissent as a gift

Instead of seeing the outlier as a problem, the way we are used to, I now see the outlier as the gift bearer – the person with issues, concerns, or ideas that are often essential for a group to consider, the one through whom they come to the group's awareness. Time and again I have seen that what drives a proposal forward towards improvement are the dissenting views. Because of this unusual relationship with dissent, proposals can change, even dramatically and as late as the last step, if new needs are identified.

The Shape of the Book

I don't believe in secrets. This book contains all that I am currently aware of knowing about group facilitation. In theory, if you wanted to apply my facilitation methods, you could do so after reading this book without needing to attend any training.[2] I am listing all the skills and principles I am aware of that can guide you in your choices as a facilitator.

Here's what you can expect as you read it.

Chapter 1: Facilitation and Group Function

This chapter introduces the overall framework about the role of group facilitation and where it fits within the overall mix of factors that support a group in its functioning. It mainly answers the overall question: Why do some groups work well together and others don't? And what does facilitation have to do with that?

---

2 Though if you wanted to, the trainings do exist. My colleagues and I provide trainings to organizations as well as to individuals who want to learn on their own. You can visit http://convergentfacilitation.org for more information.

Chapter 2: The Gift of Self: The Art of Transparent Facilitation

This chapter focuses strongly on transparency in group facilitation, which is one of the core principles of my approach. I provide detailed information about whether, when, how, and about what to be more transparent: More is not always better. What matters is whether describing to the group what is usually hidden – your inner thoughts, decision-making process, or intentions in the moment – would or would not be a contribution to the purpose for which the group came together. How to solve this puzzle? This is what this chapter addresses.

Chapter 3: Convergent Facilitation General Toolkit

This chapter introduces a number of themes that show up in most facilitation scenarios, and provides guidance for inner work as well as specific skills needed to navigate the complexities that arise. For example, every facilitator, sooner or later, will be called to facilitate a group where there is mistrust that leads people not to tell the truth. All of us have stories to tell about "difficult people," that we didn't have sufficient skill to integrate into a group. We will all be called upon to attend to the tension between a previously decided agenda and the emergence of new and volatile issues within the group. As part of attending to such topics, this chapter also introduces some general approaches that we can call on as facilitators – for example, the principle of listening first and speaking afterwards, and more.

Chapter 4: Facilitation Principles for Efficient Collaboration

This chapter provides the core principles that support reaching collaborative decisions in a group, while the next chapter provides the specific structure and flow I have developed to actually reach decisions. The main function of this chapter is to transcend the implicit dichotomy we have accepted that pits collaboration and efficiency against each other. Specifically, this chapter introduces the principle that everyone matters, along with many insights about how you can use every moment to move quickly towards greater collaboration through understanding what supports willingness within a group and thus avoiding unnecessary discussion. By distinguishing willingness from preference, on the one hand, and from compromise on the other, you can increase your capacity to engage with all that happens in a room, including the outliers, so that every divergence begins to provide the opportunity for greater convergence.

Chapter 5: Creating Breakthrough Collaborative Decisions with Convergent Facilitation

This chapter is the heart of this book. It contains a full description of the Convergent Facilitation approach to decision making. It builds on the insights, principles, and skills in the preceding chapters, and presents the specific methodology that supports groups in converging on a decision they can all move forward with willingly. Although this methodology operates in three clear steps as described above, in real life you are likely to move back and forth between the steps.

Chapter 6: Attending to Power Differences

In order to make for a smooth and simple presentation, the previous chapter was based on the assumption that you are a designated facilitator who is not part of the group, and it sidestepped a number of other more complex issues. In this chapter, I focus on expanding the skills and practices to attend to the many challenges that arise when there are power differences in the room. Those can be within the group, between you and the group (especially if you are also a decision-maker), or between you as participant in a group wanting to facilitate "from the sidelines" and the designated facilitator along with the rest of the group. In all these instances you will see how you can use skills you already learned earlier to make it possible to establish true collaboration even when power differences abound.

Chapter 7: Case study: Contested Child Custody Legislation

This chapter provides detailed information about one dramatic application of Convergent Facilitation. This project effectively serves as proof of concept that collaborative lawmaking is entirely possible, even under conditions of strong ideological polarization. Because this is a live issue, I am only providing some details and not others. I am aiming to offer as much inspiration and clarity as possible while protecting the sensitive nature of the information and the relationships within the group. The main purpose of this chapter is to provide examples of exactly how and why the principles work to create such breakthrough results.

Facilitation and Group Function

CHAPTER ONE

I'VE BEEN PARTICIPATING IN GROUPS and then leading groups since the mid-1980s. The settings I've been part of range all the way from small, one-time workplace meetings to multi-day residential retreats with dozens of people coming together several times a year. Even before I started leading and facilitating, I became increasingly interested in understanding why some groups worked so well together and others didn't, especially when it comes to making decisions.

Initially, I assumed, without ever thinking about it, that all that would be needed was a high degree of personal skill – people knowing how to interact with each other and how to be self-responsible and empathic. As a result of this, when I discovered Nonviolent Communication in the mid-1990s, I was imagining a quantum leap in terms of group function amongst practitioners. After all, I reasoned to myself, the people who comprise these groups are both skillful and passionate.

It was a painful awakening to see that the personal skill alone just wasn't enough; that sometimes it was even a hindrance, because the application of the personal skills became almost more important than achieving whatever purpose the group set out to accomplish. It was clear to me that there was something missing, and I am grateful to Jean Francois Noubel, founder of the Collective Intelligence Research Institute, for naming this insight so clearly: Personal evolution doesn't automatically translate into better functioning within a group or organization.[1] The group or organization needs to have certain things on the level of group structure and process in place in order to function well.

1 Personal communication. See also https://www.youtube.com/
watch?v=7EZeVQLdK84.

This awakening was made even more clear, and in moments distressing, when I saw groups without such skills functioning beautifully using, for example, talking stick circle process. Why were people more able to converge through this process, which at times I found irritatingly choreographed, and not through open conversation? Many years later, I now can answer this question: The talking stick circle process supports members of a group in functioning as a whole rather than a collection of individuals pulling in different directions.

When I started leading groups regularly, in the mid-1990s, I learned a new piece of the puzzle. I noticed that, for the most part, what I did as a facilitator tended to have a more reliable effect on how the group functioned than how any of the members of the groups participated. Even in groups with animosity and mistrust, I could regularly support people in hearing each other and in coming together around meaningful decisions.

Still, with all I was beginning to understand about the interaction of personal skill, quality of the process being used, and the presence of skilled facilitation, I was missing two major ingredients in the soup of decision-making. It wasn't until after the period of Occupy Wall Street that the final pieces of clarity emerged, at least for that moment.

I imagine that readers of this book cover a wide range of responses to the Occupy movement, ranging from active supporters, who may be devastated that Occupy didn't manage to sustain itself over time in the form in which it started, all the way to those who consider Occupy a problematic movement and are quite relieved that it no longer poses a threat.

Regardless of opinion about Occupy, at the level of group process, looking at the example of Occupy has been profoundly instructive for me. Specifically, reflecting on the trajectory of this movement helped me understand more about group function because the Occupy movement exemplified an ethos of functioning without leaders, a variable I had not explored deeply before. Facilitation of the assembly meetings, to the extent I witnessed it, was minimal, more akin to traffic control than to leadership of any kind. I attended several such meetings at Occupy Oakland, and was amazed by three things. One was the degree of willingness people exhibited to be in extended, often repetitive meetings. I was also surprised that any decisions were made at all in this atmosphere because it didn't include dialogue and all that happened was people expressing positions and then voting. The third was the number of decisions that weren't made.

In my mind, Occupy didn't sustain itself, in part, because of how extraordinarily difficult it was to make decisions and move forward given the degree of mistrust of leadership and power the movement exhibited, even to the point of opposition to facilitation and dialogue. The challenge of collaborative functioning was made ever more crystal clear to me as a result. The question I was most haunted with was the degree to which full-fledged facilitation was needed to accomplish effective group function. Were there conditions under which groups could function and make decisions without active facilitation? As my work in group facilitation expanded more and more outside the workshop setting and into organizational and public settings, and as I began to research these topics more extensively, two additional factors came to my awareness that helped me understand why some groups work well without active facilitation and others don't.

The first of these is clarity about shared purpose. It took me years to fully grasp how profoundly important it is, because so much of the time groups function without an explicitly articulated shared purpose. In its stead, a group relies either on clarity of purpose that resides with a group's leader, or there is no shared purpose and everyone assumes others share their purpose. When a group is not aligned around a shared purpose, any process and any decision are more challenging, because people are likely to be pulling in different directions, sometimes with great passion.

The second is more elusive and complex in its effect, and I didn't notice it on my own. I owe this insight to Carne Ross, whose book *The Leaderless Revolution* is filled with examples of groups functioning and making decisions on their own, and who was able to name the defining characteristic: These are groups that have a shared fate, which is even stronger than a shared purpose, and that have true freedom in carrying out their decisions.[2] A particularly strong example of this principle is the way the commons have operated for hundreds of years. Commons, initially, were physical resources that were managed by a group or a community for the benefit of everyone and without any legal ownership. Commons have been sustained for many hundreds of years until taken apart by modern privatization, although there are still a surprising number of resources in the world that are managed as commons.[3] Such resources are managed and operated by groups of individuals or communities that have no specific training in group process and who don't necessarily have a facilitator. Nonetheless, these

2 Carne Ross, *The Leaderless Revolution* (Simon & Schuster, 2012).
3 One particularly astonishing example is the *acequias* in the Southwestern part of the US, which are elaborate systems of canals and ditches in very arid areas. They have been managed in an uninterrupted manner for several hundred years, allowing access to water to everyone who is part of the system and contributing to the sustainability of the region. Another is fisheries in Maine, where how much fishing would be done by whom and when is decided collaboratively by the entire community of fishers.

groups function with remarkable effectiveness, with minor and manageable conflicts, and with resource sustainability for generations, often centuries. The reason is clear. Groups managing commons, and similar such groups (Ross' book contains many examples) are able to do this because they are not debating opinions or having a discussion. They are making decisions about practical matters that vitally affect all of them, and they are autonomous in terms of carrying out those decisions rather than depending on some external authority such as government or a corporation. These two factors combined create a strong shared fate which is equivalent, I believe, to what Convergent Facilitation accomplishes in its first phase or criteria gathering.

Putting all of these ingredients together, I can now state my perspective on group function. The most important variables are:

- the quality of the process
- clarity of shared purpose
- autonomy and meaningful capacity to carry out decisions

I no longer believe that a high level of personal skill is either necessary or sufficient for group functioning. In particular, in the absence of any of the crucial ingredients, I believe it's iffy whether personal skill will make up for it or exacerbate the issue.

On the other hand, skilled facilitation can make up for the loss of function that a group is likely to experience in the absence of a structure and a purpose. The less clear the purpose, the less defined the process of reaching decisions, the more is required of the facilitator to support the group in functioning as one whole and converging towards a decision.

I developed the process of Convergent Facilitation as a way to reliably support groups in converging on decisions even when purpose, process, or authority have not been sufficiently developed. Given how fractured our modern societies are, the risk of groups on all levels not coming together is too high, whether the group is a workplace team or a collection of delegations to peace negotiations. Convergent Facilitation provides a purpose: reaching a decision that works for all. It supports clarity of process by making explicit the methodology used for reaching that kind of decision. Within this framework, groups become more able to recognize where their authority lies and to make the decisions that they are able to make with far less strife.

In the rest of this book, I am focusing on the methodology and facilitation skills that can help you overcome obstacles to effective decision-making in a group. My intention, again, is to provide you with sufficient information about how to facilitate groups in such a way that the likelihood of a convergent decision continues to increase as you acquire experience.

The Gift
of Self:
The Art of
Transparent
Facilitation

CHAPTER TWO

TRANSPARENCY IS THE PRACTICE OF REVEALING OURSELVES
TO OTHERS. In the context of facilitation, this means, primarily, making visible to others the reasons for making specific choices or decisions regarding facilitation. At other times, we may choose to reveal a more inner experience that includes feelings, thoughts, or needs. In my experience, transparency while facilitating has the enormous potential to contribute to a group's ability to open up, to come together, and to function with trust and efficiency.[1]

On one level, transparency in facilitation is a stylistic choice. On another level, it can be a strategic choice that supports a group in coming together as well as a tool for building trust and removing barriers of professional distance. In addition, transparency is a key skill in Convergent Facilitation in particular, for two main reasons. One is that moving towards convergence without engaging in much discussion is unfamiliar, even confusing and demanding at times for people. As a result, being able to offer guidance and clarity about facilitation choices is key to supporting the group. The second is that Convergent Facilitation is quite directive, and transparency about choices highlights its collaborative nature in terms of the relationship with the facilitator. For all of these reasons, I am placing this chapter early in the book even though this could appear as a more advanced concept and set of choices.

Although transparency is often discouraged, based on a concern for the integrity of the facilitator's role and for the primacy of participants' needs, my own experience is that the benefits of transparent facilitation outweigh the risks. Overall,

---

1 An earlier, much longer version of this chapter appeared as "The Gift of Self: The Art of Transparent Facilitation," in Sandy Schuman, ed., *The IAF Handbook of Group Facilitation* (Jossey-Bass, 2005).

I have seen far less transparency in group facilitation than I advocate for. This is because our cultural habits suggest that a facilitator is supposed to be "neutral" and not show what's going on. I find this sad, because I think that as facilitators we lose effectiveness when we hide important facets of our inner process. Rather than deciding, once and for all, to be transparent or not to be transparent, my own path has been to keep investigating and learning about when and how transparency supports my role as facilitator, and when and how it may detract from it.

Responsible transparency requires both a high level of self-awareness and internal mastery, as well as finely tuned communication skills to convey to the group what we choose to share of our inner experience while sustaining the focus on participants' needs. This chapter addresses both dimensions.

How Transparency Can Support Trust

One of the ways that transparency can be singularly helpful to a group is in supporting trust. This trust is the result either of seeing the humanity of the facilitator or of understanding the choices of the facilitator, or both. Here are a couple of examples:

- **Bridging power differences with the group.** You can support this in happening by showing your humanity as the facilitator. For example, as an adult facilitating a group of youth, I chose to express my own experiences with some vulnerable sharing. I did this deliberately as a way to humanize myself to them and bridge the gap in experience and power. In addition, through my choice of transparent sharing, I was able to convey to the youth that their experiences matter, thereby increasing the chances that they would feel free to express their concerns, feelings, and needs. The result was a high willingness on their part to reveal their own experiences related to the topic we focused on for that day.

- **Managing "traffic" in the room.** You can do this by helping people understand your choices as the facilitator. I tend to be explicit in naming what I am doing when I facilitate and why I am choosing it. For example, instead of saying, "I am going to put your comment on a separate sheet and address it later," I am more likely to say, "I would like to come back to your comment after we're done with the current topic, as I am concerned that we already have several open loops that will be hard to juggle. Would that work for you?" In this way, the person in question knows the "why" and also that they are on my radar screen, allowing them, usually, to relax into accepting my choice.

The Challenges of Transparency

Lest you get the sense that any form of transparency is always helpful, let me say it in no uncertain terms: Trust is not the only possible result when we choose to be transparent. I myself have had experiences and been present in other situations when revealing certain types of feelings led to people having anxiety and concern about the facilitator's capacity to guide the group towards its purpose. I completely understand where the hesitancy about transparency arises from, especially the concerns about overwhelming the group with information that is not germane to the issue at hand.

This apparent unpredictability, when transparency could sometimes lead to increased trust, safety, and connection, and sometimes to the loss of trust, is one of the reasons why so many facilitators opt for caution and even restraint regarding self-disclosure. It is also one of the reasons for writing this chapter and attempting to provide sufficient guidelines to support more capacity and willingness on the part of facilitators in this area.

The trap of neutrality

Another factor that often confuses the choice about transparency is the expectation of neutrality – both external and internalized, which can easily appear inconsistent with transparency.

The result of the "requirement" of neutrality often looks like facilitators making what appear to be neutral and objective statements which include hidden expressions of self. For example, without active vigilance, many of us often take on the role of authority by deciding what is important and expressing our own impressions and evaluations as if they are simple observations. Any time we do that, we consciously or unconsciously disguise the fact that we are expressing our own subjective perceptions and experience. There is a world of difference between saying, "Let's stay focused on the task at hand" – which makes us the authority on what that is – and saying, "I am not confident that what is happening will support us in reaching our goals for the meeting" – which recognizes that we are, in fact, making an evaluation that arises from our own inner sense. Sometimes, we are "doomed" to learn to be transparent if we want to act with integrity in our role as facilitators.

In my own work as a facilitator, I have come to align myself with an emerging term in the field – multi-partiality or omni-partiality, understood to be distinct from impartiality, the hallmark of neutrality. I regularly tell groups that I am not neutral and don't intend to be: My goal is to make things work out for everyone, and I advocate for everyone. I care, and I pour my heart and soul into any facilitation task. I recognize this as distinct from many other variants of facilitation.

To fulfill my purpose of advocating for everyone, I seek, in any given moment, to have enough clarity about everyone's needs that I can sense whether something will work for them or not. I have been known to dissuade a group from accepting a proposal because I wasn't sure it would attend to some people's needs, or to speak in the name of people not even present, *even if I don't agree with their position!*

This stance helps me land more easily on the side of being transparent – albeit still with many caveats about the when, what, and how.

Conditions for Success: Know the Moment

The art of self-disclosure does not lend itself to hard and fast rules and therefore requires considerable skill and consciousness. Before risking self-disclosure, it is essential to consider elements such as the group's purpose and the capacity of the group to contain the experience of a facilitator without getting lost or anxious.

At the same time, most decision points about whether and how to reveal ourselves to the group do not announce themselves ahead of time. Therefore, a thorough understanding of our relationship to ourselves and the group moment by moment (rather than "once and for all") is also necessary. This is one of the ways in which transparent facilitation requires a high degree of awareness of our inner experience, a level of self-connection, or conscious awareness of our feelings and needs.

In short, adding transparency to the range of options available to us requires ongoing, quick decision-making – while speaking – before choosing what to say. Several factors combine to increase the likelihood that sharing ourselves with the group will be productive. I detail three of them below:

Clarity of purpose

Clarity of purpose essentially means being able to answer the question: How will being transparent contribute to the group? Having clarity about what we are trying to achieve or create by revealing an aspect of ourselves to a group is key to successful integration of such transparency with group facilitation. The more rigorously we examine our motivation in speaking, the more likely we are to support the group process rather than hinder it.

If we have not clearly identified the purpose of sharing a part of ourselves, we run the risk of *acting* on our needs without awareness. Instead, we can aim to first *connect* with our needs, so we can know why we want what we want, and only then proceed to making conscious choices about what we want to do. If we are not clear about how transparency will contribute to the group, we could explore what needs we are trying to meet and whether those needs are ones we want to act on while facilitating. As facilitators, we cannot rest with a casual choice, because in the absence of clarity of purpose, participants may interpret unconscious needs in us even if those needs are not there.

As facilitators, we are not without needs, as certain versions of neutrality and professionalism seem to imply. Rather, we bring many needs and intentions to our work which are intrinsic to the process of facilitation. Primary among them is a desire to contribute to the group, including offering process guidance, insight from our experience, and more. Without wanting to contribute, we will be unlikely to mobilize the heart and skill required to proceed with the task at hand.

We also have other needs that can seriously undermine the process if they are not met during facilitation. One key need we have as facilitators is that of self-connection.

To make our inner experience useful to a group, we need to develop our capacity for self-connection, by which I mean the capacity to be aware, as much as possible and in each moment, of our feelings and of how the many thoughts, evaluations, and judgments that occupy our consciousness are manifestations of our deeper needs. Without knowing our own inner experience moment by moment, we lose some of our capacity to make choices about facilitation. The only thing we ever know for sure at any moment is our inner response to what is happening. Everything else we believe about what is happening in the group is an inference, as there is no way to have direct knowledge of a "group." Being able to notice when a judgment arises and to discover and connect with the needs that give rise to it is a key entry point into making choices, moment by moment, about our next actions while facilitating.

For example, if we think that someone in the group is being "domineering," we are likely to react rather than respond – that is, likely to make a statement to the group coming out of unaware judgment or frustration rather than conscious choice about what would most contribute to the group. In contrast, if we inquire into the needs underneath the judgment, we can come to recognize and own our experience, allowing us more choice. For example, we may tap into wanting care and consideration for everyone in the group. However brief this exploration might be, it is often all it takes to make a conscious choice. Instead of responding in a way that might shame that one person and create more separation within the group, we might, instead, find a response that invites the entire group into noticing the dynamics and attending to all the different styles present in the room. The more we know about what needs are alive in us, the more options we have for choosing whether and how to try to meet our needs based on what now appears relevant and caring. Having more options and more awareness benefits the group and its process.

When we learn to tune into our feelings and needs, we are likely to discover many other needs that are not specific to the process of facilitation, such as our needs for acceptance, love, protection, and safety, to name a few. Those needs are there, because we are human. We cannot make them go away, and it would be a form of violence even if we could. What we *can* do, however, is to become aware of these needs, and make choices about whether and how to attend to them. Otherwise, we run the risk of acting on the needs without awareness, thereby making choices that could easily conflict with our intentions and hopes for the group.

Transparency is most effective when we have made a conscious choice to reveal some of our inner process to the group based on clarity about how doing so will contribute to the group's process. To achieve such clarity requires both self-knowledge and reflection on the connection between what we are about to reveal and the purpose for which the group has gathered.

In some instances, for example when we give a group an exercise in engaging with *their* inner experiences, transparency can be outright confusing. The specific content of our own inner experience could easily distract people from that task into anxiety about the content of what we say. With some reflection, we would likely choose not to take a turn when other people share.

Conversely, in the example I used earlier about facilitating a group of youth, sharing my own experience with the group came from my conscious assessment that it would serve the purpose for which I was there, which was to support the youth in learning tools for increasing inner freedom. I chose to give voice to my vulnerability because of a clear intuitive assessment that my doing so would bring the conversation to a deeper level and allow the youth more freedom of expression.

Simply put: What makes transparency effective is the relationship between the specific content of what we are transparent about and the purpose at hand, the content in and of itself. For example, when I teach people how to facilitate, I regularly share with them the deeper nuances of my internal process of making decisions moment by moment. In the context of people learning about facilitation, sharing at this level has been a rich and powerful model of what they are trying to learn.

However, if I were working with a group that has a different purpose – for example, to work out the timeline for a complex project – my offering the same information about my decision-making process could be enormously confusing and even irritating. Attention to process and content at the same time, the hallmark of facilitation, is most definitely an acquired skill. A group that is focused on a task, or on learning other skills, may lose track of what is going on and feel anxious, confused, distracted, or bored.

Holding the whole while sharing

The fundamental stance of facilitating is one of split awareness of self and of the group. As a facilitator, I continually track what is happening inside me and am attentive to the needs of participants and the dynamics of the group as a whole at the same time. Once I have identified a purpose for transparency, I then aim to determine my capacity to stay on both of these levels at once even while being transparent.

Even if we start sharing our inner process with a clearly identified purpose, we can easily get lost while speaking as other needs come alive in us, such as needs for understanding, connection, or acceptance. This can lead to losing our focus on the purpose of sharing in an unaware attempt to get those other needs met.

With experience, we can learn how to assess our capacity to remain on two levels at once. We can develop discernment about how much of ourselves we can touch and reveal before losing our capacity to hold the whole. Before and during sharing an inner experience, we can ask ourselves something like: "Can I talk about this feeling in myself and maintain my split awareness, or will I disappear in the feeling and lose my attention to others? Can I tell this story without losing track of the main thread of the moment? Am I certain that I can contain within myself the longing to be heard and soothed about this experience?"

Tracking participants' capacity to contain transparency

Whatever our inner experience, however relaxed, confident, and present we are in sharing our experience, we also need to be aware of the capacity of group members to hear our openness and maintain their own focus and sense of safety, trust, and empowerment.

Both before and while speaking about ourselves, we need to assess where the group is and whether participants are likely to receive what we are about to share, or what we have already shared, in a way that is consistent with the purpose of sharing. Even if we do not know ahead of time the skill and capacity of group members, our own ability to notice the effects of our sharing on the group will give us information about our next choices. If we notice discomfort in the group, we can change course while speaking or take measures afterward to increase trust in the group.

One particular risk of expressing our own experience is the possibility that group members may think that they must somehow "take care of us" or do something about what we have shared, thereby becoming distracted from paying attention to *the purpose at hand*. To address this risk, close attention to what we do with what we just shared and what requests we make of the group is paramount. If group members expect neutrality, authority, and self-control from us, they may become quite agitated and nervous when seeing our human vulnerability. People who are not accustomed to seeing the humanity of facilitators, or of leaders more generally, may derive part of their sense of safety from having someone whom they trust to be the authority. Such expectations on the part of group members do not mean that we must avoid sharing ourselves altogether. Such expectations do, however, require us to be flexible about how far to go and skillful about how to maintain the sense of safety in the group.

The most challenging feelings to reveal effectively are any fears or anxieties we experience while facilitating. Even if we are relaxed about our fears, we can lose the trust of the group if participants believe that our fear is overwhelming us or detracting from our ability to conduct the meeting effectively. With feelings of fear and anxiety in particular, but also more generally, effective use of transparency requires finding a way to bring our inner confidence across so participants can be relaxed about our expressions and trust that we can still handle the situation. Clearly, to convey that confidence requires having it in the first place, based on having enough experience and trust in ourselves to know that we can navigate the situation, including continually assessing and reassessing how much self-expression is relevant to the purpose at hand and whether what we have said already is enough to accomplish the purpose.

The Nuts and Bolts of Transparency

Once we make the decision to be transparent, knowing how to express ourselves increases the chances that our purpose will be served and decreases the risk of loss of connection, focus, or trust in the group. The heart of transparent facilitation is finding a way to express clearly what we choose to reveal in the least challenging way to participants in the group.

Our inner experience doesn't happen in a vacuum. It is both informed by what happens around us, and affects what happens in the group. This interaction with the reality in the group outside our inner experience requires a few more skills to navigate effectively. This is what this final section is about.[2]

You may remember that, in the Introduction, I talked about how this book is not a facilitation primer. This is one of the places where this distinction is significant. While I *describe* some of the skills below, reading about them here is not the same as getting direct training in how to master them.

---

2 The skills presented in this section are all drawn from the legacy of Marshall Rosenberg's work in codifying aspects of Nonviolent Communication. See *Nonviolent Communication: A Language of Life* (Puddledancer Press, 2003) for full details about the practice.

Ending expressions with a clear request to the group

One way that I know I have reached sufficient clarity about the purpose of revealing something about myself in a given moment is that I know what I want to hear back from the group after speaking. When I think I do not want anything back from a group, or do not know what it is, I see it as an indication that my choice is not yet clear enough about why I want to share of myself. In such moments, I wait until I have full clarity about what my purpose is and what response from the group would support me in knowing if my purpose got accomplished.

Knowing what to ask from the group offers us an effective feedback mechanism for assessing whether our purpose in disclosure was met already, is still being met, or is not likely to be met at all. Without asking the group for something after we express our transparency, we increase the chances that the group will receive our words as a weight, as something to do something about, rather than as a gift to them.

Even the most challenging form of transparency – our discomfort about our own situation as a facilitator – is more likely to serve a purpose if it is followed by a clear request to the group. For example, if a facilitator says: "I am a little uncomfortable stepping into Janet's group. I know that you've been with her for years and have a very trusting relationship, and I'm not sure that my leading the group tonight is an easy choice for you. Would anyone tell me if you have any concerns about my facilitating instead of Janet, so we can be honest with each other and proceed with clarity?"

This expression, although potentially challenging to the group, ends with a specific and clear request that has a clear purpose. By acknowledging that participants may indeed have concerns and inviting them to share them, the facilitator communicates to the participants that she is solid enough in her role to hear their discomfort if it arises.

Developing a habit of ending any of my expressions in the group with a clear request of what I want to hear back contributes to clarity, understanding, and movement in the group. Without it, chances increase that I will make decisions that are not fully serving the needs of the group. This can include losing some people, going in a direction that is not supporting the group without having mechanisms for the group to communicate that to me, or losing the thread of interest and connection, which is vital to the very trust people would have in my facilitation. In addition, in Chapter 4, you will see that choosing my requests as a facilitator is one of the key skills that support a group in reaching a decision.

Making a practice of ending my expressions with clear requests is useful even when I assess that continuing to reveal myself is no longer contributing to the group. I can still check my intuition with the group by requesting feedback from them about it. What I then say may sound something like this: "I would like to stop what I am doing right now and instead go back to our agenda, because I don't trust that pursuing it further would contribute to the group. Is anyone still incomplete with what I have said so far?"

However, the practice of ending each expression with a clear request is not a rule, and important exceptions exist, such as when speaking within a circle of sharing.

In addition, I want to be mindful of how often I check in with the group before proceeding with what I want to do next. If I am confident that what I am doing is contributing to the group, or if I am confident people will speak up if their needs are not met, I am more likely to continue without checking with the group. Similarly, if I assess that there isn't enough safety and trust in the group for people to respond honestly to my requests, or if my requests are likely to trigger a lengthy discussion, I may choose to rely more on my own assessments rather than checking with the group.

When and how to make requests of the group is an essential ingredient of the art of facilitation, independent of how much we reveal of ourselves. We return to this topic at greater length in later chapters that describe the specifics of Convergent Facilitation, as distinct from the general principles of facilitation we are looking at here.

Owning any feedback we give to the group

When I facilitate, speaking of my experience is in itself a powerful feedback mechanism for the group, a remarkable mirror, and an opportunity to see the effect of their actions on another. At the same time, depending on the level of experience and maturity of group members, such expressions may trigger reactions or concerns on the part of group members and have the potential to derail the group process.

Providing feedback to a group entails both observing behaviors (by describing exactly what happened as if captured by a video camera) and evaluating them. Thus, we need skills for differentiating between observations and evaluations, describing behavior in non-evaluative terms, and taking full responsibility for our evaluations instead of asserting them as if they are just "true," which is the same as taking the position of an omniscient god. Without specific competencies in all these areas, participants are much less likely to make use of our feedback and instead take offense, become upset, or withdraw from participation.

I have many times been astonished by how often people, including facilitators, express evaluations, even outright judgments, and believe that they are making an observation. In fact, one of the telltale ways of predicting that a judgment is about to come is when someone says: "I'd like to make an observation." This is no accident, because most of us are very unskilled in describing behavior, and resort to evaluations of the behavior without providing any concrete observations of the behavior that leads us to make our evaluations. Try it out for a moment. Think of a meeting you have attended recently, and of someone whose behavior concerned you. Maybe you thought the person was "domineering" or "inauthentic" or "crass." Can you remember what it was that the person actually said or did that you evaluated in this way? Let's stick with "domineering" for a moment. Did the person start speaking several times in the meeting before others were done? Did they express disagreement with any new ideas that someone else put forth?

Why is this important? A person is highly unlikely to learn anything from, or be open to, any feedback that suggests they are domineering. The more you are able to observe behavior before evaluating it, the more likely you are to contribute to people's ability to hear your feedback without defensiveness. When you facilitate, providing feedback to the group or to individuals is an essential part of your task, and being able to reduce the likelihood of defensiveness is a huge bonus.

Any time we give feedback to the group that is not a strict observation, we are, in fact, engaged in revealing aspects of our inner life, which may include our feelings and needs as they are known to us, as well as our values or our core beliefs. What this means is that much of what we say involves sharing of ourselves, and the choice we have is whether to be open about it or mask this disclosure with statements that appear to be neutral or objective.

Here's an example of something that probably seems clear and innocuous upon first read. When noticing that one of the participants is bringing up a new issue, it would be common and easy to say something like this: "Addressing what Joe said in this moment is taking us away from what we already agreed to do today. Let's stay focused on the task at hand."

This statement seems to be objective, and thus maintains the appearance of neutrality. However, it runs the risk of alienating Joe and possibly others in the group. In addition, opting for this form of feedback misses the opportunity to tap into the group's power of making agreements and then making conscious choices about whether to keep them.

To express this feedback in a way that recognizes our subjective experience might sound like this: "I am uncomfortable taking time right now to address what Joe said, because I want to support the group in completing a task as well as in keeping to our agreements. I also want to support your choice in the matter, so I am willing to address Joe's issue if this is what you all want. I'd like to see by a show of hands how many people would like to take more time now to discuss this item."

This expression owns both the feelings (discomfort) and the needs (supporting the group's process), and invites the group to participate in deciding what happens next. Involving groups not only in content decisions but also in ongoing process decisions supports group empowerment, which is one of the key purposes of facilitation. This practice also prepares the group for the challenge of standing up to the facilitator or working together without an experienced facilitator.

Fluidity in switching between transparency and empathic reflection of others

One of the key skills of facilitation not highlighted in this chapter is the skill of reflective, empathic listening (see Chapter 3 for information about this skill). The capacity to discern and check with participants our understanding of what matters to them that is expressed in their statements is vital to making progress in a group, especially in charged moments. When we also want to bring into our facilitation the practice of sharing more of ourselves, one of the key skills we need to learn is to notice when we are paying attention to ourselves and express that separately from our empathic reflection of what participants are saying. If we mix self-expression and reflective listening, we run the risk that both will lose their potential for greater connection with the group and for contributing to the group. Consider the following example which is a mixture of empathic connection and transparency:

> *Facilitator:* Jane, I really understand your concern about long-term effects of this policy proposal and how much you care about patient well-being [empathic reflection], and I am worried that taking more time with it right now will not move us toward greater understanding in the team [transparency]. How about if we come back to it later, after we have addressed the immediate issues of information sharing we are looking at?

When Jane hears this, she is not likely to experience being understood and therefore is very unlikely to be open to hearing the rest of what the facilitator says. Separating the two parts provides an opportunity to connect fully with Jane's concern, and potentially also to gather more information relevant to facilitation choices. Consider this alternative which illustrates empathic connection by itself:

> *Facilitator:* Jane, are you concerned about the long-term effects of this policy proposal because of how much you care about patient well-being?
> *Jane:* Yes. There is no point in continuing to discuss any of this now because I don't see how this policy could ever be approved.

At this point the facilitator has more information than before and may choose to change course and stay with Jane's concern, or ask her if she would be willing to hold off until the other issues on the table had been discussed. In the latter case, Jane is much more likely to be willing to wait, having already been heard about her concerns.

Integrating Self and Others

At the root of the injunction to avoid revealing our own inner experience I detect an assumption that transparent expression and supporting others in expressing themselves are mutually exclusive behaviors.

Part of my hope in presenting the possibility of transparent facilitation is to challenge this assumption. Instead, my premise is that transparency and support for others' expression can enhance each other *or* interfere with each other depending on how skillfully we navigate the delicate terrain of group facilitation. In particular, I have called attention to the following factors as key to deciding about how transparent we want to be and when:

- Careful consideration of what aspects of self involve more or less risk to group integrity, especially by relating them to the purpose at hand
- Ongoing attention to the group's responses to our facilitation and transparency, so that we can assess how well our transparency is contributing to the group
- Cultivation of a high level of self-awareness and capacity to maintain and return to our stance of holding the whole, so that we can continue supporting the group even while speaking about ourselves.

Awareness alone may not be sufficient to the task. It is my hope that, with this awareness and with continued application of the skills in this chapter and beyond, you will find your way to increasing your ability to enter and exit transparency with ease and grace, so it can become a tool that supports and deepens trust and effectiveness in groups you facilitate.

Convergent Facilitation General Toolkit

CHAPTER THREE

SUPPORTING A GROUP TO REACH COLLABORATIVE decisions efficiently is an incredibly demanding task. It will require of you a high degree of inner clarity and presence, along with a capacity to think quickly and adapt to rapidly changing conditions. On this foundation, some specific intentions – all an elaboration of the quality of faith I discussed in Chapter One – can support you and the group to remain focused on the prize of a solution that works for everyone. Finally, even before the specific skills that are unique to the focus on collaborative decision-making, there is a vast set of core competencies and facilitation skills to master. This is what I cover in this chapter, thereby concluding the preparatory section of this book before moving to the specific principles and skills for decision-making.

The Inner Work of Facilitating Collaboration

I have been facilitating groups since the early 1990s, and I absolutely love doing it, both when combined with teaching and when it is the entire focus. This love and pleasure fully coexist with my knowledge that facilitation is an exacting and demanding human endeavor: The amount of things to track, the guaranteed presence of repeated surprises, and the intensity of the commitment to supporting everyone within the group are taxing.

This task becomes next to impossible if you are someone who finds it hard to stay present in the face of challenging circumstances or if you tend to take things personally, for example. This is because facilitating a group is an ongoing process of making one choice after another under stress and without full information. Becoming emotionally upset interferes with making choices, leading us, instead, to *reacting*.

The ramifications of reactivity in a facilitator – or any leader for that matter – are far more pronounced than reactivity on the part of any one participant, simply because the facilitator is holding the whole, and because the group is looking to a facilitator to hold the whole. Although in general I encourage people to experiment with facilitation and learn as they go, a history of trauma that has not been attended to sufficiently to be able to remain calm under stress seems to me to be inconsistent with taking on facilitation as a primary occupation. I would urge you, if you know yourself to be susceptible to reacting under stress, to engage in trauma healing before continuing on this path.[1]

In the remainder of this book, I am assuming a certain baseline of capacity to access inner calm and choice.

That said, I want to stress that where we draw the line about this capacity is not easy to discern. There is no facilitator I know who's never lost their calm. It's certainly happened to me that I have lost the capacity for choice on more than one occasion. I am not talking here about reaching some kind of perfection before embarking on facilitation. I am only talking about knowing yourself well enough to be able to assess how likely it is to happen, how able you are to recover and continue, and what your plan B can be for those times

---

1 There are many modalities in existence that have been tremendously helpful to people with trauma. I will name just a few: NVC itself, especially the practices that integrate NVC with neurobiology (see Sarah Peyton, *Your Resonant Self: Guided Meditations and Exercises to Engage Your Brain's Capacity for Healing*, W.W. Norton & Co., 2017, and Eric Bowers, *Meet Me in Hard-To-Love Places*, Eric Bowers Publishing, 2016); EFT (Emotional Freedom Technique) (see Gary Craig, *EFT Manual*, Energy Psychology Press, 2008); Somatic Experiencing (see Peter Levine, *Waking the Tiger*, North Atlantic Books, 1997); David Weinstock, *NeuroKinetic Therapy*, North Atlantic Books, 2010; *Becoming What You Need: Practices for Embodying Nonviolent Communication*, independently published, 2017); and Trauma Release Exercises (see David Berceli, *Shake It Off Naturally: Reduce Stress, Anxiety, and Tension with TRE*, CreateSpace Independent Publishing Platform, 2015).

when you do lose capacity. For myself, I know it's quite rare; I then am almost always able to recover very quickly; and I have someone with me in most instances that are potentially charged so that I can get immediate support.

This section focuses elsewhere, on some other core areas where developing yourself on the inside would be highly advantageous to your capacity to facilitate groups, especially in complex and demanding situations. They are neither specific skills nor particular intentions. Rather, they are general qualities and approaches to connecting with yourself that can be embraced at any time in your life. They just happen to be immensely useful when you facilitate, because they give you more strength and self-trust overall, which you can then use when you facilitate and the inevitable challenges arise.

Self-connection and intuition

Because facilitation is irreducibly linked to intuition, one of the capacities you will need to develop is to establish, maintain, and regain connection with yourself. I see self-connection as the ground of everything that we do, and I define it simply as having the clarity to know, moment by moment, where I am – what I am experiencing including what's happening in my body, what feelings live in me, what's important to me right now, and what I want to do next. This is quite different from the ongoing chatter of judgments of self and other, thoughts about what I should be doing, doubts, insecurities, and protections that most of us live in most of the time. Such disconnected processes, if they run the show, could easily compromise what you have to bring to any situation. In particular, when you are facilitating, anything that you do has far-reaching ramifications for the group, because you are a major source of guidance and energy in the room.

In my own work, I have come to embrace the extreme humility that I never *know* anything: Not what is truly happening in the group; not what will serve the group; not what the best outcome is. The *only* thing I know for sure is what happens inside of me. This is my primary source of information if I am honest about what's going on, since everything else is filtered through my perspective, my worldview, my interpretations about what is happening, and more.

As a result, I use every bit of what happens inside me as a source of information. Most especially, this applies to my intuition, which I use as my guide to action. Of course, what happens inside me, including my intuition, is *also* informed by everything that's happened before and my worldview and perspectives. Still, it's all I've got. So I dip into the humility of not knowing, and then I pretty much constantly check in with myself about what is going on. Based on that, I choose the next thing, the next thing, the next thing, freshly each time. Because I use it as a tool in this way, I devote significant energy to engaging my intuition and to cultivating it over time.

For example, one of the aspects of facilitation about which I am continuing to develop my intuition is the sense of whether or not the group is with me or with someone else who's speaking. This is important to me, because I find it wasteful to have anyone speak, whether it's me or anyone else, when people are not listening. Here's an example. At a workshop I was leading, someone wanted to ask a question and it looked to me like he didn't have awareness of how little willingness there was in the group to hear him. I had no way of knowing, and, indeed, it turned out that I was mistaken. Still, in the moment of facilitating, the *only* thing I could go with was my intuition, which is my primary instrument as a facilitator. And so I obeyed it, as I always do (the *only* thing I obey, in fact). And then I learned. What I did was give the group a signal about this awareness by saying: "I'm not sure the group is ready to hear one more question from you, and I want to check with them before you ask your question. Are you OK with that?" I then turned to the group and checked with them. When everyone then affirmed that they were fully with him, he felt angry at me for what he thought was my bias against him. What I learned from that was that regardless of how strongly I believe my intuition, in my speech I want to be more tentative, and, in the case of an individual who may be challenged by a group's response, affirm more strongly my commitment to their needs. Here's what this might have sounded like: "I want you to ask your question when everyone is fully on board to hear it. Do you mind if I double-check with the group before you proceed?" Hopefully, over time, this will be integrated to such a degree that my intuition will shift.

Given this example, it is as good a moment as any to affirm again that it is never your role to make everyone happy and comfortable. If you think that your job is to keep everyone happy, you might want to reconsider being a facilitator, because you will accumulate too much stress.

Instead, I see the role of the facilitator as being committed to awareness of more and more needs, to giving significance to all the needs that you're aware of, and to attending to them in the best possible way that you know how. This is different from making people happy, because it's a far broader focus, and because you can attend to people's needs by letting them know they matter even when you are unable to actually meet their needs.

It's often easier *after* a moment is over for you or other people to notice what you could have done or think of some other, better way of attending to people's needs. Maybe. In the moment, all you can do is be aware of as many needs as possible and come up with the best possible path forward given the needs and the purpose as you are aware of them. Nothing more and nothing less.

If you are new on the path of honoring your intuition, it is likely to show up as a very tentative voice, easy to dismiss. This is where cultivating it has been so important to me. I always listen to my intuition, and I act on it almost invariably, even when it doesn't make any sense to me. After the fact, if I like the results, I take them apart to understand what contributed to the outcome, and deepen my commitment to those principles, choices, or practices. If I don't like the results, I aim to understand what my intuition omitted, and then to integrate new learnings into my inner core of knowing.

I have found that the more I listen to my intuition, the easier it becomes to follow it and to discern the difference between intuition and figuring things out, on the one hand, and impulse and reaction on the other. While I follow my intuition, I engage differently with my reactions, listening to them for clues about what's important to me so I can choose with consciousness.

For many people, one of the blocks to building intuition is a perpetual sense of insignificance that so many of us walk around with all the time. Cultivating your intuition requires digging underneath that layer of hesitancy to find something that you can *know* is true and that you can trust would be a gift. Some people call that place "the God in us," or you can think of it as the source of Life within you, or clear purpose and wisdom. Whatever the name, it's the deepest truth, which cuts through any insecurities. Following Dawna Markova's poem "Wide Open,"[2] I refer to this willingness to go with what you find there as the act of risking your significance.

This is one of the essential elements of facilitating. We all need to learn to move and respond and assert irrespective of our insecurities. What I have found ends up happening is that facilitation becomes a fast-track course in personal growth. Along the way you are likely to learn that your insecurities are just there, and you learn to give them less power, and eventually they become smaller. What's more, this can happen without you having to cry for years about what happened to you in childhood; you simply gain strength through the doing and then facing and surviving the consequences.

Self-care and support

I have a lot of sadness about the many people I have encountered who do a lot of facilitation and don't have adequate support systems. I want that for every human being on the planet, and definitely for those who take on leadership challenges for the benefit of larger wholes than themselves. This is consuming work, and I want those of us who do it to be able to show up fresh and resilient for the next time, and the next time, and the next time. This is especially critical in the times of great difficulty in which we live, as more and more people are called to collaborate and yet don't quite know how. A lot of responsibility is likely to come to you, and support is truly essential.

This will require you to step out of an ethos of self-sufficiency (if it exists in your culture) and to embrace interdependence as a lived principle rather than just an idea. After all, if you

2 "Wide Open" by Dawna Markova, Ph.D., www.PTPinc.org. This poem is most commonly known by its first line – "I will not live an unlived life" – rather than its *actual* title.

want to facilitate collaboration, interdependence is an integral part, and modeling it in your own way of being will support a higher level of integrity for you.

Similarly, you will likely need to overcome any notion that having needs or limits is a problem, so that you can grow in your capacity to care for yourself and honor your limits. This ranges all the way from learning to say "no" to too many assignments to doing the activities that nourish your soul so you have the necessary energy to show up as a facilitator.

Willingness to live with the consequences of your choices

Facilitation is risky business... There is no way that you can make everyone happy all the time. While this is always true in life as well, it's particularly crucial while facilitating that you have the capacity to make potentially unpopular choices.

One simple and intensely uncomfortable truth is there is no action without consequences. Put more bluntly: There is no action that has the potential to only meet needs. Everything that you do, that any of us does, has some combination of meeting needs and not meeting needs, regardless of how much you care and how much everyone's needs matter to you. And the question is how conscious you want to be about those choices. The more conscious, the more free you are.

If you know yourself to be risk-averse in the area of interpersonal relationships, this would be an important area to develop. As with most qualities, you can build capacity through taking very small steps in the direction of more risk – small and steady, so you can learn to continue to live in peace with the potential negative consequences. It is only then that you can discern what consequences make sense to risk, what your true limits might be, and where you might choose to create change in how you operate to reduce the risk of such consequences. In this way, you might become stronger and clearer as a result of experimenting.

Making room for "difficult people"

Every single one of us has people that are easier for us to deal with and others that are harder. As a facilitator I have made it a deep practice to take ownership of my difficulties instead of putting them on people and judging them. I have trained myself to speak, and also to think, in terms of people who are currently beyond my skill level: I don't have enough capacity *to find ways of responding to them that serve them, me, and* the group. This framing both leaves open the possibility that tomorrow I will know, and also puts the responsibility on me.

Whether it's particular views or certain interpersonal styles, or the nebulous and impossible-to-observe "energy field" you pick up from a particular person, it is your task to train yourself to be able to engage with, care about, and incorporate the needs of every person in every group you facilitate. That is, indeed, a tall order, and one that is fully consistent with my values. Whether through spiritual discipline, through role plays, or through doing healing work, this is essential inner work that is required for the kind of facilitation that is truly committed to everyone's well-being. I have it as my goal to be able to connect fully and have full empathic presence with anyone in a group, and I know that even after many years as a facilitator, I am not fully there. The practice continues. This is as good a moment as any to come back to an earlier point: It's not about being perfect. As Marshall Rosenberg, creator of Nonviolent Communication, suggested, it's about getting better through practice.[3]

Learning from mistakes

One of my colleagues and a dear friend has been a source of immense inspiration for me in this area. Before seeing his journey, I had never imagined how profoundly helpful mistakes can be if used to their maximum potential.

What my friend has been doing for years is to investigate deeply every event he has facilitated. When successful, he celebrates the results, and rigorously looks at what made the success possible that he can learn from for the future. This applies to everything, not just the facilitation itself, though he reviews as many of his choices as he can remember for their rationale and outcome. In addition, he also reviews the relationship with the client, the preparation, the work before the event with client staff, the physical setup, the conditions under which people show up at the event, and the follow-up work. His intention: to identify what he can do more of in future events to achieve more reliable positive results.

When the facilitation engagement doesn't yield the desired results, he reviews, similarly, every decision he made, and applies the same method to it. Given that some of his choices clearly didn't yield the intended outcomes, he also takes time to consider what he could have done instead to be more likely to reach the goal. This is painstaking work, and he does it with joy and dedication.

The result of this thorough approach is twofold. On the one hand, he rarely "attacks" himself, even when he makes significant mistakes. Instead, he has compassion and deep

---

3 The actual words used by Marshall were provocative, as was often his style for making things memorable. That's why he talked about becoming "progressively less stupid."

understanding for why he chose what he chose, coupled with mourning his unsuccessful choices and having immense curiosity about how to improve them in the future. On the other hand, because of this methodical approach, his path has been a steady movement in reliability, presence, and charisma as he continues to do his work.

This is directly related to the willingness to face negative consequences, because without the openness to the risk, it is far harder to engage with what happens. Instead, I have seen in myself and others the tendency to just skip over negative consequences and jump on the next project or event without pausing to learn and integrate.

Sometimes negative consequences happen, and even after a serious review you realize there is really nothing you would change. That is, then, an opportunity to more fully embrace yourself and your integrity and courage, which, still, makes the next time ever so slightly easier to open to. Without this willingness to incur negative consequences, discernment is hard to come by. Ultimately, what you want to aim for is growing in your capacity to remain peaceful when negative consequences happen, while at the same time developing more understanding of what you do to contribute to negative consequences, so you can consider what you might do differently to reduce the chance of this kind of consequence while maintaining your own integrity with your values.

Leading with your strengths and compensating for your challenges

No two facilitators have the same strengths. Your capacity to facilitate will increase the more you learn to look at yourself with honesty and see where you shine. Is it in being able to receive people with warmth and appreciation? Perhaps you always remember to reflect the essence of what they have said with poetic words? Or maybe you have strong graphic sensibilities and can create useful diagrams? Whatever it is, capitalize on your existing strengths and build your facilitation practice around them.

Because you're human, you're not going to shine in all areas. Part of developing your inner capacity includes reaching a state of being able to own, with calm acceptance, all the places where you don't shine. For example, I know that I tend to overestimate people's strength and capacity, and have on many more occasions than I would wish asked people to stretch further than they can truly hold during some of my workshops. Once I understood that, I began to work on increasing my awareness in this area, which is still work in progress. I simultaneously have been training myself to shift my internal discernment (the hardest part of this process!), aiming to remember to check in with people more fully before inviting them to stretch, and asking for feedback and support from others. The result is that it's happening less, and I am hopeful about managing to get to enough awareness that this pattern shifts.

As you begin to take an inventory of your own strengths and challenges, you will find areas that, for you, will require work and commitment to grow into.

In some instances, however, you are likely to discover a challenge that cannot be outgrown. For example, while I am highly skilled and capable in tracking within meetings, which requires only short- and medium-term memory, I don't track well between meetings, because my brain's ability to form new long-term memory was impaired during chemotherapy and menopause. My memory will not expand again. This means that if I want to engage with a group as a facilitator and ongoing consultant, for example, I need to proactively recognize this limitation and find alternate strategies for tracking other than relying on me to remember. It doesn't have to be a pie in the sky. Even something as simple as this would do: "I'd like to take this up in the next meeting, after we handle x, y, and z, but I am not confident that I will remember. Would you be willing to take the responsibility for bringing this up again next week?"

What are some of these areas for yourself? What might you learn to fully accept as a permanent limitation? How will you develop the willingness to ask for support to make up for the challenge? What might that support look like before, during, and after facilitating a group?

Lastly, you may have more challenges than you have capacity to work on in self-development. Those areas that you cannot make a priority at present would also then become opportunities to ask for support to compensate for the present lack in your repertoire of capacities.

Orienting Toward Your Role as a Facilitator

Whatever you do to develop yourself outside the context of facilitation increases your capacity and resilience when you facilitate. Such resilience allows you to be in much more choice about how you facilitate, especially how you respond to unforeseen circumstances and challenges that arise in the room.

Bear in mind that, like any person who writes about facilitation, I am biased in favor of my approach to facilitation, which is highly transparent, flexible, and active. This bias colors my own choices when I facilitate as well as what I focus on here. My greatest hope is that you can look at what

I describe below as resources to you rather than the gospel of facilitation. As I discussed above, you will need to follow your own style, rely on your own strengths, and compensate for your areas of weakness rather than attempt to emulate anyone else.

In this section, then, I provide a collection of ways of focusing your attention and choice-making energy – both of which are your most precious resources – that I believe can support you in being available for a group you facilitate.

Recognizing and utilizing your power

As a facilitator, you are in a never-ending practice: to decide, moment to moment, what you want to do next with the group, and invite the group to then decide with you. This spells a dual aim: to shape a direction, and to leave room for input. Truly *any* time there is a decision point, such as someone asking a question, you are called to decide whether or not you want to take the question and open a new loop. Most of the time, this is a decision that you will want to make on your own. Some of the time, you will want to include the group in making it. Even that choice is one you will need to make. And, some of the time, you will be caught in the dilemma without knowing.

Whatever happens in you affects the group, because as a facilitator you have power (much more on that in Chapter 6). Simply put: Any time you turn to the group – when you have a dilemma, or when you have a preference – *how* you frame the moment and what question you ask has a huge influence on the group. Because, except in unusual circumstances, groups entrust themselves to the facilitator, whatever you ask for, the group will tend to grant you. Be mindful of this, and utilize it for supporting the group's purpose.

You are the only one who decides what your own preference

is and how widely you are going to open to hearing dissenting views on the matter at hand, if at all. If you are not sure, ask for space, and use it. It's easier for a group to wait, even a whole minute, when you tell them what you are doing than for you to just stand and think without them knowing what's going on; for example, "I'm not sure where to ask us to go next. We could stay with what we were talking about or we could turn our attention to the last comment. Please would you hold on for 30 seconds while I figure out what I want to ask the group?"

Once you know what you want to do, frame it clearly and transparently, ideally by tying the dilemma to the group's purpose and also presenting it as a choice. Depending on what you think will serve the group and how strongly you feel that, you will ask different questions. A group will respond very differently to "Is this something you still have energy to discuss? Please raise your hands if you do" than to "I really don't want to go on until we address what just came up, as I am concerned about trust in the group. Is there anyone who can't accept that?"[4]

The choice of what thread to follow and what question to ask is a constant process of decision-making for a facilitator. In order to make useful choices for the group, you will need to become familiar with yourself to know where you might want to overcompensate. For example, some of us tend in the direction of directive intervention, some in the direction of expressing care for anyone who might possibly need it. Be aware of which direction is the stretch for you, and learn to exercise that stretch as one of your options.

---

4 A full discussion about the differences between these questions, and the overall art of how to invite dissent or willingness, is presented in Chapters 4 and 5.

Willingness to reconsider plans

Planning is an essential ingredient in preparing for facilitation. You want to have an idea, before coming into a room, about the steps you want to take to achieve the group's purpose. Without a plan, you will have nothing to lean on when the inevitable "disruptions" arise. That said, your plan, by definition, happened *before* knowing the conditions in the moment, and cannot, therefore, be the only guideline for how to respond to what happens. If you prioritize plans over and above the specific individuals in front of you, especially when they are struggling, you are likely to lose their trust. You will also lose their trust if you drop the plan every time something happens in the room.

What to do, then? For me, the art of facilitation includes aiming for a way to weave what is happening, the unexpected, *into* the intended purpose as a way of revising the plan without losing the intent and without losing the people. The purpose will influence what I listen for when I listen, how I would determine when to check in with the group, and what I might say to the group at that time.

If the purpose of the meeting is to create criteria for success of a project, for example, then I would listen to what the "disruptor" says to hear either hidden criteria that are expressed indirectly, or to hear reasons why focusing on the criteria may be premature and there is other work that needs to be done first. For as long as I continue to hear new criteria, I can capture them and stay engaged. The second option, whenever that appears to me to be more aligned, is to change the plan and do something else first, not instead. Here, the skill of transparency that we looked at in the previous chapter is what I would draw on as I clue the group in on why I no longer believe that the necessary conditions are in place for having an effective discussion about criteria for success, and invite the group to decide with me instead of deciding for them.

If the group is coming together to decide on a budget for the project, then I would focus on gleaning, from whatever appears as a distraction, more information about what would support a budget decision that works for all *even if this is not what the person is consciously offering*. In fact, they may be criticizing another department for profligate expenses, and I could still extract useful information for the budget from what they say. As in the previous example, I remain open to the possibility that something else needs to happen, such as talking about how to improve relations with the other department before making any budget decisions.

At times, this dance can be quite tricky, because it relies on being able to stay open both to what you came in wanting to do and the purpose of that while at the same time being open to what is emerging and what people want. Imagine, for example, that a group you are facilitating is drifting in a direction that isn't aligned with your own sense of what would most contribute to the purpose for which they are there – perhaps by engaging in some discussion that is clearly meaningful for them and yet isn't moving the conversation forward towards a decision.

This might require a complex dialogue with the group. For that, you will need to know clearly what is inside you and honor it sufficiently to be in dialogue with the group, with what it is that the people want to do. When I am in this kind of dialogue I experience it like a dance – on the one hand I know I want to be fully open to what the people want, and on the other hand I want to maintain my own clarity within me of what I believe will be a gift to the group, ultimately finding a way to bring the two together. On two ends of this dance are two risky situations. One is that I have so much clarity about where I want to take the conversation that I am no longer attentive to whether it works for the people or not, thereby subtly giving them an experience that they don't matter. The other end is that I so much want to be supportive of where people want to go, that I completely lose track of what the voice of clarity in me points me to in terms of where I want to go next. In this instance I can easily disappear and just follow people and associative threads without having the focus that would bring the group to closure. Both inner clarity and flexibility are essential for completing this kind of dance.

Patience

Patience on my part allows the group to slow down and to grow in acceptance of what is happening. If I demonstrate capacity to stay the course with an outlier, for example (a topic I return to more fully in Chapter 5), it supports the group in having more trust that there is something of value in what that person says.

In the same manner, my own impatience, if and when I have it, can be destabilizing for a group. For example, if someone expresses an objection to a potential decision, and I respond impatiently, this will affect the entire group, not only that one person. Everyone will take in that this could happen to them – that if they express an objection, it might be dealt with impatiently. Impatience on my part consumes energy from the group. Everyone looks to the facilitator to understand what happens in the room, to get a sense of what behaviors are accepted or not, and to have a sense of who matters and who doesn't. To put it in dramatic terms: Impatience on my part interferes with the optimal conditions for dialogue and trust within the group.

Embracing uncertainty
by releasing attachments

As a facilitator, I have learned to overcome a great many forms of attachment that initially were interfering with my ability to simply be with a group and support them to move towards convergence. This is inner work initially, and subsequently an ongoing commitment while facilitating about how to show up and what conceptual and even spiritual frame to hold for my work.

- *From what's fair to what's possible.* I have come to see the idea of fairness as divisive, often used as a weapon of separation and an attempt to gain the upper hand, which is generally inconsistent with the radical notion that guides my work with groups: a solution that can work for everyone. I share this with groups, to the extent possible without challenging norms beyond their trust level. I put it on the practical level, not in terms of what is right, and that usually helps people accept my choices. They can see that putting much effort into what they may think is "fair" when it's clearly not possible is not a wise choice.
- *From what's right to what attends to purpose and needs.* Similarly, one of the ways in which I can cut down on unnecessary discussion is by avoiding the trap of discussing the merits of different ideas and trying to argue with each other about the right approach. Instead, I once again focus on the practical aspects. For example, when someone expresses concerns about a proposal that some others are favoring, I could imagine asking that person: "What would be your proposal to improve on this while maintaining the qualities that the proposal you are concerned about has?"

- *From the all-knowing facilitator to a person sensing things.*
  This is a topic I already covered in significant detail in
  the previous chapter. I am including it here because it's
  a significant part of the overall framing of my role and
  way of being as a facilitator. Thus, for example, instead of
  saying "This conversation is irrelevant," which places me
  in the position of God, I vastly prefer saying: "I don't see
  the relevance of what you're saying to our overall purpose.
  Are you open to writing it down and bringing it up later
  with me at break?" This is also about how we might recover
  from having said something that implies that I know: "I
  noticed that you withdrew from the conversation right
  after I labeled what you talked about as irrelevant. I regret
  how I said it and the effect that it had on you that I see
  now. I don't regret that I brought up the topic. I obviously
  did something that didn't work, so I am asking for your
  feedback..." This way of speaking puts me on the same plane
  as everyone else, and that's likely a big part of why this
  form of transparency tends to work so well to achieve trust.

Attending to group energy

One of the images that has worked well for people who've
been at my facilitation trainings is the image of a ball that
it's our task to keep in the air at all times. That ball is group
energy. Although we can never *know* anything about what's
truly happening in the group, only intuit it, there are a few
elements that regularly affect group energy that you can
cultivate and educate your intuition about through practice
and attention. Below are a few of them; you will learn and
discover more over time.

- *Discussion.* Even if a discussion is really animated, it tends
  to polarize and to keep some people engaged at the expense

of others. For the group as a whole, discussions are taxing. This is why I rely so much on show-of-hand questions instead of open-ended ones. It's also what informs the particular type of questions I use in looking for whether the group is ready to convert a proposal to a decision. (See Chapter 5 for more details on that.)

- *Focus on one or a few individuals.* When what happens in the group begins to focus on one or a very few individuals, the others can easily become restless. This is particularly tricky, because as the facilitator, it could be tempting to imagine there is high energy in the group because *your* energy may be engaged with that person.

- *Group process fatigue.* After a while, groups lose their energy regardless of what you do. Being in a group, even with a facilitator that holds the whole steadily, consumes a fair amount of energy, because it focuses attention in very particular ways. Just the fact that most of the time most people are not able to speak because only one person at a time can speak means that much accumulates internally that has little to no outlet.

- *Challenges and conflict.* When there is a lot of challenge or strife in the group, that, too, takes a toll. Most people have some degree of conflict aversion, so even if you and the people who are more comfortable with conflict are tolerating it well, many people may have at least low-grade anxiety.

- *Confusion about process.* Any time there is lack of clarity about what's happening or, especially, what's expected from the group at any given moment, the energy quickly drops. This is why making requests is so helpful for a group: By asking a question and letting people know how to answer it (hopefully, mostly, through a show of hands, as you will soon learn), you are attending to this element and keeping the energy higher.

- *Open loops.* Open loops, such as requests not attended to, shifting to new topics without finishing a previous one, or people whose needs are unattended for a while, tend to tax group energy even if they are not consciously remembered by the group. As much as possible, aim to close loops as close to when they open as possible. Closing a loop doesn't necessarily mean attending to all the details of an item. Putting things up on a list that's visible to all is enough so long as a mechanism for getting back to such lists is known to all.

So what to do if you notice the energy dropping? How can you lift the ball higher in the air? Broadly speaking, you can do it by shifting the activity (a dyad activity or a break), reconnecting people to purpose (explicitly tying what's happening to the purpose), infusing faith into the room, or naming what is happening and inviting the group to reflect on how to address it.

If at any point in time you are not sure how to attend to a drop in energy, give the group something to do while you figure out your next choice instead of keeping them focused on you and waiting, which is taxing for them and likely stressful for you.

The Nuts and Bolts of Facilitating Groups

The inner work prepares you for being able to be present and free to choose when facilitating. Even with the full commitment to this approach, including adopting the particular orientation to your role as a facilitator I present here, there are still a host of specific types of challenges that call for specific facilitation skills. This section covers a number of those skills without aiming to be exhaustive. The next two chapters cover principles and facilitation skills that are more narrowly focused on supporting collaborative decision-making.

Making requests in a group

One of the core skills involved in facilitation is the practice of making requests in a group which I introduced in Chapter 2. Making requests is the way in which you can make decisions with the group instead of for the group. They are your primary way of knowing whether or not the group is ready to make a certain decision – whether about its purpose or about a next step in a process. Making requests in a group is also your way of getting quick feedback about what's happened so far, thereby also supporting you in assessing what to do next.

Making requests in a group calls for different skills than making requests of an individual, because the potential for runaway discussion is ever present in a group the second you loosen the reins of the process.

In order to keep the process moving with efficiency and care for everyone, the art of it is about finding a way to make the response as easy as possible while providing as much information as you need as a facilitator in order to know how to guide the group and the process next – and to do that with high efficiency relative to the current goal. Overall, aim to ask questions that will minimize discussion when you don't want discussion, or that will make room for it when you do want it. This is the art of making requests in groups.

While doing this is an art form, there are still a couple of guidelines you can use to support your experimentation.

Questions with yes or no answers. Whenever possible, make a request to the group that invites people to raise their hand instead of implicitly calling on them to speak – that provides efficiency.

To make that happen, I aim for a question that's clear enough so that people can say yes or no to it, and invite them to raise their hand if they want to say yes. I avoid open-ended questions like, "I want to know how people feel about our lunch break." Those questions are unlikely to give me the information I want, and easily devolve to chaos.

On the most practical level, the practice is to start the question with "How many people...?"

Drawing people out with requests. One of my own least favorite kind of group to facilitate is a room full of nice, polite people. This is because nice, polite people need a lot more support, and thus require more work of me, in order to speak truth. Without everyone's truth, we cannot get to a solution that *truly* works for everyone, not only on the surface. Here's one way you can approach a group in order to draw out the silent people who appear to go along with everything.

> I'm surprised that only one person has raised their hand with concerns... If you're not sharing what's on your mind, I worry that the decision will not be as robust. Don't worry about rocking the boat. I truly believe that you will serve the group well by saying what's on your mind.

What if no one still raises their hand? If you are still really concerned, you can surely ask again, and then wait.

I'm waiting because I am still concerned. I would love to hear from more people.

If you're still concerned, you could – though it's even more uncomfortable – ask specific individuals to give their opinion about the matter at hand. If they say they are OK with the proposed decisions, and they are not telling the truth, there is really nothing more you can do, and the group will need to learn the hard way what happens when not everything is shared up front. One other strategy is to go around the room and have everyone speak, which reduces the pressure on any one individual, and tends to bring out much more feedback. *Why, then, not do it always? Because it's the most resource-*consumptive way of responding to a proposal in terms of time and group energy.

Weaving needs together with requests. One of the ways you can serve a group in your role as a facilitator is to directly move towards convergence. For example, suppose you're trying to decide, with a group, whether to wait for latecomers or start at the agreed-upon time, and you're hearing opposing opinions. You can aim for convergence from the very first moment. If Martha expresses her concern about waiting, from which you gleaned that she wants to maximize learning time, you could turn to the group and say:

> Hearing that this is Martha's concern about maximizing our learning and movement, is that enough for you to shift? Are you willing to go ahead and start? Or is there something important about waiting that you'd like to express?

Let's say that Jamal then expresses his concern about people coming in and not being able to participate. Here's what you might say then:

> So you want to wait so the people who are not here have the chance to participate with us from the start. Does anyone have a suggestion that would address both concerns?

If you experiment in this way, you will gradually discover that groups can be amazingly creative if invited to do so. One group, in this exact scenario, created an elaborate system of buddies for the latecomers, and then got to work with everyone on board.

Responding to challenging moments

The facilitation challenge related to emotionally charged moments is to decide, moment by moment, how much attention to give to the specific situation and how much to the overall purpose of the group. Not attending to emotional challenges at all and staying focused only on purpose reduces trust and safety within the group. Attending to it to full and utter completion is at cost to purpose; groups sense that and tend to lose trust with that choice, too.

The frame that I use for myself is aiming to reach sufficient partial completion or connection so that everyone involved can shift focus to the purpose at hand without emotional "casualties." Like much of everything else about facilitation, you will need to develop your own intuition and discernment which will take both knowing yourself and experimentation.

Part of knowing yourself has to do with recognizing your own habitual preference in terms of finding the "sufficiency" point, which then allows you to experiment more consciously. Over time, you increase your range of options and you can then find the sweet spot for *you*.

For example, if your tendency is always to prioritize following the thread of unresolved emotion, your discernment and learning would likely be in the area of learning to notice and attend to the loss with regards to the group's purpose. For example, you might learn, over time, that it's possible to notice that someone is uncomfortable and name it as an observation without necessarily choosing to do anything about it. Similarly, when someone in the group asks, directly or indirectly, for attention to their own or someone else's emotional state, it doesn't mean you "must" do what they want if you assess that it's at cost to purpose.

Conversely, if your tendency is always to prioritize the purpose of the group without giving sufficient attention to emotional charges, it may mean that groups you facilitate reach their goals at costs that are too high for the well-being of the group. In this case, you will need to learn how to open your heart and mind more easily to what may appear to you like distractions, and use the fact that you already know how to stay focused on purpose to support you in responding efficiently. You can do this in one (or both) of two ways after doing some reflection. One is to help the person get to a request, so the person with the challenge is the one leading the group with your support. The other is by taking the lead yourself about what to do next, being transparent about that, and soliciting feedback from the group. In other words: You end up deciding how you want to respond and which way to go while still having enough information to take into consideration the person's wishes and caring for all needs present.

Here are two examples to illustrate these possibilities.

Imagine that a participant, Jorge, takes the floor more often than anyone else, repeatedly saying, "There's no way to prioritize the issues and complete the presentation before the board meeting." Here's how you might lead them to a request:

> I get a sense that you want the group to be ready for the board meeting. Would you like to see if others are willing to focus on two or three issues and have at least those ready for the meeting?

This kind of wording may well register with Jorge as supporting him by recognizing the likely limitations and offering him a way to move forward without getting into a whole discussion about whether or not the group can attend to all it was asked to do.

Still, even this might take more attention from the group than you would like, so, as always, you have other options for how to respond. Here's what the second option – transparency about your own preference and making your own request – might look like:

> Even though this is challenging for you, I have total faith that we can move through the entire agenda. Would it work for you to wait until lunch and evaluate our progress then?

One particular point of discernment is about recognizing the difference between your own personal satisfaction and completion of an interaction and the degree to which continuing an interaction would serve the group's purpose.

If you are not sure, there is always the option of checking with the group. Without explicitly checking with the group, you don't know whether they are connecting or benefiting from it or not. If you don't check with the group, you still only have your own internal experience to gauge by. You may be seeing something on their faces, and yet it's still your interpretation and your assessment.

Like everything else in facilitation, both checking with a group and not checking with a group have potential consequences. In some instances, checking with an individual or with the group can increase trust that people's well-being is held. In some other instances, it's taxing for the group to be asked and to process yet one more decision. Part of the art of facilitating is to develop an intuition about when and when not. Only your own experience will train you sufficiently.

For now, here's an example of a sequence that you might follow after attending to a challenging moment.

You might start by looking back to the people who raised the issue and check with them: "Do you feel heard about your concern?"

Assuming the person is complete, you might next check with the group: "Raise your hand if you have a sense that what we did was sufficient to attend to this concern." Depending on the result, you might ask one or the other sub-group to stretch. If only a few raise their hand, you might ask them for willingness to continue with the topic – even if they sense it's enough – because it's not sufficient for others. If most raise their hand, you could ask the others if they are willing to shift focus even if they are not entirely complete.

If you decide to proceed to some other topic, you might choose to make yourself available to feedback later:

If anyone has feedback for me about what I've said or what we've discussed, I'd be glad to receive it at a break.

One important consideration that many facilitators forget is that there is no "rule" that you must get to a point where everyone feels completely heard and resolved about whatever has transpired. All you need is their willingness to shift focus if that's what you aim for, especially if you sense that the group is saturated with processing emotion.

How to listen to participants in a group

One of my fundamental commitments as a facilitator is to make use of every moment and everything that happens. A corollary of this is that I see having people speak in a group without anything happening with their words as a sadly wasted resource. When someone speaks, and you as a facilitator don't say anything, that drops the ball. In other words: *Speaking* is part of how you show that you are *listening*. Go beyond only saying "mmm" as the person speaks. Experiment with different forms of speech until you find your own way. It could be something as simple as: "Let me take that in and then see what I want to do about it." That is enough to keep the group's attention.

With that, I then focus on harvesting every bit of wisdom and information that is hidden in what people say. Sometimes, it takes excavating to find deeper layers of meaning that can truly serve the group. Doing it is one of the keys that open the door to convergence. Conversely, I find that being non-directive and letting people speak to each other with minimal intervention tends to polarize or to create unidimensional group coherence that doesn't address complexity.

This may go against the training you have received as a facilitator, which often focuses on making room for people to speak what's on their mind and heart. I understand fully why this training is in place: It's an attempt to give people a sense that they matter and are being heard. My concern is that speaking by itself doesn't necessarily give people the experience of being heard. If I focus on the deeper need – to be heard and to matter – those can often be attended to more effectively by certain specific forms of verbal reflection. When done well, such reflection can deepen the conversation in the room and give even people who haven't said a word the experience of being included.

The key: I focus, in my reflection, on something positive that I sense the person speaking wants, and, whenever possible, couch it in terms that speak to the group as a whole – what everyone might want for everyone – rather than in terms that speak just to that individual – what the speaker might want for themselves.

Focusing on the positive – what people want, and why they want it, rather than what people believe is right or true – makes it easier to converge, especially when the concern is couched in terms that everyone can relate to. In addition, I have found, repeatedly, that the focus on the positive helps a challenging conversation settle faster. I tend to think that the reason is that the very act of focusing on what's wanted begins to feel like movement in that direction. Conversely, focusing on what we don't want, keeps us locked in those conditions.

Here are some examples of things people might say, and a possible reflection that aims to be positive, more universal, and noncontroversial.

Context	Speech and Reflection	Comments
Facilitating a process of reshuffling people's seating arrangements in an office	My desk is too small. I imagine what's important to you is that everyone have the physical conditions to do their job well. Is this why you want a bigger desk?	Extrapolating from the specific category of desk to the larger category of physical conditions – as close as possible without focusing on the speaker's individual issue.
A team-building retreat, where people speak about their concerns with their team leader	I want John to stop being abusive. Are you saying this because you want a sense of safety at work, a respectful environment that fosters trust?	Others can recognize themselves in what's wanted whether or not they agree that John is abusive.
Staff meeting	We can't offer comp time anymore. Everyone has to work a 40-hour week. And no overtime, either. So just get used to it. I get a visceral sense of how important this is to you. Is the issue that you want human resources to be utilized in an effective and fair manner?	The broadening allows more people to join in and diffuses the tone of accusation that could easily polarize a group.

To sum up: The positive and expansive frame of reflection works by allowing both the speaker and the rest of the group to recognize themselves. Especially when working on decision-making, to which I turn with more focus in the coming chapters, you want to identify enough specificity for your reflection to be recognizable by the speaker and to serve as a guide to action and solutions later, and universal enough to be recognized by all. You want to give the individual a sense of being heard while making it relevant for the group. In a polarized setting, this form of listening is like a "zing" in the group, because suddenly they see that they all want something that this person wants.

Here are some more tips about listening:

- *Show don't tell.* Instead of saying "I understand" or "I hear you," you can show your understanding by identifying what's really important to them, expressing it in noncontroversial language, and checking with them to see if your expression matches what they wanted to be heard about.
- *Listen without responding.* Stay with the person speaking until they are fully heard. Any time you shift focus and respond in any way, such as arguing, reassuring, presenting more data, or sharing your own opinion, *it shifts the energy* from the other person to you. Stick with them. In particular, resist the temptation to try to convince them of anything. In short, it never works. Listen first, and only speak when you truly have the other's attention, which rarely happens without being heard first.
- *No buts or ands.* If you want to respond to what the person is saying rather than simply hearing them, which is rarely helpful to someone who wants to be heard, separate your response and wait till later. Most especially, avoid sentences such as "I hear that you want ... but (or and) we still need to ..." Instead, confirm with the person that you hear them accurately, and only then offer what you want them to hear.
- *Take people at face value.* If you can cultivate, on purpose and on principle, a practice of hearing people at face value, you will soon discover that people trust you and lower their protection around you, because it's so powerful for any of us to be heard in that way. If you're thinking about their agenda, you're losing the ability to just be with a person and see what happens next.

Stepping in – cultivating interruption skills

As much as many cultures frown on interruption and admonish us to respectfully wait until someone is done, as a facilitator you will likely discover that such waiting usually doesn't serve the group, and often enough doesn't even serve the person speaking. When a person speaks in a group, it commands group attention, which is a highly "expensive" resource when facilitating a group. This is why I make a point of stepping in to capture what is being said and use it for supporting the group's purpose, and work hard to minimize discussion between people in a group that doesn't get such focused reflection.

There are several key aspects to learning how to step in effectively, covering the why, the when, and the how. There is a reason why many of us feel anxious and uncomfortable about stopping someone. It's because being stopped, in and of itself, is an experience that stimulates pain for many of us almost independently of how gentle the stopping is. As best I understand it, the pain that is stimulated is related to the fundamental need of wanting our needs to matter to others. If you can remember this as you think about your choices, you are more likely to speak in a way that serves the group and the individual.

Why? There is essentially one core reason to step in: You sense, inside yourself, loss of energy or purpose in the group as a person continues to speak. Marshall Rosenberg speaks of it as learning to "interrupt a dead conversation to bring it back to life."[5] Before choosing to step in, though, bear in mind that even if you yourself are not enjoying or appreciating what someone is saying, if you sense that others are with the person

---

5 *Nonviolent Communication: A Language of Life*, p. 122.

and that the content of what they are saying is contributing to the group's purpose, then your task is to work internally to make sufficient room for the person speaking so that when they are done you will be able to then summarize and reflect what it adds to the group's purpose. You might still choose to step in if you lose trust in your capacity to track or retain what the person is saying sufficiently to make use of it when they are done.

On occasion, you might need to step in to protect the group or an individual from harm. This kind of situation goes to a level of challenge that is beyond my current focus which is, primarily, on facilitation skills designed for supporting groups in reaching decisions.

When? Marshall Rosenberg's wisdom about this question is unequivocal: "The best time to interrupt is when we've heard one word more than we want to hear. The longer we wait, the harder it is to be civil when we do step in."[6] I want to step in when I can do it with enough love, generosity, and care to extend beyond the discomfort and even shame that might arise for the person whose words are stopped for me to speak. Ideally, I want my stepping in to be a connecting experience for all. If you wait too long hoping that it will get easier, you run the risk of reaching a state of just wishing for the person to disappear. They become an obstacle to get through rather than a person to connect with. From that internal state, it's mighty difficult to step in and do it compassionately. What I call "non-generous listening" rarely converts back into genuine interest. You may as well not let it get there.

---

6 *Nonviolent Communication: A Language of Life*, p. 122.

This is the key thing that we need to work on to make our interruption a gift rather than a sore spot for another person. It's why I believe that "letting people speak" can be a disservice even to them. If you just go through the motions and wait for the speech to be over, it's a form of violence to yourself, and by extension to the person speaking. Even if you don't say it, if you're full of judgments, the energy of that often comes across. Similarly, if you have waited too long and *then* you aim to step in, you're likely to do it stepping *over* your fears and anxiety rather than walking *through* them to the other end of freedom and spaciousness inside. This will dramatically increase the chances that the other person will have an "Oh, I did something wrong!" reaction, which is definitely at odds with what you want to create as a facilitator. If you've waited too long, you will likely need to pause for a while, regain your compass and compassion, and then speak.

How? What I aim for when stepping in is to find a way to convey care for the person speaking, my purpose for stepping in, and clarity about what I want to see next. I want my words to be quick enough to dance with the flow and thorough enough to allow the person to settle. Here are a few examples:

> I want you to speak when I am fully able to give you my attention, and I am not quite there in this moment. I am noticing that there is some worry coming up in me about whether the rest of the group is still with you, and this worry is interfering with my ability to stay present with you. So that I can be present with you, are you OK with me checking with the group where they are before you continue?

I really want to understand fully what you are saying and what you want about it, and I am struggling a bit with that. It will help me immensely if you'd take just a moment to pause and see what the crux of this is for you? I think that would be easier for me to hear and understand.

Hang on, before you carry on, I'd like to pause for a moment because I think you completed something. I want to make sure I capture the essence of that before I forget, because I see it as vital to our success to take in what everyone says. [Then reflect / summarize.] Was this it? *Is there more that you want to say?*

I want to tell you what I heard so far and I'm not going to use the same words that you did. [Then proceed with a reflection/summary.] Is this what you wanted me to hear?

Stepping in is not necessarily comfortable, for all the reasons I mentioned earlier and probably others, too. I still believe it is essential to learn how to do it with the most elegance and care possible. Whatever I said above, and with all the examples I provided, it's still something you can only learn through experimenting. My own learning, still incomplete, has taken a lot of trial and a lot of error, too.

Leaning on purpose

Given how important shared purpose is for the group's ability to function well, one of your key tools is the shared purpose of the group and of the specific meeting. This is one key piece of the glue that keeps the group together. That said, it is something that you will need to track on your own, because groups pass this responsibility to you and often can get lost in the heat of the moment. If you, too, lose track of the purpose, then the group is lacking a key resource for its functioning.

Just as much as I will try to redirect a group away from doing personal healing when the purpose is to make a decision, I will aim to redirect a group away from making any business decisions when the reason why the group is meeting is for mutual support, when personal healing may be just exactly what's needed.

I aim to maintain humility, since I don't actually *know* what is or isn't on topic; I only have an intuition, and until I check with the group and decide with them, it's still under investigation. When I believe what's happening is off topic, I consider this a call to action, and present it to the group. I have noticed many times in groups that unconscious priority is assigned to intensity, for example, and I want to support groups in truly choosing whether to follow the thread of intensity of expression or the initial plan for their time.

Here are some of the instances where calling on purpose might be particularly effective in addition to other approaches we may have already covered.

Dealing with emotions or conflict during a business meeting. Often enough, groups get lost when a conflict or some other intensity erupts and all the attention goes to it. Unless the purpose of the group is learning how to deal with conflict, or related purposes such as personal growth, you can serve the group by reminding people of the purpose and working to establish just enough connection for everyone to be present for the purpose at hand. Essentially, your goal in such moments is to acknowledge and address the tip of the iceberg so you provide enough care and connection to deal supportively with these "bubbles" without shifting the overall focus of the group.

Once again, making clear requests will be a key tool. Look for a small pause, a kind of "parking place" – which can easily happen after offering basic acknowledgment and a little bit of empathy to whoever is involved – and then follow with a request such as one of the following:

1. "It looks like you got some understanding – is this enough? Are you comfortable moving back to the purpose of our meeting?"
2. "Is there anything else you want me to hear before we shift our attention?"
3. "Anything else important for me to hear before we go back to our previous discussion?"

Even if there is a lot of intensity going on, it doesn't mean that the entire group must change its focus.

4. "I can see there is a lot going on for you. I'd like us to choose together what to do – get some support right now in the meeting so you can return to the topic, or leave the meeting with someone else and get to the bottom of it, understanding that you'll miss part of what's going on here until you get back."

In all of these examples, I am aiming to describe what is happening to give the other person and the group full information to help with *their* decision-making, which is separate from my own. As a facilitator, I aim to be open to whatever the response is, trusting I can meet it with the same tools, and knowing that I do not have the job of solving the person's problem; only to care and do all I know to do to attend to needs.

In all of this, I want to remember that while I want to prioritize the original purpose, it is also the case that purpose can shift if the conditions are such that it's no longer possible to attend to it. Otherwise, I am simply being dogmatic. This possibility, too, I want to bring to the group to decide together.

> Emotions are so high I would like us to deal with them. I don't trust our planning under these conditions. Anyone seeing it differently?

Lastly, be aware of your limits. Remember that facilitation is not designed for healing or reconciliation although they do sometimes happen; pause, change course, or continue based also on your own capacity to continue giving and being present, not just your assessment of the group.

Matching your style to group norms

There is a fundamental empathic orientation that is intrinsic to facilitation. I see it as vitally important for each of us, when we walk into a room, to remember that we're facilitating *this* group for *their* purpose, not for *our* purpose. This orientation is an integral part of the commitment to holding the whole and attending to all needs.

Let me illustrate with my own challenges. As a facilitator steeped in the paradigm of collaboration, I have a particular challenge of learning to work with groups which are far less interested in collaboration than I am. This is a style mismatch, and if I don't tend to it with care, it could create a trust issue with the group. This is particularly challenging for me, personally, because I truly have a not-so-secret mission to create a world that is 100 percent collaborative, which puts me at odds with people in the room, and could easily lead to me slipping into my own "agenda" of educating the group about collaboration rather than supporting them in achieving their purpose, whatever it is.

When I know that the context is different from my own habits, I adapt to the group norms without compromising my integrity. If they're used to operating in a top-down manner and I'm not adjusting, I'm useless to them. The adaptation is not a wholesale abandonment of my collaborative style. I change things like the frequency with which I engage the group, how far I open the way for them to express dissent, and what kind of language I use. This is a way to still be collaborative and give people a sense that someone is in charge and there is structure, if that's what they're used to.

With regards to the language, I listen carefully to how the people in the room speak, and aim to stay, as much as possible, within their range of comfort about language. I know that the process itself will provide ample opportunities for stretching and discomfort; there's no need to stretch them around language or manners that may seem "touchy-feely," or to impose a level of vulnerability that is unfamiliar and not part of their group norm.

So, instead of "I'm wondering where that leaves you?" – which is perfectly acceptable in many personal growth groups, in a business setting I might say, instead, "Is this a good place to stop or is there more?" Vulnerability is something that people protect fiercely in a setting in which everything can be used against them.

In Summary

I've been facilitating groups for at least 25 years. No one ever taught me how, and I often am amazed at how I managed to get up and keep going when encountering challenge after challenge without guidance or even a whole lot of support initially. I wrote this chapter, in part, in the hope of sparing you at least some of this pain as you make your own experiments. My intention was to provide a basic roadmap knowing the road will still have its bumps. There is no way of avoiding them altogether.

However experienced you are or not as a facilitator, learning Convergent Facilitation will invite you into new discoveries. First and foremost, you will get in touch with your own intuition, as you learn to see, moment by moment, what you are drawn to do, and continually test out that sense against reality. Second, you will be called to be ever more transparent and collaborative as you learn to make requests of groups and involve them in process decisions just to the degree that your intuition suggests. Lastly, you will learn how to stretch to hold with care every person in the group as well as the group's purpose as you navigate the impossible and necessary dilemmas of being with groups.

With that, we can now turn to the specific application for which Convergent Facilitation was created: supporting groups in making collaborative decisions about matters of significance to them. Everything you've learned so far will come in handy, and you will also encounter new principles and skills that deepen what you learned already.

Facilitation Principles for Efficient Collaboration

CHAPTER FOUR

There are three ways of dealing with difference: domination, compromise, and integration. By domination only one side gets what it wants; by compromise neither side gets what it wants; by integration we find a way by which both sides may get what they wish.

— MARY PARKER FOLLETT[1]

INCLUDING PEOPLE IN DECISION-MAKING is often a challenge because most people don't have successful experiences combining collaboration with efficiency. Convergent Facilitation was born from the conviction that fully collaborative decisions are entirely possible. Moreover, my experience tells me that, with skillful facilitation, collaboration often yields *better* decisions without compromising efficiency. The requirement to reach a decision that works for everyone, combined with complete confidence and openness, often results in creative solutions that no one would have been able to think of on their own, when only holding their own perspective and needs. In addition, the decisions tend to be more robust, buy-in increases, and productivity in implementation is fueled by high morale. In short: This commitment results in the group reaching its highest common denominator.

The catch is, of course, with how the group is being facilitated. Because the skills are not widely spread, because of deeply ingrained habits of either/or thinking, and because of short-term focus, decisions are still routinely made by one person, a management team, or a majority vote. That process appears faster and more efficient, and thus more appealing, especially when tension arises and most acutely within the fast-paced environment of modern businesses and workplaces.

I consider this state of affairs tragic under the best of circumstances, because everyone is deprived of the wisdom and generative energy that accompanies well-managed collaboration. When decisions are made unilaterally, often issues, gaps, and problems don't surface until implementation time, and can delay or even block implementation. Often

1   Mary Parker Follett, *Dynamic Administration: The Collected Papers of Mary Parker Follett* (Martino Fine Books, 2003).

the issues are known earlier, but those making the decisions don't hear about them in time, as people don't speak up for fear of consequences, are discouraged about being heard, or don't trust that their needs and perspectives matter. For example, a company had to recall an entire shipment of a product because no one had the courage to tell the company owners of a defect in the production process that had been discovered much earlier. Hundreds of thousands of dollars could have been saved!

Furthermore, people who are involved with carrying out a decision they were not active participants in making are unlikely to be committed to the success of the strategy chosen, even when they are committed to doing their job well. This is even more pronounced if they are not happy with the decision or believe it would interfere with delivering a quality product or service. It is not uncommon for a person in the field to make unauthorized changes or to obstruct implementation of decisions and agreements made to the point of even engaging in what is commonly called "sabotage."

Lastly, even if implementation can proceed, the absence of explicit buy-in up front for a decision can often show up indirectly as conflict, resentment, or sarcasm down the line, affecting morale and therefore productivity.

Despite these high costs, more often than not unilateral decision-making continues to be the norm. Deena (not her real name), a small business owner, articulates clearly what may be an underlying reason for this practice.

> I don't take the time to get the buy-in and really hear them ... because I feel that if I hear them I need to do what they want... [This] somehow takes power away

from me... a little bit of fear comes up that I'm giving up some control.

Like Deena, the management of many organizations continues to employ unilateral decision-making out of a concern that the only alternative is abdicating power altogether. More and more leaders are taking measures to hear the perspectives, needs, suggestions, and preferences of those they supervise and incorporating such input as they reach their decisions. However, the final decision still remains in the hands of the leaders, and others have no *ultimate* say in the decision, even when their input is taken into consideration.

Our times are not the best of circumstances. We are in the grip of multiple global crises, and the continued reliance on unilateral decision-making is now a bottleneck in the possibility of turning around any of the exponential processes that are on their way to ending life as we know it.

This is, indeed, why more and more organizations and individuals within them are learning to operate collaboratively. Leaders and others are learning to use power and resources in such a way that everyone's needs are included and they have an explicit say in the outcome. The process I describe below is dedicated to all these people, known and unknown, who are bravely taking steps to shift the paradigm of decision-making. My own part in this global attempt at transformation is to offer you the process of Convergent Facilitation in support of your efforts.

The bulk of this chapter covers the key principles that are at the root of using Convergent Facilitation for supporting collaborative decision-making in a group. These principles are organized in terms of the breakthrough insights that I named in the Introduction. The next chapter provides the how to: the detailed steps and skills of the process.

To make things simpler to digest, the discussion in this and the next chapter assumes implicitly that you are a designated group facilitator who is not also a decision-maker with structural power. The same process can be used by decision-makers in a group or organization, provided attention is put into navigating power differences with care to create an environment where everyone's needs matter and they know it. I come back to this added layer of complexity, along with other potential wrinkles, in Chapter 6.

Core Principles

Let's face it, most of us sit in many meetings simply waiting for them to be over. Energy can ebb when each person expresses their opinion, agrees or disagrees with whoever spoke before, and adds their own thoughts to the mix. So often meetings devolve into a series of disconnected monologues that don't build together. All the while no new information is added to what's already on the table, and the group is not making any progress towards a decision.

Although efficiency is about increasing the ratio of useful output to energy expenditure, and is therefore about reducing wasted energy, in our modern times efficiency is most often equated with whatever takes the least amount of time. This habit of equating speed with efficiency often results in low willingness to engage with others, because it seems to always take longer than making a unilateral decision.

My own view of efficiency, in the context of facilitation of decision-making processes, rests on the original definition. What I want to minimize is use of group attention that isn't directly contributing to the purpose for which the group came together. I want every moment to count more than I want to reduce the total number of minutes a process takes. The result is an experience of productive use of resources. Along with the transparency that accompanies this process (see Chapter 2 for extensive notes about transparent facilitation), what I am proposing here often reduces anxiety and meeting fatigue by making visible to the group the progress towards a decision. In my experience groups have often found this process to be highly interactive and engaging, even fun.

There is no specified amount of time for reaching a decision. As I mentioned in the preface, I have facilitated a group of 300 people that, within 10 minutes, reached a decision about whether and how to revise the schedule for the last day of a conference. Everyone agreed with the outcome. I have also worked with one group over more than two years to complete a process of collaborative lawmaking (see Chapter 7). Ultimately, I believe that any group can make a collaborative decision about anything; it's just a question of having an effective structure within which to operate and then having the time, skilled facilitation, and willingness to include everyone's needs and perspectives that are necessary in order to get there.

Facilitating a collaborative decision-making process takes a shift in our attitude towards this elusive thing we call time: Instead of saving time up front and losing it later, the choice is to invest time up front and harvest the results later.

The usual outcome of this process is a decision everyone can accept as their own. Another possible outcome is a shared recognition that a collaborative decision cannot be made within available resources. The group can then choose to change the time constraints, willingly accept a non-collaborative decision-making process, or let go of making a decision.

How is all this possible? Simply put, it's because people tap into their deepest creativity and find true willingness once everyone trusts that their own needs and perspective matter. These remarkable results emerge from a strong commitment on your part to two basic principles, not just to following steps; because these principles are different from the ones we've been using for hundreds of years. The differences are deep enough that bridging the gap often requires a kind of faith about who we are as human beings.

We all want the same things. One part of this faith involves trusting that all of us want the same things, even though superficially we can be at war. In fact, one of the core skills you will learn later on rests squarely on this assumption: the skill of finding the noncontroversial essence. Time and time again I have seen that people with directly opposing views on a matter of significance to them can easily agree on underlying principles.

Human beings can shift. The second part is to remember and believe that when we humans are really heard, shifts happen. We remain attached to our own narrowly defined self-interest only because of lack of trust that anything else would work, or that anyone else would care.

Knowing that shifts can happen, without trying to force them to happen, without predicting or planning where they will happen or who will shift, your only business is to be present for what is in the room, trusting that fundamentally we're all human beings who want essentially the same things.

Here, in brief, are the core principles which provide the core framework for this process to unfold. The rest of the chapter explores additional principles and insights that support you in applying these core principles.

Everyone matters

Your goal as the facilitator is to support the group in reaching a decision that everyone can accept as their own. It's extremely unlikely that you can reach such a decision without letting everyone in the group know that they matter: What they want, their perspective, what concerns them, and their ideas can all affect the outcome. It is this felt sense, which every part of the process works to enhance, that supports all the shifts and possibilities that the process invites.

This understanding that everyone matters to this degree and in this total way means that to increase the chances that everyone will embrace a decision that may not be their preference, we need to rely on trust and willingness rather than fairness. Although fairness is a core value for most people, quite often people disagree about what is or isn't fair, without moving any closer towards a strategy everyone can endorse. Conversely, a direct focus on willingness, on what people can truly accept, and on what's possible to do with the available resources, yields faster and more sustainable movement towards a decision.

For example, imagine that you are facilitating a group in which a large majority favor a particular outcome, and in which a few people favor another outcome, feel very strongly about it, and thus are less willing to shift their position. In the end, the group may choose the outcome that fewer people favor because there's more willingness on the part of the majority to accept it than the other way around. The numbers per se don't add up to an outcome that works for everyone.

This is a practical commitment, not a moral one: It's about what's *possible*, which isn't always what anyone would consider the same as what's *fair*. When the minority is overruled, as is so often the case, their motivation to support the outcome and implement the decision is diminished. Conversely, when you engage with the minority group to find what's truly important to them, goodwill is unleashed. I have seen, many times, how powerful it is for the majority to be awakened to the world beyond majority rule and invited to let go of the assumption that just because their numbers are larger, they get what they want. This is why whenever there is a big majority for a particular small decision, even when to take a break, I often ask if there is someone who feels strongly enough to advocate for something else. This both brings the minority people to the reality of where most people are and, at the same time, provides them with assurance that their needs and views *do* matter, and if significant enough can potentially sway the outcome. Indeed, in my ongoing groups, it does regularly happen that people advocate for a different outcome and, in the end, that outcome is accepted by all.

Distinguish between the "what" and the "why"

In my experience, most people, most of the time, are not invested in their preferred outcome (the "what") provided they are heard fully for what's behind their preferred outcome or objection (the "why").

This distinction is vitally important all through this process. A key part of your role as facilitator in this particular process is to continually translate and capture the many "whys" that are present in such a way that they can be owned by everyone. In the criteria-gathering phase it's the bulk of what you do. In other phases, it's what happens whenever there is any objection – always relating things back to the underlying needs, most often in the form of the noncontroversial essence that can support convergence.

Needs are distinguished from specific outcomes in that

needs refer to an abstract quality, aspiration, value, or purpose rather than specific people, location, actions, time, or objects (think "Plato" to help you remember). Here are two examples:

- Efficiency is a need, while a particular sequence of production steps is a specific strategy for attending to it.
- Team cohesion is a need for which weekly staff meetings are a particular strategy.

This distinction is key to the success of this collaborative decision-making process: You can include and consider everyone's needs, because when we reach that level, needs are not in conflict; only strategies and the meaning we assign to them can be in conflict.

Hold the process tightly, and the outcome lightly

You don't have to walk in having it all figured out. Entrust yourself to the logic of the process and to the truth of the moment, not to any predefined notion of what the outcome will be or how you will get there. This requires cultivating flexibility and a relaxed attitude about what will happen and allows for creativity with regard to strategies that are likely to work for everyone.

I am holding the process tightly in order to attend to everyone's needs. I am holding the outcome lightly because I am not so concerned about the outcome in the sense that if we reach it together through true willingness, I am confident it will work, because the more collaborative the process, the more collaborative the outcome.

For the same reasons, I can never give people any assurances about the outcome. I do, however, *want* to give them what

I might call "process reassurance": I can assure them that I intend to track everything, to hold all that matters, to attend to their needs, and to keep my eyes focused on both the people and the movement towards outcome.

Breakthrough Insight: Cultivating Willingness

Willingness is the core ingredient that makes Convergent Facilitation work. One way in which I see my role as facilitator in groups that are trying to reach a decision is that I am doing all I can to support more and more willingness, until the creativity in the group expands sufficiently to meet the level of willingness, at which point convergence has occurred.

In order for you to fulfill that role effectively, I start with teasing apart willingness from two other states which do not lead to truly collaborative solutions: preference and compromise. Preferences don't lead to collaborative solutions simply because the range of possibilities is too large to converge. We are too idiosyncratic to be able to reach a magical state in which all of us *want* the same thing. To find willingness, in other words, we may need to stretch. Compromise, on the other hand, doesn't lead to collaborative solutions because it doesn't unleash goodwill, and often leads, instead, to agreements based on resentment or impotence which are less likely to be kept.

Willingness and preference

Understanding the difference between willingness and preference, and what may support people in finding willingness to let go of their preference is one of the keys to the possibility of convergence. Here's why.

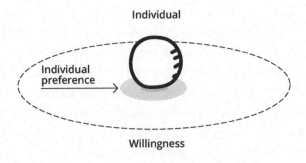

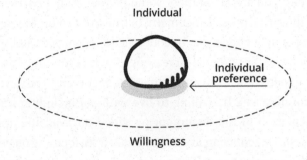

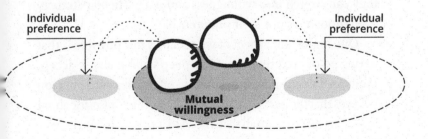

Stretching beyond preference into willingness and not beyond
is how we can find convergence instead of compromise

When a conversation is focused on finding something that everyone *is happy* with instead of what everyone is *truly willing to live* with, discussions often bog down as we try this or that strategy hoping that it will align with everybody's preferences. If, instead, you focus on willingness, you invite people to stretch towards each other to find something they can all willingly accept. This is the key action that you will be taking when facilitating this process, and I provide much more guidance about it when discussing Phase 3 of the process in detail.

For now, let's look at only one example. Let's say that in a group you are facilitating, some people want a particular wording in an official document, because of a commitment to transparency. Others may be concerned about manageability in response to the potential increase in volume of communication that would come from publishing that document. The former group may well be willing to live with *not* including some information in the document provided it's available upon request. This convergent strategy arises from focusing on both *needs* (transparency and manageability) instead of focusing on preferred *strategies*. This focus helps people discern whether they can stretch into willingness about a particular strategy even though it's not their preference.

One important aspect of what makes this possible is that letting go of preference means a deep willingness to accept imperfect decisions. The irony is, often, that each person believes that the particular proposal they are enthusiastic about is the perfect one, and all that's needed is to convince everyone else that it's so. Once people shift – with your support – from perfect preference to willingness, and shift their intention to serving the common good rather than advocating for their own position, the outcome can then work, sometimes indefinitely, without anyone questioning it again.

One small and essential example of a very workable imperfect solution is the perennial question of temperature in a room full of people. Do we open the windows or keep them closed? Turn the A/C up or down? There *really* is absolutely no way to find something that works for everyone all the time. Nonetheless, so far I haven't found anyone who cannot embrace this simple strategy in a group. Whatever the setting is – open windows, closed windows, this or that temperature of the A/C – I ask everyone to agree to keep it without any change for 10 minutes. Then, after at least 10 minutes, if anyone feels uncomfortable and wants to change it, they simply go ahead and do it and then let the group know they changed it. At that time, the new setting remains for at least 10 minutes, until someone wants to change it again. Although people may not *like* being slightly warmer or colder than is perfect for them, everyone can easily stretch for 10 minutes before changing, especially when they are spared all the annoying interminable discussion about it.

On another occasion, I was one of the facilitators for a five-day training in a group that had three separate languages that required translation. I noticed that the group was getting bogged down with attempting to find a perfect solution for the translation issue, and I could see it wasn't going to happen. Instead, I brought the dilemma to the group – that aiming for a perfect solution would take more energy and effort away from the main focus of the group. I proposed some elaborate arrangement that was clearly not ideal, and yet I could see that it would attend sufficiently to most of the needs and considerations I had heard. Then I took the crucial step of asking people to try it out and to bring it up again later if anyone felt it wasn't working. We completed the discussion and arrived at the imperfect solution – in a group of over 100 people – in less than 30 minutes, and, in the end, no one ever brought up the question again. I had heard that in previous years of the same training the question kept coming up again and again and stimulated enormous pain because everyone was still busy looking for a perfect solution.

Willingness and compromise

On the other end of the challenge about maximizing willingness is the habitual belief that the best we can get, short of forcing a decision, is a compromise. Compromise is very costly for a group. It is the product of a process of negotiating an outcome, which usually takes place at the level of positions that each party is assumed to continue to hold. Rather than being about a coming together to embrace an outcome, compromise is usually a form of giving up on having something that truly works for everyone. When I facilitate groups, I make sure to let them know that I am not aiming for a compromise, because a compromise is a lose-lose outcome – "an agreement or a settlement of a dispute that is reached by each side making concessions"[2] – and Convergent Facilitation is about a win-win outcome where we make the decision together. To use Mary Parker Follett's words, Convergent Facilitation leaves behind domination and compromise as ways of attending to differences, and, instead, aims for integration. An integrated solution tends to honor a wide range of issues, whereas compromise still maintains the either/or nature of the original

---

2 Google dictionary definition. I want to acknowledge that there are times when the word "compromise" is used without the usual connotation of "giving up" on something. In this chapter, I am excluding that particular use of the word for the sake of maintaining clarity. I choose, instead, to use the word "compromise" for any agreement that is entered into with less than full willingness. This is because I want to point to the radical goal of seeking to include everyone's needs in shaping the solution, so it can truly work for everyone.

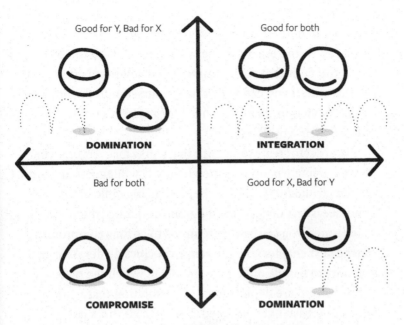

Good for Y, Bad for X   Good for both

DOMINATION   **INTEGRATION**

Bad for both   Good for X, Bad for Y

COMPROMISE   **DOMINATION**

We can do better than domination or compromise

challenge. As Follett suggested, a compromise is quantitative, so that the difference is divided, or people give up something to get something else.[3] Compromise is rooted in a worldview that is based on scarcity and separation. An integrated solution, on the other hand, is qualitative, so that the difference is transcended. Integration is rooted in a worldview that's based on togetherness and abundance of possibilities to explore. This worldview supports convergence and the emergence of a solution that works for everyone. It is the power of an integrative process that results in what in pure math wouldn't make sense: finding the *highest* common denominator for the group.

3 Mary Parker Follett, *Dynamic Administration: The Collected Papers of Mary Parker Follett.*

Bear in mind that for most groups you are likely to work with, given the reality of the world, *you* will be the one to hold the faith that such an integrated solution is possible. In this way, if you can truly throw yourself into the process with conviction, there's no need for members of the group to shift *their* worldview.

In order to create something that works for everyone, your task is to invite people to stretch only *to* willingness and not *beyond* willingness. This can be particularly difficult to hold if the issue is very divided and the group has limited resources. At such times, you can be very tempted to go for a compromise. In the next chapter when I get into specifics, I offer some tips on how to handle difficult moments in which the resources of the group are depleted and yet a solution that works for everyone hasn't yet emerged. For now, all that's important is for you to recognize the pivotal nature of this distinction.

This distinction can be tricky, because the same strategy may be adopted willingly or as a compromise. As a facilitator, it's vitally important for you to be able to discern the difference even when the people in the group may not. You cannot tell the difference from the solution itself, because the difference is about the inner state more so than the specifics of the agreement.

Most of the time, when people change agreements – explicitly or de facto in their actions – it's because they never entered them for real. This is one of the key ways that energy is drained in so many workplaces. If I'm concerned that this kind of "going along without agreement" is what's happening, I question it. This could look like this: "Josh, I'm feeling a little concerned because we are on the verge of making this decision and I haven't heard from you. You have a key role in this project and your opinion and your wishes and needs are really critical, so I'm wondering if you'd be willing to say how you see the issue?"

If we either don't discern it well or don't engage with it when we do, we run the risk of what's happened to untold number of facilitators, myself included. When it finally becomes clear that the apparent agreement wasn't truly wholehearted, there can be a lot of cleanup to do afterwards to regain trust, which often in any event means revisiting the issues. This is why I am presenting below some of the factors that lead to increased willingness, so you can put conscious attention into attending to them and discerning whether they are actually in place.

Factors contributing to willingness

Over the years of working with Convergent Facilitation, I have been focusing, specifically, on the question of what increases willingness, because true willingness, and nothing less, is what creates convergence.

The more these conditions are in place, the more easily people find the willingness to shift. The less these conditions are in place, the more likely people are to give up on their needs and agree to what they experience as a compromise, without true willingness. When that is the case, the price is often paid later, as I already discussed earlier.

The fundamental function of your facilitation is to attend to these factors throughout the entire process. Although there are many different things that facilitators do, I generally see the role of facilitator in Convergent Facilitation as, in essence, supporting people in being fully heard, in hearing and opening to the needs of others, in shifting their intention to serving the common good rather than advocating for their own position, and in trusting that they have true freedom to choose.

Being heard: Especially in a high conflict and low trust group, the experience of knowing that our needs matter and are held with care is a strong prerequisite for any kind of willingness to shift to occur. Focus on hearing people's needs to their satisfaction, not only yours! A person is heard only when they experience being heard, regardless of whether you believe that you hear them.

Otherwise, people are so occupied with being heard that they literally can't make room for anything else, least of all being affected by hearing others' needs. This factor is the sine qua non for the *possibility* of willingness to shift.

Hearing others' needs: Instead of arguing and convincing, in my experience one of the keys to collaborative decision-making is that people shift their positions and their willingness to live with a particular outcome when hearing other peoples' needs. This is a different form of trust: It's about trusting the true motives of those they may be in disagreement with. So often the lack of willingness to shift comes from attributing bad faith to others. Hearing and believing other people's needs, and, especially, being supported in integrating, accepting, and caring for those needs, is what creates the *motivation* for shifting.

Togetherness in serving the common good: The more confidence people have that they are all working on a joint problem and are not at odds with each other, the more goodwill they will have, and, with it, the willingness to shift towards something that will address the totality of the needs present in the group. People rise up to the occasion of serving the common good much more often when the common good is expressed and trusted.

Sense of freedom: One of the things I love about all of us humans is that we have such a deep need for freedom. What this means, in the context of collaborative decision-making, is that the more people believe they are free to make their own decisions, the more likely they are to find willingness to shift. To the extent they pick up any direct or subtle attempt to force a decision on them, they will have less willingness.

Working Towards Efficient Collaboration

Before moving to the next chapter and the details of what happens in each phase of Convergent Facilitation, I provide a few more guidelines to consider and use in any of the phases. As you begin to experiment, you will gradually develop your own understanding about what's most important to focus on when.

Where's the opening? Where's the obstacle?

Overall, when using Convergent Facilitation, I continually hold my sight on the ultimate goal: reaching a decision that works well enough for everyone. With that in the forefront of my mind, the entire process of facilitation begins to look like a dance. As I continue to support the group towards that outcome, I rarely move in a straight, logical, linear manner. Instead, I dance with what's happening in each moment to see where to go next. When I see an opening, I would immediately consider that next: someone expressing goodwill, a moment of generosity, a partial convergence, a new idea. For as long as the opening exists, we keep going in that direction. Until an obstacle arises: opposition to an idea, a moment of tension, re-polarizing in the group, an outlier showing up. At that point, I choose whether to attend to the obstacle directly or look for an altogether different opening. How do I attend to an obstacle? By hearing a person, revising a proposal, naming a new principle, or any one of an indefinite array of options that learning to facilitate uncovers. Everything in our facilitator toolkit is an option for responding to such obstacles. How to respond to obstacles is the craft. How to know whether to pursue an obstacle or look for a new opening is the art. Both increase with experience.

Make strategic use of every word

The process of facilitating a group is highly verbal – both you and the other people in the group are continually speaking or listening to words that others are speaking. Because efficiency is about how you and the group use resources rather than simply about how long the process takes, this means that you want to have as many ways as possible to maximize the usefulness of the words that are being said. The core principle here is one of no waste. For example:

- Say everything only once unless you learn from the group that something you said was not clear. If you repeat yourself, it's more draining for both you and the group. I have been training myself for some time now to ask somebody else to paraphrase what I said, rather than repeat it myself.

- Consider how what you're about to say or ask can truly move the group forwards. And when you're unsure or not clear about what to do or say next, return to the big-picture intention: either to get to a decision or to have clarity that the group can't make a decision at this time. In each phase this will result in a different focus, and will help you reorient.

- End everything you say with a clear request to the group (see Chapter 3 for more details about that). In general, any statement (except a response to someone else's request) without a request leaves too much room for confusion, and usually disperses the energy. The level of group energy is what you work with. You can think of it like a ball that you are trying to hold in the air or pass to others, and never put down on the floor. Making a statement without a clear request is akin to dropping the ball.

- Focus on hearing every *need* in the room, not necessarily hearing every *person*. Keep asking if there is anything *important* that's not already captured, and let the group know that you are not necessarily going to hear from everyone. At the same time, put extra care into not missing the quiet people who are quiet because of not feeling sufficient trust to speak.

- Make requests that people can respond to without speaking. Any kind of yes/no question reduces the possibility of a discussion that gets out of hand. The aim is to maximize hearing from people at the same time as minimizing discussion that isn't contributing to purpose.

  When talking to one individual, framing requests as yes/no ("Did I capture it accurately?") as opposed to open-ended ("Tell me what you would like to add") achieves that purpose sufficiently.

  With a group, the way to achieve the same purpose is to use a show of hands (e.g. "I would like to see by a show of hands who is in favor of the strategy that was just proposed").

At different points in the process it may be tempting to hear from everyone, or at least from more people, instead of focusing on a show of hands. While this approach deeply enhances a sense of "we" in the group and increases trust and mutual understanding, it is the most time- and energy-consuming strategy, so make this major investment only if you believe it will give you a lot of necessary information, or when there is spaciousness and what's most important is to weave connection in the group. I usually hear from everyone only at the beginning and at the end of a significant chunk of time, depending on the size of the group.

One other significant context when I might choose to hear from everyone, even if it's not *directly* moving the group towards a decision, is when the people in the group are not accustomed to participating. More often than not, this would be in contexts of power differences, such as when attempting to involve employees or youth who are not in any decision-making position, or in community settings when class or race differences are present. My choice then would be to go around the room and ask everyone to speak to the issue. Although such a move doesn't add value directly to decision making, it adds tremendous value to trust and engagement, which are essential if I want collaborative decision-making to happen.

- Ask for information only when you need it in order to move forward. For example, if you can reach a decision without hearing all the reasons behind positions, because everyone is willing to accept a certain outcome, there's no need to know the reasons. Sometimes, just knowing there is a strong preference is enough to generate willingness from everyone else. The whole backstory may not be necessary.

There's also no reason to hear about why people like a proposed agreement, only what's in the way of reaching the goal. Otherwise people go right back to explaining why their viewpoint should be adopted, which reduces the goodwill. Those who also agree can get exhausted, and those who don't agree are likely to have *less* willingness and to feel more alienated the more they hear why they "should" accept the proposal.

- Invite brevity from the group by specifying the length of time you want people to speak, knowing that whatever you ask for, people are likely to talk longer, because most people want to be heard. If you ask people to say a couple of sentences, for example, you are inviting more discussion than fits within the narrow parameters of most meetings that are not discussion groups. If you invite people to say a couple of words, then you are likely to get your two sentences.

- Minimize the chances of hearing information twice from people by asking people to only speak if they have something to say that hasn't yet been said.

Follow a trajectory of meaning

Many groups tend to follow a rule that people speak in the order in which they raise their hand. My own experience is that this method of running meetings contributes to inefficiency. The reason is twofold. First, there isn't necessarily connection between the speakers, and therefore what people say doesn't build something together. Second, the specific contribution that each person is making isn't necessarily harvested.

What I propose to groups, instead, is to follow a trajectory of meaning. As each person speaks, I tend to reflect and capture what they said to their satisfaction. Then I focus on those people who have something to say that is related, until that particular thread is complete, and therefore digested by the group. Only then do I ask for other threads to be started.

If you come to a group that is habituated to working with a "stack" such that people speak in turn, it may be a little unusual for them, which will require more transparency from you in each moment about your choices as a facilitator. For example: "I've seen your hand up; are you wanting to say something about the topic, or is it something new?" I have never experienced a problem in this way if I'm being fully transparent about what I am doing and why I am doing it, and especially if I remember to acknowledge the people I am not calling on to speak.

Make convergence visible

Since the goal of this process is to create convergence, any time you sense that some people may have shifted in their openness or willingness, or in their attachment to their own preferred outcome as needs are expressed, check this out explicitly. This is powerful feedback both for you and for the group, since convergence might come from unexpected corners.

In addition, if indeed convergence is happening, and everyone sees that some people are moved by hearing what's important to others, this in itself brings them closer together, and turns up the volume on general goodwill, along with collective ownership of everyone's needs.

For example: "Hearing this now, how many people have

more of an interest in finding a way for us to increase our visibility in the market?" Since convergence often happens at the level of needs/criteria first before there is convergence on a particular outcome, stay away, initially, from asking for willingness to go along with any particular strategy. The specific example I just used is about collective ownership of needs, not any particular outcome. Trust may increase if people have a sense that they are not the only one caring about their needs.

Take full responsibility for the process

There are many ways you can share responsibility for the process and for the outcome with the group, and the more you do it, the more the group can take final ownership of the outcome. You can mobilize the group for tracking time or other elements of the process; reflecting what needs are being brought up; and coming up with proposals to address the needs.

Still, the ultimate responsibility for the process resides with you; you are the one who is explicitly there to look after the group as a whole. Others may join this leadership framework, and they go in and out of it while your role means you occupy this position explicitly for the duration of the process. This is precisely why facilitating is so demanding.

This is directly related to the core principle of holding the process tightly and the outcome lightly. Even in those instances, and they often happen, when I myself make a proposal to the group based on what I hear from different people, I am only offering it for purposes of movement. Even when making a proposal, remember that your goal is only to move the process forward towards finding something that works for all concerned.

As needs are named and ideas are generated, for example, it may be helpful for you, as facilitator, to focus part of your attention on the question "What strategy is most likely to fly?" whether you personally like it or not. If you wait for it to emerge from the group, that sometimes may take forever. Aim to cultivate alertness to the emerging strategy while being completely not attached.

Tend to the energy in the group

As I discussed in Chapter 3, one of the most important things you can do as a facilitator is to support the group in maintaining its energy and focus. Since the process tends to go through many moments of micro-convergence followed by micro-divergence, there are likely to be times when people are not fully engaged or are discouraged. In addition to the general tips I shared in Chapter 3, and what you discover for yourself, here are a few more ways you can attend to this that are specifically about being in a decision-making process such as Convergent Facilitation:

- Reminding the group of where they are in the process, what's coming, and/or what the purpose is. The momentary ups and downs of group process can be taxing for people, especially if they are not process savvy. You can shift their experience by providing a context. For example, if you sense a level of fatigue and tension in the group, you might say something like: "I sense some strain in the group, and I would like to speak to that. We've just finished reviewing the concerns about this proposal, and I am optimistic about our ability to get through the rest of the process today. How about we pause the process for a moment and take a breath. Remember: We are not going to go anywhere without everyone." Speaking to what you believe is going on and inviting people to rely on your faith likely provides them with just enough energy to proceed to the next moment of micro-convergence along the path.

- Appreciating people, either individuals or the group as a whole. For most people, aiming for a collaborative decision is hard work. They are asked to stretch, to articulate their needs more fully, to hear other people's needs, to set aside their favorite scenario, to believe people they previously mistrusted, and more. Any time you notice anyone, or the group as a whole, doing any of those things, you can simply name it and continue. Each time you do it, the level of energy and willingness tends to increase. I come back to a longer discussion of appreciation in the next chapter, when talking about how to start a meeting.

- Naming explicitly the goal of a decision that everyone can accept as their own rather than majority vote, decision by leaders, or unfocused discussion. Within this context, you can also remind people of their role as stewards of the whole instead of advocating for their own positions.

At this point, you have some familiarity with many of the principles and skills related to Convergent Facilitation, including how to maximize willingness, and how to enhance the efficiency of the collaboration. The next piece to master is the actual flow of the process from start to end, which gives you a structure for how to apply the principles, insights, and skills you have learned so far. That's what we turn to in the next chapter.

Creating Breakthrough Collaborative Decisions with Convergent Facilitation

CHAPTER FIVE

... The point of the process is not to persuade the community that you are right, as in a debate; rather, the point is to bring you, as an individual, to understand as much as possible the reasons for opposite opinions. Your responsibility is to see the views of others, their concerns and their reasons, which will help you to choose willingly and intelligently the steps that will create a solution – because it is in your own best interest that all needs are addressed in the community.

— JEANNETTE ARMSTRONG

IT'S ONE THING TO UNDERSTAND a whole array of principles. It's a whole other thing to know what to do when you walk into a room as a facilitator to support a group in reaching a collaborative decision about a topic of significance for them. You know that your task is for all of them to experience that they matter and to support them in speaking and hearing each other so fully that an integrative solution can emerge that all can accept as their own. This chapter provides you with the nuts and bolts of exactly how to do that, step by step, from the moment of starting the meeting to the finish line of having a decision that all can accept.

Like the previous chapter, this one, too, takes the position that *you are a facilitator who is not a member* of the group, certainly not someone with structural decision-making power. I cover that and other layers of complexity in the next chapter.

Starting a Meeting

Many facilitators I have trained have confessed to me that they have the most anxiety about how to start a meeting; that once the first few minutes are over they are able to relax and be in the flow much more easily. For myself, even without anxiety and with years of experience, I tend to dedicate a disproportionate part of the design time to the first few minutes.

The reason for the anxiety of many and for my particular focus during design is one and the same: The first few minutes are often hugely important in terms of setting a tone for how the group will function, beginning to establish trust and flow, and giving people something they can lean on as the process moves forward into the often unsteady waters of collaboration.

While there's no set formula for how to do this, the elements I present are particularly important to attend to as you begin a meeting in which you aim to use Convergent Facilitation for guiding a decision-making process.

The primary question that guides me moment by moment as I navigate the process, starting from the moment I walk into the room, is: What can I do in this moment to support the movement towards convergence? Since I want every moment to count in this process as a way to increase efficiency in the deepest sense of the word, I want to be that intentional right away. At the beginning, in particular, I want everything I say to have inspirational value and/or operational value.

For example, saying something like: "Thank you for coming, my name is _____, and I will be facilitating a dialogue around the issue of _____" is so familiar and predictable, and with so little actual content, that people can easily ignore your words and continue their own thoughts and distractions. They would just be waiting for your words to be over and for something to "start."

Instead, what you would want to be looking for are ways to get people to be compelled to stop and listen to you, and for the meeting to already start to be meaningful. In that moment and in every moment.

This will require you to be your full human self even while you are playing the crucial role of facilitator. The cultural norms about what it means to be "professional" conditions you, me, and all of us, to be separate as facilitators. It takes effort to "unseparate" yourself, because the role is protective and makes you less vulnerable to whatever others might do in response. If you step out of this protection into more of a present connection with people, the power of your person is then enormous. This requires of you to overcome your fear of being uninspiring, and nudges you to be as visionary as you can ever be.

All the content presented below is aimed to support you in offering this gift to the group you will be facilitating.

Appreciating people

From the beginning of any facilitation, I make a point of verbally and frequently appreciating people, so long as it's genuine. This is especially important at the beginning, and even more so if I am in a context where I have reason to believe there is stress, mistrust, or non-voluntary participation. In those settings, just being in the room is an effort.

This is probably a key reason why we so often say "thank you for coming" at the beginning: This phrase points to something of vital truth, which is the tangible effort that people make in choosing to make themselves available to a process of collaborative decision-making. The more charged the topic, the more divergence there is, the more unspoken challenges, the more power differences, and the more mistrust, the more effort it takes. As a facilitator, you are stepping into this effort.

Because of all this, I want even the opening to be something of meaning that will grab people's attention instead of any kind of generic framing that people can tune out while waiting for my speech to be over. This generally gives people some sense of affirmation and respect and humanizes everyone at once. If you do this, your words can begin to help them settle in and experience some degree of trust, because people know that you see something about their reality. Even if you know nothing, you can always guess something. For example: "I'm so appreciating that all of you made whatever effort it took to be here, whether it's getting childcare, getting someone to cover for you at work, or anything else I don't know, so you could be here and participate in this process of decision-making."

In naming, acknowledging, and appreciating people for the effort, you are humanizing both yourself and the people, at once, and, in this way, you are establishing a connection. This connection is not just between you and them, it's also among them, because this is also the moment in which they realize that they are not the only ones who made the effort.

You are also increasing people's motivation to keep focusing, committing, and stretching. In simple terms, when people are appreciated, it's easier for them to do more.

In order to do this, you will need to overcome the cultural conditioning to be separate as a facilitator, so you can bridge the artificial divide between being a "professional" and being fully human. My own approach to this is to deliberately step into being present, human, and even vulnerable, and that allows me to be in connection with the people I am facilitating. This has enormous positive power.

Establishing shared purpose

I can't think of much that is more galvanizing for people than a meaningful connection with a purpose that excites them. Because of that, as facilitator, what's most important for you to share is the why, because it carries the most meaning. Alas, in reality, that is the piece so many of us often leave out, without offering it or asking for it from those in the groups we facilitate.

Just think about the difference between the sentence I used above as an example – "I will be facilitating a dialogue around the issue of _____" – and the sentence I would far rather use – "We're here to come up with a decision about _____ that everyone can truly accept as their own." Which one is more likely to get you intrigued enough to listen to what comes next?

The more you know about the specifics, the more you can be specific in what you say. Bear in mind that while you, by virtue of being a facilitator, are most likely very interested in the process itself, you are unlikely to get people excited about the process – in this case "dialogue." Most people are far more interested in results than in how we get there. This is part of why the second sentence works so much better – it focuses people on the product of your time together with them.

The second option does one more thing, which is that it creates a vision. The idea of reaching an outcome that truly works for everyone is radical and novel for most people. While some might react cynically when they hear it, all will be somewhat provoked and hence more alert, readier to engage, either to satisfy their hopes, or to see if they can prove you wrong...

Describing your role as facilitator

There is nothing sexy about being a facilitator, so just saying something like "I will be facilitating" is not likely to create substantial contact. What you might consider, instead, is to name something specific about your role that excites you, and by virtue of that has a greater chance of engaging the people in the group.

For myself, what I almost invariably aim to emphasize is my own passionate commitment to everyone's needs, what I earlier referred to as being an advocate for everyone in the room getting an outcome that works for them.

Because so many people are habituated to thinking of facilitators as people who don't do much and who are trying to be neutral and unobtrusive, framing your role in this way can, once again, be a provocative way to invite people to engage more fully.

Providing an overview of the process

I generally tend to keep this part of the Introduction as brief as possible, because I am never expecting people to be able to make full sense of it or remember it for later. I imagine to myself that people often bring into the room confusion, discomfort, distraction, and the common lack of interest in participating in what so many people experience as a charade of collaboration.

My own purpose in reviewing the process is to provide as much inspiration and surprise as possible. Here's what it might sound like: "In the first phase of the process I guide you to identify all that's important to you regarding this decision, with the goal of coming up with a list of needs that you will all take collective ownership of for the rest of the process. Then we'll come up with proposals that attend to as many of these as possible. Finally, we will aim for a decision that incorporates enough of what's important that it can truly work and everyone in the room can accept it as their own."

This way of framing it includes within it the radical and unusual nature of the process while speaking about it as if it's completely ordinary. That is what I aim for, because I want people to be prepared for later and to be intrigued in the moment.

Naming elephants

One way that you can increase your sense of credibility is your willingness to name challenging dynamics and conditions that the group will need to face. When you walk directly into uncomfortable territory, the message that people receive is that you have enough confidence to handle it and won't shy away from complexity or tension. They can then relax.

Here are some of the common elements that you might want to acknowledge if you know about them:

- *Anything that's contentious*: This may include power differences, either between you and the group, or, more commonly, within the group. Naming issues of power is a relief to those with less power and a wakeup call for those with power. You can also name any tension that you are aware of, such as active conflicts, the recent departure of someone who was important in the group, or any other from a host of issues that could be present. Your task is to present them without emotional charge, and in a way that will imply to everyone that your intention is to care for the group and not for some people only.
- *Constraints:* If there is anything that is non-negotiable, name it upfront, so the group can be in choice about where they put their attention. For example: "We are asked to come up with a new seating arrangement for the department, and the constraint is that no walls can be moved." Having non-negotiables doesn't eliminate the possibility of collaboration, because whatever power structures exist outside the room, within the room, and within the constraints, there can be full collaboration about everything else that is negotiable.
- *Decision-making power:* One of the more demoralizing experiences for both individuals and groups is to participate in a decision-making activity that leads nowhere because they don't actually have the power to make the decision. If there are any limits to the participation of the group you are facilitating, let them know right away, so they can decide whether to invest their energies in the project. People are much less creative and willing if they are just

being asked for input than if they are fully entrusted with making the decision.

Creating group agreements

Many groups want to start a process by agreeing on what are usually called "ground rules." My own position on such is quite ambivalent. While I recognize the significance of having agreements, I have two main issues with the typical agreements I've seen groups make.

One is that the agreements are often vague to the point of my truly not knowing what specific behavior is expected of people. As an example, what exactly does "speaking with respect" look like? Being a bicultural person, I know for a fact that respect looks very different in different cultures. If a group is taking the time and energy to make agreements about how to operate and what processes to use, I want to support it in making *behavioral* rather than *value* agreements. Respect could look like waiting until someone is done speaking before saying anything; it can look like summarizing what someone said before responding; or it can look like expressing appreciation after each time someone speaks.

The second is even more subtle. Many of these kinds of agreements are hard for anyone to integrate under any conditions, let alone the intensity of trying to work on a project or a decision together. If there is no explicit agreement about what to do when someone breaks an agreement, they tend to be used as weapons against people when it's convenient to do so, in the very process usually breaking, again, at least one of the agreements that the group has taken on by doing so.

Instead, what I want to do when making group agreements is to aim to cover some core areas of group function with clarity, care, and transparency. I support the group in coming up with agreements that are concrete and behavioral and thus can be measured without another layer of arguing. And I want to have utmost clarity on what we agreed to; to be very clear that the agreements are voluntary and not imposed; to aim to make them all within capacity rather than subtly inviting people to stretch, even if they are willing; and to agree on what we plan to do in the eventuality that an agreement is not kept. In the absence of such extensive clarity, the familiar structures of top-down decision-making and punitive responses will likely be the implicit norm. I want to do everything in my power to establish a norm within any group that I work with that the violation of any agreement is likely to be received with love. *Ultimately, nothing less than loving presence creates* sufficient trust for collaborative processes to flourish in our current global reality of mistrust.

This commitment to loving presence is an aspect of a larger frame through which I see my role: I am there, in part, to support the conditions that would allow each person to speak freely and to have their needs included in what happens.

Confidentiality. Because of how charged the topic of confidentiality is, I want to take a moment to discuss it specifically. By common habit, the decisions about confidentiality are made by facilitators and handed down to a group. I find it almost invariably richer and even bonding in a group, especially a group where vulnerable experiences might be shared, to examine what is important to people about confidentiality or lack thereof and to create an agreement that's crafted to accommodate the specific needs in the room.

Although each group is, ultimately, different, after doing this exercise in a number of groups, I have identified a particular level of confidentiality that has worked for most groups. In the interest of efficiency for many groups, I'd like to describe it in the hopes that it supports you in groups that you facilitate. The agreement is this:

- No identifying information of any kind is shared.
- Any story that has details about specific people is not shared.
- If sharing, individuals focus on what they learned or experienced, not on what other people said.
- At any point in time, someone can say, "Don't repeat this in any form whatsoever."
- If anyone pushes to hear details, the individuals from the group respond by expressing their discomfort and saying something like: "I wish I could tell you and I made an agreement in the room and I want to honor that agreement."

In my experience, this allows for more flexibility and for the richness to flow out without compromising people's privacy and dignity.

Establishing connection and presence

Depending on the size of the group and the total time of facilitation, you might want to include a go-round in your opening, so that everyone speaks to a question you ask them. The value added by this is enormous, and so is, often, the cost to the group. What you can get is a sense of where people are, what their hopes or concerns are, and many other valuable pieces of information. This exercise can also support the sense of shared purpose if your question invites people to reflect at that level.

That said, often enough the benefit is felt only by you, however large it is. Others, especially if they know each other well, may be predisposed to be impatient. One way to attend to this is to ask a question that people are unlikely to have answered for themselves or shared with others in the group. When I have chosen effective questions, I have often heard, at the end of the day, some version of surprise and pleasure at getting to know coworkers or community members at a different level.

Having set the tone of the meeting – deep, alive, engaging, and honest – you can now shift to the criteria-gathering phase and begin to collect needs from the people in relation to the decision that they have gathered to make. Depending on the question that you may have just asked of the group, you may end up beginning to collect items for the list even before officially announcing it.

In the rest of the chapter, I describe skills where they are most relevant although most of the skills can be of service at any part of the process. For example, the skill of identifying the noncontroversial essence which is described below (see shaded box) is completely foundational to any attempt to hear someone, anywhere in any process of facilitation. It's particularly important in the first phase because this is where the foundations are built, both of the content, which is the list of criteria, and of the process, through creating collective ownership and trust. Both of these rely heavily on this particular skill.

Similarly, I present the three phases of Convergent Facilitation as if they are completely distinct and linear, because this is easiest to digest. In applying the process, there are likely to be endless variations. For example, many decisions arise in the moment and can begin directly with the third phase and only go back to Phase 1 and 2 if a challenge arises. Why? Because they are small enough and short-lasting

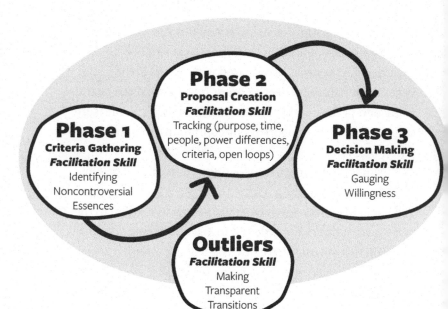

Here, again, is the diagram that describes the flow of Convergent Facilitation, this time with the relevant facilitation skills highlighted for each phase. The core question associated with each phase appears within the description of that phase.

enough that there is enough reason to believe that the entire process won't be necessary.

Phase 1: Criteria Gathering

Core question: *What is important to everyone in the group?*

It's time to get to the heart of the process. For a while, now, you will be working with the group to come up with the list of needs, criteria, principles, considerations, or guidelines that everyone will recognize as describing all that's important to the group in reaching a decision. This list is owned by everyone, and guides the rest of the process. It has a direct practical function of supporting the creation and evaluation of proposals. It also has the vital and intangible function of sustaining the sense of goodwill in the group. I have rarely seen it be "too often" for a group to come back to the collective ownership of the needs.

Given how important the "why" is for bringing people together and for creating trust, I start every part of the meeting with the "why" of the process, and with the "why" of each step. When people know that, they have more patience for the specific details. You can remind people of the "why" any time you sense attention flagging.

Instead of just saying: "I'd like to make a list of what's important to everyone in the room," you can gain more momentum by saying: "The first step to a decision that works for all of you is to come up with a list of what's important to everyone so that we can together address as many of them as possible. To create that, I'd like to ask people to say what's important to them and then capture the essence on the board for all of us." People are going to be much more motivated when they see the goal that's being served.

Bear in mind that, at least initially, it may be a while before someone steps forward. This kind of silence may be awkward, which is probably why, on average, teachers wait at most three seconds before they provide the answer instead of waiting longer for the students to come up with it on their own. If you want to support the group in taking ownership of its decisions, you will need to demonstrate a relaxed attitude. If you can let people know that you're planning to wait until someone steps forward, sooner or later, someone will.

From then on, you will be in a dance with the group to identify as many of the needs present in the room as possible before heading for solutions. Finding, capturing, and taking collective ownership of all the underlying needs at the level of the noncontroversial essence makes it possible for people to come together to solve problems. When they trust that their own needs matter and understand others' needs, they can get mobilized to serve the greater good.

The flow itself can be quite varied, depending on your facilitation style, the specific constraints of the group, and the general mystery of unpredictable human behavior. You will find your own way of asking people for what's important to them and capturing it in one collectively-owned list.

Breakthrough Insight: Finding the Noncontroversial Essence

If you were going to learn only one thing about Convergent Facilitation, this insight would be my top choice for you. The reason for it is simply the powerful effect on everyone when you are able to do this. For the person heard, they now trust that they matter, because you reflected what they say and it's now on the board. For others, because understanding the noncontroversial essence reduces tension and brings people together. Even if they disagree with the person's initial position or proposed solution, once they see the underlying commonality, they are able to see the person as being part of the solution instead of a problem.

How then do you do this magic?

Working with needs

Your main task here is to hear the underlying noncontroversial essence behind what people say and reflect it back to them in a way that captures for them what they intended to be heard about while at the same time framing it in such a way that everyone else can take ownership of it.

Because none of us are habituated to speaking at this level spontaneously, this requires you to train your ears to listen for the essence. You can help yourself a tiny bit by being precise in what you ask people to speak about. Instead of asking them for their positions, opinions, what they believe is the way to go, or anything else that points them to the "what," your goal is to help everyone get to the "why" or, at least, to the most essential level of the "what." You can do this by asking questions such as:

- "What's important to you about this issue?"
- "What's at the heart of this for you?"
- "What difference does this decision make?"

Most people are not accustomed to making the distinction between the "what" and the "why." In addition, because the "why" is often more vulnerable, it's also less comfortable. As a result, even when you ask for the deeper layer, most people are still likely to supply a specific strategy, express a "should," or even become tongue-tied. This is where your own ability to translate becomes essential.

The translation has two moves to it. One is to shift into what's *wanted* from whatever people say. This often comes in one of three ways that tend to hide the "wanting" energy.

- "Should," "have to," "must," "can't," "won't," "don't," and other similar constructs
- Fears, concerns, worries, warnings, and their many cousins
- Facts

My goal is always to focus on noticing an internal move *towards* something that is actively desired instead of any of the above. This is because a "should" invites resistance; fears invite reassurance and dismissal; and facts invite disagreement.

The work of the facilitator is not finished with finding what's wanted, because that, too, can be minimized or criticized. The second move is about moving from the "what" to the "why," which is the core aspect of this insight. How deep you will go depends on many factors; what's most significant is that you *know* there can be more depth, and that you recognize when you have reached the depth that captures enough of the essence with enough acceptability to all.

Once you have a sense of what the "why" might be, check it out with the person who spoke before putting it in on the board. Remember, you are looking for something that captures the essence and that is, at the same time, noncontroversial. If you reach something that feels really obvious and yet truly speaks to the person who articulated it, that is the most satisfying way to bring the group together. Oftentimes what will make something noncontroversial is the move towards something that's wanted for everyone, and thus is easier for anyone to embrace.

Over time, with experience in Convergent Facilitation, you will likely develop an intuitive and swift way of assessing how noncontroversial the language is. Until then, you may need to check with the group.

How to Get to the Essence

1. As facilitator, ask yourself these questions:
   a. "What's really important to this person?"
   b. "What does this person need?"

    c. "Why does this matter to this person?"

    d. "... and if this person had this, what it would it give them?"

2. Does the answer you've come up with have these characteristics?

    a. is noncontroversial

    b. can be evaluated (subjectively)

    c. uses positive language – what is wanted rather than what is not wanted

    d. is relevant to the context

    e. is operational – can in principle be made to happen

    f. applies to everyone – this is a need that everyone can recognize, not just one person's need

    g. doesn't have a specific outcome (as long as it's non-controversial, this is the least important criterion)

3. If so, check in with the person by saying, "So what you want is..." or "Is it that you want ..."

4. If it isn't, keep engaging with the person until you have found the words that match their intent and are noncontroversial needs at the same time.

As you engage with people, both here and everywhere else in the process, remember the principle of taking responsibility. *You* are the one doing the work of translating while creating the conditions in which people can speak as freely as possible. There's no need for them to work harder than is absolutely necessary. Just exposing themselves to say what's true for them is a lot. At the beginning of a process of collaboration, especially if there is contention in the room, people may simply be afraid. The fewer restrictions you put on how they're supposed to speak, the more likely it is that you will hear from them at all.

For example, suppose someone says: "I don't think we need to do any strategic planning. It's a total waste of time. We should just stop the freeze on hiring. That person we almost hired before the freeze suddenly came down – she has what it takes to completely revamp our products. This is so obvious." This is a moment in which, if you don't step in quickly, the room can devolve into accusations and debates which can only increase mistrust. Instead, you can bring people together right away by saying something like: "Let me see if I got the essence of what you're saying. Are you saying that focusing on innovation is truly important to you?"

One way that you can begin to train yourself to find the essence is to listen to two things at once. One is that you listen to every word as a clue, though, in the end, most of the words will be discarded when you formulate the noncontroversial essence. The other is to listen, first and most strongly, for where the highest emotional charge is in the message or in yourself. In this case, the strongest emotional charge I am picking up is the last sentence: "This is so obvious." It's clear to me that this person feels somewhat on the outside, and is likely often experiencing themselves as not being understood or alone. This is vital information for me as the facilitator, and has, in my initial intuitive assessment, no bearing on the content of what the group is discussing. So I trace it through its pointer to what the content is that matters most; in this case I land on "completely revamp our products." Maximizing innovation was one way of making sense of this phrase. You are following the *emotional* thread, not the logical one, remembering that emotions have their own logic which, in modern societies, is often undervalued.

While many people are likely to disagree with the specific strategy for how to achieve innovation (hiring a particular person), it's almost certain that everyone will recognize innovation as something vital to their organization. This may not capture *everything* that the person said, and that's not what you are trying to do. You are only after the noncontroversial essence. That's what all the words are pointing to: One or two core bits that you can capture. If you capture it to the person's satisfaction, then the group comes together and the person becomes more ready and open to hear from others.

There is absolutely no science to this, only a honed craft. If you sense the emotional charge elsewhere, you will likely have a different translation. As long as you are attentive to your mistakes and learn from them to refine and deepen your intuition, you will continue to get better over time. If you picked up the charge around "total waste of time" you might reflect something entirely different, such as "efficient use of resources." I personally look for what is of the essence, what has emotional charge, and what I believe can move the group forward, which is more likely to happen around content (innovation) than around process (use of resources).

Another part of how I work it out is to check, internally, with an imagined "other side" within me to see if what I am about to say as a reflection would be noncontroversial for them. If I feel inside that my internal imagined representation of someone else in the group is unhappy with the wording, it's a good chance the real someone in the group will also be unhappy, and it's worth continuing to explore to find something less controversial.

Part of how the coming together happens is that in the reflection I uncouple the criterion or need from the person who spoke it. It's not Jane's concern or Bruce's need; it's part of what everyone will hold from now on, so it belongs to everyone. When you come back to it later, leave out the name of the person who raised a particular item, as this can easily repolarize the group.

Here are two more examples of how this skill can be applied in the moment.

> *Shirley:* The problem is with one of my direct reports. He rose through the ranks, and he's often... I hate to use this word, and it's sadly true... He's sometimes abusive to the workers.
>
> *Facilitator:* I am guessing that what you most want about this is to create an environment across the company that's truly respectful of employees. Is that it?

This reframe provides enough specificity to be recognizable to Shirley, can still serve as a guide for action, and is universal enough to be recognized by all. Shirley can now be heard and this is made relevant for everyone.

> *Owen:* I don't understand how for nine months we have no financial statements. I can't execute fiduciary responsibility without financial statements.
>
> *Facilitator:* You want the information and tools necessary to assess the financial integrity of the agency?

This reframe removes the blame, which in this case is directly expressed, and sometimes can be completely embedded, and invites people to notice that they would want the same thing too. This reframe broadens the nature of what's said, and that's one way of getting a wider and easier agreement.

There's a piece of inner faith here that I want to make explicit because it can otherwise be so seamless that you won't notice it. It's the core assumption that whatever anyone says is an expression of the same fundamental core values and wishes that every human being has always had. It may be expressed in a controversial, annoying, even harmful way, and it still is an expression of something essential that can bring people together.

Another way of saying it is that I essentially don't look for any hidden agendas or underlying motivations that are kept secret. I take people at face value on purpose and on principle. I know that if there is anything hidden, it is likely to *come closer to the surface* because it's so powerful for people to be heard for face value that they'll lower their protection. This is an area that for many facilitators may need focused attention to shift a habit. If you are preoccupied with figuring out people's ulterior motives, you immediately lose the ability to just be with the people, to meet them as full human beings and see what happens next.

Engaging people to find needs

Over time, you will get better and better at finding the noncontroversial essence right away. Even then, there are always likely to be times when you don't see it. What can you do then? Here are a few options I have found over the years.

- Ask for more time to reflect instead of responding instantly. "I'd like to take another moment to reflect on what you said to see if I can get the essence of it." This is a way to overcome the "awkward silence" anxiety, and often will give you enough space to find something you can then check with the person.

- Reflect any part of it that you do understand and makes sense to you. Usually, this will result in the person saying more, giving you additional clues to the essence.
- Ask the person to help you: "Can you tell me what's important to you about what you just said?" Although what you are after is, invariably, the "why" behind what they are saying, "why" questions tend to generate defensiveness. This is why I used a "what" question here.
- Ask the group for help: "Does anyone have a clear idea about what's important to Jamil in what he just said?"

As much as you try to follow the principle of using every moment well, make sure you stay with each person who speaks until you either have truly heard and captured them fully, or have an explicit other plan for doing so outside of group time. If you leave someone in a vulnerable state of not being fully heard, they are going to be less available to the rest of the process, and you are likely to lose more energy later. In addition, when you make a genuine attempt to understand one person, everyone in the group begins to trust that you might be that interested in what they have to say too. Your goal, always, is to reach one or more statements that are about what's wanted, in positive language, which is also accepted by everyone else.

Dealing with putdowns

Every once in a while, the level of tension in a group can be so high that someone will criticize and put down someone else for what they want. The most painful of these can be something short and snappy such as "That's stupid!" What can you do then? The first thing to recognize is that in those instances you have a very small window in which to acknowledge both parties. This means that economy of words is vital. What you most likely will want to do is start by acknowledging the person who did the putdown before the other one loses their dignity. This can take the form of saying, for example: "I want to hear more and I'll come back to you in a moment." This tells the person they matter without shaming them for shaming someone else!

At that point you can turn to the other person and say something like: "I want to check in with this other person and I want to reassure you that I won't change what's on the board without your consent, because I want to have what's important to you on the board. Is this OK with you?"

This sequence gives both people something to stand on while you are sorting out the complexity. You then transition back and forth until what's important to both of them is fully captured without any further controversy.

Tending to the List

As you hear from one person after another, find the noncontroversial essence, and add it to the list, you are gradually building what will serve as the basis for the rest of the work of the group. From time to time, especially towards the end, you may encounter controversies you will need to address. Every step of the way, you consciously cultivate the shared ownership of the list.

Creating shared ownership

Shared ownership of all the needs is key to the possibility of reaching a decision, and even more significant if you have time constraints. This is because it de-polarizes a group and invites goodwill. Although you are not likely to ask for a reaffirmation of the collective ownership at every step, after each new criterion is added to the list, it's still vitally important that internally you continue to hold the list as belonging to everyone together. Every time you add a new item to the list, do it only if you have confidence that it's likely to be noncontroversial enough that the entire group can adopt it without challenge.

From time to time, you are likely to want to recap the list of needs that's growing on the board. Whenever you do that, state the needs without reference to who expressed them and what specific strategies they represent. It takes some internal discipline to leave it at that without even looking at the person, and this discipline pays off. It helps those whose needs have been named already as well as those whose concerns haven't yet been heard, because they can sense that everything will be included. If, for whatever reason, there is no board for you to capture what you are hearing, this would be a great opportunity to solicit support from the group to track everything, so that no one has the alienating experience of being "left out" because their criteria or needs were forgotten.

As you review the needs, and especially towards the end of this phase, you can explicitly invite people into shared ownership by saying something like: "Since we're aiming for a decision that everybody can accept as their own, we will need to attend to all these criteria." That helps everyone be a steward of the whole rather than an advocate for their own position. And because their interests are included in the list, it's not at their own expense. It's vitally important to remind people that there isn't going to be a process of ranking the needs, since this immediately diminishes the sense that people matter. It's only proposals that are going to be evaluated, later in the process; the needs, the list itself, is accepted as a whole for the remainder of the process.

Right before you officially end the first phase, it's vital to find out if the shared ownership is truly there. There are two pivotal questions here that are important to address to the group. One is whether there is anything significant that's missing from the list, and the other is whether there is anything on the list that anyone is struggling with. If there is, welcome it as enthusiastically as you can – the more open you are to controversy, the more quickly you will get to the convergence that lies at the other end of finding its essential characteristics, namely the noncontroversial list.

Dealing with controversy

Whether at the end of gathering criteria, at an earlier time when you explicitly ask if there's an issue with any item on the list, or when your intuition will miss something, there will be controversy in a group you are facilitating. What can you do then?

Every objection contains within it the desire to be heard by the person who expresses it. Your first task is to find out whether the objection *also* has specific content issues that require tweaking the needs list. The only way to find out is to listen with full attention to the person who has the objection. Be curious to learn and see if there is, indeed, anything that you will want to do something about. Sometimes it truly is the case that the objection is only about wanting to be heard and nothing needs to be changed.

Once you have ascertained that there is specific substance to the objection, there are three ways in which it can be addressed. Sometimes, after listening to the objection, you or someone in the group will think of an easy way to change the wording of the criterion in question without changing its content. You will still need to ask again if the new wording works for everyone. Bear in mind it's no longer owned only by the person who first articulated it, so it's really important to ask everyone, so that both those who supported the original principle and those who objected to it can be on board.

Sometimes tweaking the words isn't going to be enough, and you will need to find a deeper need or a more abstract principle that is at a level on which there is no controversy. This is not a trivial maneuver, so I want to give you two examples.

1. Even though "fairness" is often cited as a core principle, it can be divisive because of different understandings of what is fair. Find an underlying need that satisfies the person who mentions fairness. This could be, for example, "making sure that everyone is included," or it could be "holding in consideration past harm to people" – it all depends on context.

2. "Consideration of my working style" can be too personalized. It would be easier to own "Attention to differences in working styles."

3. There are two ways to deepen, or universalize, a need that's been named. One is about finding a common denominator that supports a decision that applies to everyone and works best when it's important in the end that everyone will do the same thing. For example, a criterion such as "Ensuring that no one is exposed," if found controversial, can be taken to "Minimizing risks to all participants."

4. The other way is to find a frame that supports a dispersed set of self-selected decisions, and is a better fit for when the group can make room for multiple parallel strategies. In this case, "Ensuring that no one is exposed" could be taken to "Allowing everyone to find their comfort level."

You will know which to use based on the context of the group; it's not intrinsic to the content.

One of the more surprising experiences of working with Convergent Facilitation has been the frequency with which, when I do something like that – either change the wording or take it to a deeper layer – the new version works better for everyone, including the ones who had initially expressed the criterion in question. In that way, the search for a deeper need seems to be part of the magic of bringing people together to own the list.

The last option available is to add another need or principle to the list that sufficiently captures something for those who object to create a balance with the original that was challenging for them. This is one of the ways that gathering the criteria supports the final decision by creating a strong list of constraints. The more needs and criteria are collected upfront, the more robust the final decision.

Sometimes it can be really tempting to attend to a controversy by removing something from the list. I can count on one hand the number of times I've done that. The cost of doing it is that someone is now less sure that they matter, which can backfire strongly later even if they don't say anything now. The gain is usually minimal, if any. Although some of the items may be redundant, they are all at the very least placeholders for specific interests. You don't lose anything by redundancy except at most a minute later when proposals are being evaluated.

If you find an important reason to remove something, then it will likely come as no surprise to you that you can only do it after checking with the entire group and finding no hesitation. It's certainly not the first thing I would try. I am, typically, interested in having more rather than fewer items on the list, provided they are relevant to the issue that needs to be decided.

Because of that, up to the final minute of this phase, I potentially invite more controversy by inviting more needs, especially from the people who are silent, those I have any reason to suspect are not speaking in full. I have seen countless times that someone finally is willing to speak what they've been holding, and it turns out they were the only person aware of certain considerations, without which any decision made would have been much less useful to the group as a whole. Sometimes I have even quickly scanned a room all around, looking at each person individually for a second, to see if there are any other needs not yet spoken. As I said earlier: There's no need to hear from everyone, only to hear all the needs.

Once you have heard all the needs and done all the work to address all controversies to everyone's satisfaction, the group is ready to begin looking at proposals. Ask them one final time if there is any controversy or anything missing, maintaining your full presence, with a relaxed and curious attitude, and then celebrate with them. It's a huge accomplishment, and in my experience people feel it tangibly.

Variation: Creating a list ahead of time

I don't always wait for the beginning of the actual meeting before beginning the process of gathering criteria. Once I know that I am going to work with a group (or multiple groups), every conversation I have with any stakeholder is a source of information about what's important to that stakeholder, and therefore what would need to be included as a criterion on the list if we are going to find a solution that works for everyone. In fact, even when I am not engaging in a decision-making process, I find that tuning into the noncontroversial essence of what someone is saying, what is truly important to them, deepens the quality of listening and brings clarity to a conversation rapidly.

When I gather criteria ahead of time, I then present them to the group as a draft that I gathered from various conversations, and invite them to reflect on the list in the very same manner as I would if the criteria were gathered live. This has the advantage of beginning the convergence without any effort on the part of anyone, because criteria from divergent perspectives are already on one list. It also gives people a sense of what information we are looking for and can thus *focus and streamline* the process. One time when I did this I knew I was successful because a man who was previously quite adversarial looked at the list for a long moment and then exclaimed, with evident confusion: "There's nothing here to disagree with!"

Phase 2: Proposal Creation

Core question: *Does anyone have a way forward that addresses all the criteria (needs) on the list?*

It's now time to mobilize the creativity of the group as you invite them to come up with one or more proposals for addressing the needs gathered in the previous phase. Whereas the previous phase was quite tightly managed by you, in this phase you take a step back and invite people to engage with each other more than with you, so that they can brainstorm and synergize.

This is by no means equivalent to saying that you have no role to play here. Although this phase is facilitator-"lite" compared to the other two, at least in terms of others' experience of you, the responsibility is still in your hands, and there are two primary functions that remain exclusively or primarily yours. The first is to support the group in creating the committee(s) that will work on one or more proposals. The second is to maintain a careful eye on how each committee is functioning and to support them in staying on track and in dealing with controversies when (not if, usually) they arise.

This phase can be the longest chronologically in the life of a decision-making project. If there is research about how to implement anything, this is when it will happen. If there are legal issues to sort out, this is where it will happen. By the time this phase is done, your hope is to have pretty detailed and implementable strategies for attending to the criteria gathered, so that the group as a whole can gather one more time and finalize its decision (the third phase later down in this chapter). Because these kinds of considerations are very content-specific, I am not discussing them in this context, except to say that if you facilitate a group over the life of a complex process, you are bound to become somewhat of a content expert along the way, and may, on occasion, be the one to propose a solution to a specific tangle. This happened to me a few times in the course of my longest project so far, where I actually came up with legislative drafts as part of facilitating the process. You can read about this in Chapter 7, where I describe in some detail this project as a case study.

Who will work on a proposal?

One fundamental insight that has guided my choices about how to support a group in coming up with proposals is that when we truly trust that our needs matter, many more of us than I would have expected are surprisingly happy to have someone else make the decisions even though when "required"

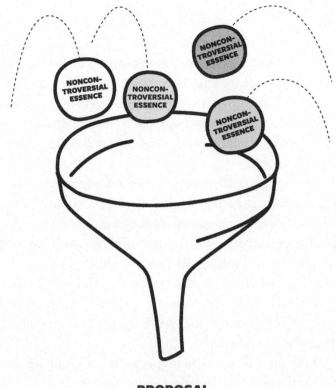

PROPOSAL

to have an opinion we will generate one and even become attached to it. I think we are all secretly traumatized from many experiences of decision-making processes turning sour, and want to protect ourselves from those disappointments, so there is relief in being less involved. Watch out, though, because a very common pattern is for people to stay away from participation until it comes time to implement, when they will criticize or interfere. It only works to entrust others when the basic trust really exists.

This insight has helped me free myself from equating the value of inclusion with the particular form of having everyone participate in every decision. It's extremely unwieldy for a group larger than six to ten people to be involved in the details of searching for an initial strategy that attends to the needs of all, not to mention the scheduling. What's important, instead, is to have those who are the active engineers of the proposal be exposed, in the process of proposal creation, to as much of the needs and reasoning of people who will disagree with them as possible.

If the group is small enough, tremendous gains can be made by having them all participate. Having all of them wrestle with the constraints and manage to come up with something they can all agree to, creates cohesion and the exhilaration of active participation and accomplishment. In addition, there is no need for a separate phase of reviewing the proposal, because the decision is being made step by step along the way, and everyone comes along. They reach the finish line together, all informed, and all active.

At the same time, the more people in the group who're crafting the proposal, the more active your facilitation will need to be in order to bring enough divergence to the group to elicit sufficient creativity. Eventually, the benefit of having everyone participate dwarfs in comparison with the added stress. For example, you will need to be vigilant to catch the people who are quiet from decision fatigue or mistrust rather than because they are fundamentally OK with what's happening. Depending on the group, somewhere between eight and ten people it becomes unwieldy, and you will very likely want to form one or more committees.

The committee or committees are entrusted to come up with proposals that address the most criteria and meet the most needs. The proposals are then brought back to the larger group for further discussion and a final decision.

Forming multiple committees

If the group is large enough and/or if there is enough tension and mistrust, multiple committees/small groups to work on proposals can give more people a sense of involvement as well as more chance overall for creative solutions to emerge.

Multiple committees are useful, in particular, when the task at hand is substantial and can be divided, and/or if there are multiple stakeholders that want to be involved in all phases or if the final decision would benefit if *everyone* is involved with proposal creation. In that case, make sure that each committee is comprised of people who have different perspectives and expertise.

There is no "science" to the decision about whether to have multiple committees working on the same problem, resulting in more than one proposal at the end, or have each committee work on a different part of the problem such that the resulting proposals add to each other rather than run in parallel. Dividing the problem requires, in general, more trust, and more consideration of matching skills to tasks. On the other hand, it leaves each committee with less work. Another consideration is that multiple parallel committees do allow more voices to be involved in holding all the needs, which is why it may work better when there isn't enough trust.

If there are multiple committees, another option to consider is for each one to have a volunteer facilitator, and for you to only support the facilitators rather than to work with each of the committees. When doing so, the committees may not get as far as they might with facilitation; however there may be more creativity in what they attend to on their own. For a more detailed example about this approach, read the chapter about the Minnesota project I facilitated.

Selecting one committee

There are many situations in which the option of multiple committees doesn't exist. This can be for any number of reasons such as that there aren't enough resources, including your facilitation presence, to support multiple committees, or people are simply either not available or not willing to commit to doing the work. In such cases, you will have the rich and complex task of selecting one committee to do the work.

The temptation is often to pick the people who are most agreeable and moderate, and that can lead to complete disintegration when a proposal is presented to the larger group. Instead, aim to pick the people who are least likely to accept the proposal at the end. You want to have the diversity of needs and the most intense attachments to outcome in the committee that's doing the work. Others will then more likely follow. In other words, consider selecting the people with the strongest opinions and greatest potential to block the process, so that you can have the most potential for controversy in the committee.

To begin with, it's simplest if you can get people to volunteer on their own. Give them strong guidelines for self-selecting. Here's what I usually say to groups in this moment: "Please volunteer for this committee if one of the following is true for you:

- you're concerned that if you're not there, something will be missing;
- you have strong opinions;
- you have something to contribute to the functioning of the committee; and/or
- you will be challenged to trust what the committee comes up with if you're not part of it."

In addition to these, you will likely want to consider additional elements specific to the situation you are facing. For example, if there are multiple layers of structural power within an organization, you want to make sure that people with less power are part of the committee. There are two basic reasons for this intention. One is that they are likely to be closer to implementation and therefore know things that people in higher management are more likely to be oblivious to. The other is that they are more likely to believe (and often with good reason!) that their needs and perspectives will be dropped. For similar reasons, if there are multiple organizational roles and perspectives, you might want to see to it that the committee includes a variety of those.

If there is someone you believe is essential for the committee to be able to function, make that known to them in the form of a question or a request, not a command. For example: "I'm concerned that if you are not part of the committee you will not be satisfied with the results. Are you open to joining?" Or "... they will be missing your years of experience. Are you confident that the committee has enough knowledge to carry out its task without you?"

The process of forming the committee is a delicate moment during which your focus is on keeping the togetherness reached at the criteria-gathering phase. Your language counts, here as elsewhere. For example, instead of "I want to make sure that all the different opinions and positions are represented" – which can re-polarize – I focus on the needs, and say "I want us to have a committee that represents all the different needs" – which brings people together. This is one of the many moments in which a subtle shift in your words can have significant difference in outcome.

Ultimately, your goal is to have everyone on the committee

**Please volunteer for
this committee if:**

- You're concerned that if you're not
  there, something will be missing

- You have strong opinions

- You have something to contribute
  to the functioning of the committee

- You will be challenged to trust
  what the committee comes up with
  if you're not part of it.

add value to it. If they don't add value, they are likely to add weight. It's another application of the principle of efficiency. Just as much as there can be people missing, there can be too many people, in which case you will want to invite people to de-select for where you see the redundancy.

One last consideration is that sometimes you might not be able to have all the needed people on the committee for logistical or other reasons. In that case, for the committee to do its work well, they will likely need to learn enough about what's important to the people who are unable to attend. "Enough" means both that the committee members feel confident and that the person who cannot attend is satisfied that what's important to them has been heard and understood.

Breakthrough Insight: Reaching a Shared Commitment to the Whole

However you choose who will be making the proposals, once the work of proposal creation starts, the purpose of the process shifts. You are no longer looking for additional criteria, though they may still surface, at any point until a decision is finalized. Instead, the task now is to come up with a proposal. If the key focus of the first phase was on finding the noncontroversial essence for each thing said and creating a whole in this way, the key focus of the second phase is finding solutions that can attend to that whole.

Now that you've got the committee(s) that will work on the task, it's time to support them in doing so. There are a few more set-up tasks, and then the big unknown.

Moving towards proposals

First, you will likely want to remind people that they are now stewards of the whole, not advocates for their own position.

Just as much as I am reminding you time and again, they are likely to need the reminders and the support about how to do it. What they are stewarding is both the concrete list of the needs that they all participated in generating earlier, and the felt sense of the totality of the group, its dreams, its trust, however tentative it is or isn't. I've often been asked how it is that people shift from being advocates to being shared problem solvers. The frequency of the question, to me, is a sign of what our culture has done. We are all habituated to believe that it's unlikely. In my experience, again, when people are truly heard and trust that they matter, they spontaneously want to care for others. If you keep reminding them that the goal is solutions that work for everyone, not just for some people or for some other people, they will at least be intrigued. Although most of us accept the ubiquity of war, we don't want to be at war all the time; it's really not pleasant. This process gives us a way to transcend conflict, and people are hungry for such hope.

Second, if the process was set up to be an either/or decision, the likelihood of successfully converging diminishes. It's way more likely that hybrid solutions will work. As an example, colleagues of mine were doing a training in Pakistan for Afghan refugees. The training was so successful, that people were bemoaning not having had such a training earlier which could have prevented some war or bloodshed. Being so moved, some of them spontaneously invited my colleagues to come to the mosque on Friday. Instantly, a few others were deeply offended about how anyone would dare invite people from the US to the mosque. Sadly, within seconds they were having a big and heated argument. My colleagues slowed down the action, and supported everyone in expressing and hearing needs. At the end, they were left with what to do after everyone understood everyone's needs. Then, with all that knowledge, they were able to craft an elaborate path whereby my colleagues were able to get into the mosque and not be in view of the people praying. There would not have been a way to have everyone agree to the original "yes" or "no" debate, because there truly were needs, in either direction, that would not be met. It was only the ability to step out of the either/or paradigm that we are so used to that allowed the group to find a true solution.

Third, invite the committee to push the proposal forward as far as possible. This means getting all the research done and all the necessary stakeholders involved so that the proposal addresses the "how" in sufficient detail that if the proposal is accepted action steps are already clear.

In search of specific outcomes

Just as your central facilitation question for the criteria-gathering phase is what's important to the different individuals in the group, the central question for this phase can be phrased this way: "Does anyone have a way forward that you believe can address all the needs (criteria, principles, etc.) on the list?" As you will soon see in more detail, one of your key functions during this phase is to track whether this task is actually being done.

If, for example, a proposal that someone put on the table does not address a criterion that was named before, give it back to the person who proposed it. You can refer back as often as necessary to the list of needs you are holding with the group, and name the need(s) that you don't see addressed by the proposal in question. Most importantly, don't wait for the person who named that need to have to object again. This increases trust, because people see that their needs are held by you and they don't have to be so vigilant about them.

The flow in this phase is the most organic and open-ended, and the most difficult to orchestrate in any structured way, because the main asset here is the creativity present in the room. Here's an example of how this may unfold.

Imagine a team that got together for figuring out how to engage with a new production procedure. Rather than going through a separate criteria-gathering phase, the group may even start the process directly with proposal creation, choosing to identify the needs through exploring a variety of options and the objections that come up. Here are some of the needs they may discover:

a. order and coherence in the production sequence
b. staying on the cutting edge of the industry
c. respect for employees' experience
d. ease of implementation
e. sustainability for the company

Initially, there may be a tug between two strategies on the table. One strategy may be to invite a newly hired production manager, with an advanced degree in engineering, to design the full implementation. This strategy is likely to address a, b, and d above, but not c and e. (This person may be familiar with state of the art processes, but not as fluent with the internal systems within the company in order to know who to involve in the planning and what the ramifications are for the sustainability of the company.) The other strategy being considered may be to adopt right away some of the steps of the proposed procedure, assess their effect, and then decide again about other steps. This strategy is likely to address a, c, and e, but not necessarily b and d.

As the team reviews and assesses the proposals, it can

easily happen that someone will suddenly pop up with a new proposal that attends to all the needs. This might be to ask the new production manager to partner with a senior floor worker and with a representative from finance and form an implementation committee with them. With the two additional members, the implementation committee can now ensure that the needs for respect and sustainability are addressed alongside the other needs.

Because you are in a position of facilitating the process and not part of the group, the outcome doesn't affect you in the same degree, and you can have more creativity as a result. If nothing else, you are likely to have less anxiety about the outcome, and that in itself will give you more space. Accordingly, even though a proposal that comes from the group is preferable, if no proposal addresses the needs sufficiently, and you see a way to modify an existing proposal or create a new one that incorporates more needs, you would be serving the group. If there is a lot of contention in the group, you might tie the proposal more explicitly to the needs you believe it addresses. Making the proposal is a way to check your understanding of where the group is – you essentially try it out to see if the proposed strategy indeed addresses sufficient needs.

As the exploration proceeds, you can keep adding needs and principles to the list as proposals are being shared, especially as you hear objections. If the criteria-gathering phase was thorough enough, the group is less likely to discover new needs at this point, which is why I put so much focus on drawing people out and surfacing as many needs and principles as people can be conscious of in the first phase. If you do add new ones, keep recapping the whole and re-invite people into shared ownership of the new and expanded list.

The proposal creation phase ends when there are no new tweaks and the committee generally agrees that this proposal attends to as many needs as possible and is ready to be brought back to the larger group. If the entire group is involved with the proposal creation, then this phase and the next one are merged. In that case, the group needs to be more meticulous because there is no further process to discovering any errors. This means that you would be supporting the group in giving much more attention to how it decides that it's done. More on this in the section further below on the decision-making phase.

Tracking

During the proposal phase, when much of the work is being done by the group, you will likely be using many of your overall facilitation skills to support them in focusing on their task. In part, this is because on their own they are more likely to get bogged down in discussions that don't converge. Your main task, then, is to keep them on track with an ongoing invitation to come up with a proposal that attends to as many needs as possible.

At all times, in any phase of this process, it's part of your role as the facilitator to assess what is happening in the group and respond to it. This capacity to track what is happening is the most significant facilitation skill for this phase, which is why I am presenting it here even though this is a skill that you will likely use in any form of facilitation and any part of the process. This skill is crucial in this phase in particular so you can keep the process going and focused, and to support people's confidence and trust in the effectiveness of the facilitation.

I focus on tracking six elements: purpose, time, people, power differences, criteria/needs, and open loops. If you have a concern about any of these elements, which I elaborate below, you could propose a way for the group to refocus, or you could bring the issue to the attention of the group to support *their* decision about what they want to do. The choice about which way to go depends on how the process was set up and how much active facilitation you gravitate towards.

Tracking Purpose: *Is what's happening related to the group's purpose?*
There is no activity that I consider intrinsically fitting or not fitting while facilitating; it all depends on the purpose. To the extent that I am conscious as a facilitator, I am constantly checking what is happening in relation to what we are here to do.

In the context of Convergent Facilitation, the purpose is always clear: Move as efficiently as possible towards a solution that works for everyone. This overarching purpose takes different forms in each of the phases. In the first phase, the purpose question is about whether what's happening is contributing to getting all the criteria to be on one list. In the second phase, I focus on whether what's happening is supporting the emergence of a proposal. In the third phase, it's most about whether we are moving towards a solution. When dealing with outliers, as will become clearer later in this chapter, the purpose is convergence, togetherness in facing the gap between the outlier and the group. Here's an example of how you might try to redirect the group: "I want someone to note the point just made by John. It seems important to the overall functioning of this group, and I don't see it as directly related to what we gathered for today. Is someone willing to write it down and bring it up at another meeting? ... Thank you! John, are you OK to drop it for now so we can stay focused on reaching a decision?"

Tracking Time: *How much time is left in the meeting? How much time did the group agree to discuss this topic? What do you want to focus on given the amount of time left?*

In case you haven't noticed, I don't believe in right answers that serve in all circumstances. One of the circumstances that most affects my facilitation choices is awareness about how far we are from an agreed end time. Closer to the end I am likely to be less flexible, open to less discussion before trying to reach a decision, and, specifically for this phase, less willing to support efforts to find a more perfect proposal.

Here's an example of what you might say under such circumstances: "We now have only a few minutes left, and I want to make sure that we consciously choose how to proceed. There may be more tweaks we could make to the proposal being formulated, and I am concerned that if we continue in this way, we will not come to closure so we can bring a proposal we feel good about to the larger group. So I want to hear additional tweaks only if they are absolutely essential to someone."

Tracking People: *Who is waiting to speak? Who hasn't spoken at all? Is the person complete with a topic – both the content and emotion underneath it?*

The larger the group, the harder it is to track people effectively. This is one of the reasons why I advocate for committees/smaller groups for the proposal-creation phase. If the group is small enough, the person who doesn't speak stands out more easily, for example. It may be a bit challenging, and, still, I hope you can train yourself to have sufficient comfort with saying things such as the following two examples.

Patty, I just want to check in with you, since I haven't heard anything from you since we started this meeting. I'm not sure if that's your choice or if you're sitting on something that you haven't told us.

Mary, I am aware that you've been wanting to speak for a while, and I want to come back to you in a moment after this thread is complete. Are you OK to wait?

If you are working with a group over time, tracking people extends over the life of a project, not only in this one meeting. For example, if a decision is arrived at by one person stretching a long distance to support the group, note this down to track it in some way for the future. You want to ensure that the group doesn't always align in the same way, with the same people stretching. If, for the next decision, the same person is offering their willingness to stretch, you might want to remind the group that this already happened, express your concern, and raise the threshold for everyone else before accepting this person's willingness.

Tracking Power Differences: *What are the power relations in the room and how do they affect the process?* Tracking power differences, and attending to them, are so important to me that the next chapter is entirely dedicated to this topic. For now, what's important to say is that power differences affect the process of decision-making at all the phases, depriving the group of useful dissent, of essential criteria, and of creative ideas.

Tracking Criteria/Needs: *Is the discussion focused on the criteria/needs that have been identified? Are there needs left unattended as a group is forming proposals? Does a change in a proposal meet more or fewer criteria/needs?*

Even when I sense that the group is on target, I want to track, separately from purpose as a whole, whether what the group is doing is attending to the task that has been defined by the list of needs that was created.

Here's the kind of thing you might consider saying: "It looks to me like in all the discussion that we've had so far we haven't touched on the need for teams to be sitting close to each other for maximum efficiency. Let's take a moment of silence for everyone to reflect on this need and then see if we can modify any of the existing proposals to attend to it."

Tracking Open Loops: *Are there requests or topics on the table that haven't been closed yet because you attended to something else first?*

The reason I suggest that you track open loops is because when you say to someone "Is it okay to talk about this later?" they are entrusting themselves to you. They are not going to hold it in their awareness and ask to speak again, because they believe that you are tracking it and they want to respect your choice about when to come back to it. Then, if in the end you didn't go back to it, they will lose some trust. As a facilitator, people's trust in you is of vital importance, so do anything you can do to maximize the sense that if they entrust themselves to you the loop will be closed. If you don't trust yourself to loop back, there is no loss if you ask the person to be responsible. For example: "I really want to come back to your question and I am holding so many threads that I am not confident I will remember. Can you remind me after lunch?" This attends to the trust, because then there is no implicit expectation that you will take care of it.

There are plenty of ways to track open loops, including creating a "parking lot" for open items and checking in with that list periodically. How you do it is secondary. Focusing your attention on making sure the open loops are closed is what's important.

Here's an example of how you can bring up an open loop: "Gary, hang on a second. Before you start, this seems like a new topic, and we already have something we agreed to talk about that Susan brought up earlier. Do you mind waiting until after we've handled Susan's concern?"

Phase 3: Making the Decision

Core question: *Can the group come to a decision that everybody can accept as their own?*

The moment of truth is finally here: Can this group come to a decision that everybody can accept as their own? The choreography of this phase is the most complex and tight, and takes a fair amount of practice for most people to truly master. The core question that guides your choice in this phase is simple in itself: "Who do I invite to stretch towards willingness so we can find convergence, and how far do I ask them to stretch?" The difficulty lies in the fact that there can be so many different openings and there is no way to know the path ahead of time. Like every engineer, your path forward with the group can only be continual trial and error.

This phase is when you harvest the fruit of the seeds you planted in Phase 1, where you focused on creating coherence, goodwill, and trust within the group as you put together the list of criteria/needs.

The mantra you can keep reminding people of in this phase is that they cannot all have their preferred outcomes if there is going to be a decision everyone can embrace. Most likely, everyone will stretch some, and some people are likely to stretch more than others. Still, no one will be asked to stretch beyond what they can. This is also the time I usually remind people that the process is not about what's fair, only about what's possible.

With that reminder, we embark on evaluating the proposals relative to the needs, picking the proposal to work with, gauging willingness and inviting dissent at the specific level you deem useful, and then showing up to receive what comes back so you can continually integrate what is happening and move the group towards convergence. Each part of this journey contains information about new skills to master.

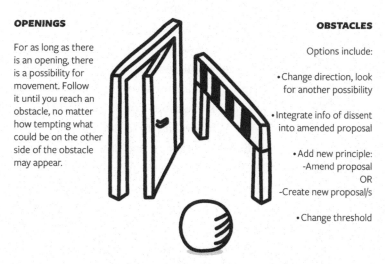

OPENINGS

For as long as there is an opening, there is a possibility for movement. Follow it until you reach an obstacle, no matter how tempting what could be on the other side of the obstacle may appear.

OBSTACLES

Options include:

• Change direction, look for another possibility

• Integrate info of dissent into amended proposal

• Add new principle:
 -Amend proposal
 OR
 -Create new proposal/s

• Change threshold

Follow openings and engage with obstacles using questions/thresholds that give you information

Applying the principle of looking for openings before obstacles to Phase 3. See page 127 for more information

Evaluating proposals

The first step in this process is to evaluate the proposals that the group now has, so as to choose which one to start with in trying to come up with a decision. This process can be done manually through a series of hand raises. It can also be done using a web-based app that was developed specifically for Convergent Facilitation which enables all participants to evaluate proposals in relation to previously entered criteria.[1]

Because not everyone would have access to internet while facilitating, especially anyone working with communities who lack access to resources, I describe fully how the manual process works.

There is no way around it: It is a tedious process, because each proposal is evaluated against the entire list of criteria. The longer the list, the more proposals to evaluate, the more times people will be asked to raise their hands.

Still, the amount of feedback that a group and you receive from this simple exercise is enormous relative to effort, hence efficient by definition. Just looking at the evaluation grid provides an instant way to know which proposal attends to the most criteria and is therefore the one to start with for a decision or modification. If there's only one proposal, this process of evaluation supports the group in seeing quickly where further refinement is needed so the proposal has robust support.

Because we are all habituated to voting, both you and the group can easily imagine that the evaluation *is* the decision. Despite repeated reminders, I still regularly hear people talk about "voting about the proposal." Remind yourself, and the

1 See Next Steps for further information about how to access the app, which is available without a paywall, and has a variety of functions, including gathering criteria and raising concerns in addition to evaluating proposals.

group, that the purpose of evaluation is only to offer guidance about how to proceed towards a decision: "This is absolutely not a vote; it's a tool to help us determine where to focus and where to go next." If there's only one proposal it's to see where sticking points still exist and focus attention there. If there are multiple proposals, this evaluation helps you figure out which proposal to attempt to convert first into a decision, knowing that you and the group may end up returning to another one later.

In a moment we will return to how you utilize the information that this grid gives you. First, here's a simple flow for how you might generate these kinds of responses.

You might start by saying: "Now we'll see how closely the (first) proposal attends to the criteria. We're not voting on adopting any proposal. We're seeing how closely the people in this group believe it comes to meeting the criteria and we're going to use that information as a jumping-off point for decision-making. Raise your hand if you believe this proposal attends to Consideration 1." Then record the number of hands raised.

Now repeat for the other direction: "Raise your hand if you believe it doesn't." Again, record how many hands are raised.

Along the way, let people know, as needed, that if they see this proposal as neutral with regards to this criterion, or for any other reason don't know how to evaluate it, then they simply don't raise their hand in either direction. Also let them know that there is no need to agree on whether and how any proposal attends to any criteria; it's only people's perception of that which is being evaluated.

Ask the same questions for all the considerations, and then for other proposals if they exist. In the end, you may have a grid such as this:

Criteria/ Considerations	Proposal A		Proposal B		Proposal C	
	Attends	Doesn't	Attends	Doesn't	Attends	Doesn't
Consideration 1	13	5	10	3	9	15
Consideration 2	10	4	5	4	12	3
Consideration 3	6	2	11	1	11	2
Total	29	11	26	8	32	20
% No		27.5%		23.5%		38.5%

As you see, the grid itself is quite basic, and will be different depending on how many criteria and how many proposals there are. You see in the example a reminder that it's completely fine and to be expected that the numbers don't necessarily add up to the total number of people in the group when people don't raise their hand for either option. I have always seen this happen, because people don't know, or don't bond with the particular consideration, or don't think that the proposal is relevant to that need, or for any other reason.

Making this determination is, in itself, an intuitive facilitation task. You are trying to find the proposal with the least opposition based on the following:

- Number of people who believe that a proposal attends to the list of criteria
- Number of people who believe that a proposal does not attend to the list, and the proportion of the "doesn't attend to the criterion" for each proposal
- Number of people who engaged with evaluating each of the proposals
- A felt sense of the strength of objections based on previous steps of the process

In the example above, although Proposal C has more people who see it as meeting needs, the level of concern about how well needs are met is high enough that Proposal A appears like a better candidate to start with, cautiously. Again, as you begin to gauge how much willingness there is for Proposal A and engage with the dissent, you might discover that although fewer people thought it would attend to sufficient needs, their concerns are very compelling to them, possibly enough to create a shift in the group, and certainly enough to try another proposal before inviting a larger stretch from anyone. In the end, Proposal B, with the least amount of active support, might be the one chosen precisely because at the same time there is the least amount of opposition. *None* of this can be known in advance. All you need is to have your own intuition about where to start.

If Proposal C were the only one, then the place to zoom in on would be Criterion 1, because that's where the prevalence of concerns appears to be. More generally, if it seems from the evaluation grid there are many sticking points, you can find out which criteria are the priorities by asking questions such as: "If we figure out this one, who would support this proposal?"

When you are done deciding where you want to start, make this decision on your own, without involving the group, as the level of complexity about deciding on a proposal as a *process* decision before working with it as *content* is likely to be beyond most groups' capacity. Still, let them know why, for example: "I'd like to start out with Proposal A not because it's better but because it has less opposition to it." Try to make everything be really practical and clear, not "right."

Bear in mind that since we are looking for a solution that works for everyone, not necessarily the "best" solution, we may never get to the other proposals if the first one manages to become a decision.

Now that you have chosen the proposal you want to attempt to convert into a decision, it's time to help the group make a decision.

Breakthrough Insight: Inviting Just Enough Dissent

The ultimate outcome of Convergent Facilitation is a decision that everyone agrees with. Most often, we refer to such decisions as "consensus." So, is Convergent Facilitation just a fancy name for a consensus process? The reason I have stayed away from using this more familiar term is because of the way that Convergent Facilitation proceeds: Rather than focusing on how to find agreement, when I work with groups to reach collaborative decisions, I focus on surfacing and engaging with dissent. It's a counterintuitive aspect of Convergent Facilitation: I overall want to know, and therefore to ask, where is the energy that wants to go in a different direction from the proposal on the table, so that we can engage with it. This is a key feature of the process, and one that no doubt requires some unpacking to grasp how it works to create an agreement in the end.

Gauging willingness/dissent – basic flow

Your fundamental task in this part of the process is to continually assess whether or not there is "enough" willingness in relation to any one proposal. Bear in mind that the proposals brought in from the proposal-creation phase are only starting points, and may be completely discarded. You gauge the level of willingness, mostly, by finding out how much dissent there is.

This is the part of the process that is most like art and the least available to step by step instruction. It relies in an irreducible way on your intuition about what "enough" willingness is, and, therefore, what kind of question you will ask the group in order to gauge this. Because of this challenge, you can think of the entire section about gauging willingness/dissent as information to shape your intuition rather than as specific guidelines to follow.

Once you find and ask the question, if there is no dissent, then the decision is made, and all that's left is to recognize and celebrate that. If there is dissent, then you will need to engage with it. Engaging with dissent is vitally important for guiding the group towards true willingness to accept the decision rather than compromising. This is when you and the group can find out whether the group has sufficient resources to reach a collaborative decision and, if not, decide together how to handle this.

Another way of looking at this part of the process is that you are always trying to find the sweet spot where you maximize both efficiency and collaboration. You do this by finding out exactly how much support a decision has, so you can decide if you want to slow the process down or speed it up, aim for convergence or for recognizing a limit on the resources of the group.

It would seem, on the face of it, like asking this directly would give you the answer: That if I want to know how much support a proposal has, I would ask for a show of hands of how many people are sufficiently capable of accepting this decision. In reality, though, it's the exact opposite that supports movement towards a decision. Asking about levels of *support* can give you some information about where the group is. It cannot give you information about what you need to work with in order to reach a decision; what the distance is between where the group is and reaching a decision. The only information that is directly related to the movement you are seeking with the group comes from questions that are designed to assess the level of *dissent*. This is why inviting dissent is so crucial to Convergent Facilitation.

Gauging willingness/dissent - setting thresholds

Dissent tells you how far away the people in the group are from making a truly collaborative decision. It's your main instrument for supporting groups in converging on a decision. The way I assess dissent is always by choosing questions that can be answered by a show of hands and don't lend themselves to discussion. My aim is to help a group make decisions by progressive approximations rather than by hearing from people, because discussion often diffuses group energy. Instead, I get group input by carefully crafted show-of-hands questions.

Some questions make it easy to express dissent. I call these low-threshold questions. Others make it hard, and I call them high-threshold questions. Lower threshold questions, by making it easy to dissent, encourage more discussion. Higher threshold questions make it harder for participants to dissent, thereby promoting a faster decision-making time.

You can imagine an invisible threshold that people have to cross in order to express a "no" or voice an objection. For example, you will get different responses if you ask, "Is there anyone who absolutely cannot imagine living with the proposed strategy and would leave the group if we decided this way?" or if you ask, "Is there anyone who has even a minor discomfort with the proposed strategy?" Below, in a shaded box, you can find more examples of the language you could use in asking low- and high-threshold questions.

The spectrum of possibilities is wide. The closer I get to how many people are dead set against a proposal, the faster I get to a shared agreement. Why, then, not always use that end of the spectrum? Because the high threshold to cross to express dissent is costly for the individuals in the group. These are the two variables I work with: care and efficiency. I aim for the exact spot that will give the relevant opening to dissent that will support the current goal.

Overall, it takes a careful consideration about how much energy the group has to make a decision. How long can we take? At what cost would a quick decision come about? As a facilitator, you need to make these assessments so you can pick where on the spectrum you are going to position the question you are about to ask. At one end, the less discussion, the quicker the decision and the higher the cost to the group. At the other, the more discussion there's likely to be before reaching an agreement, then the more buy-in if you do reach it, because it's less costly to the group.

Both high- and low-threshold questions have costs, which is precisely why it's an art and not a science. The cost of a high-threshold question is that it may require too much stretching, thereby leaving people in a state of less than true willingness, resembling the usual unilateral decision-making more and more the higher the threshold. People can lose trust that they matter, especially in a context in which they didn't have much trust to begin with. High-threshold questions also reduce the level of creativity because less dissent is invited into the room. Lastly, since power differences affect the internal thresholds that people have to cross in order to speak, higher thresholds tend to disproportionally affect those with less power. They do, however, yield decisions faster.

Low-threshold questions are not without costs either. Almost by necessity, they make the process longer, more volatile, and deeper. This generally means an end result that's more robust and can be accepted by more people. However, the challenge of staying in the unknown longer, and the general distaste for process that so many people have mean that, along the way, some may be lost to the process.

Nor can you always find medium-threshold questions or trust that they can always solve the challenge. Because just as much as they could lead to a fast-enough decision with enough *discussion and creativity*, they could also lead to a decision that's both too slow and without enough creativity. There's no way around investigating the exact set of circumstances that you're in with a group, and choosing, within those constraints, what you intuit would most serve the group.

There are two basic principles that you can use to guide your inner exploration:

- Set the threshold high enough that you can get the information you need with just one question, so that if your intuitive sense was correct, you might get a decision with one question only;
- Set the threshold low enough that if you misjudged willingness, there's an opportunity for the group to correct it.

In addition to these very broad principles, here are some more specific guidelines that can help you cultivate your intuition. You can use these guidelines for sifting through quickly in the moment as you decide or for learning after the fact. I tend to believe that the best learning is to reflect on each success and failure in finding a question that would work, and learn from it for the future.

- *Your own openness:* Because your presence is a vital asset to the group, your own limits are a very significant consideration in making facilitation choices. In the context of setting the threshold, your presence will diminish rapidly into resentment if you make it too easy for people to dissent relative to your level of interest and true willingness to engage. Make sure you are really honest with yourself and invite only as much dissent as you are truly prepared to engage with.
- *Group stamina*: How much stamina does the group have for remaining in uncertainty and continuing to explore options vs. how much urgency is there about reaching a decision? The more urgency or less stamina, the higher the threshold. If there is true urgency, you are likely to only want to hear very serious concerns.
- *Timeline within the process:* In general, you will find that early in the process you will want to lower your thresholds so you can have more creativity, and later in the process you are likely to raise the threshold so you can reach convergence within the existing timeframe.
- *Balance of numbers:* How many people are favoring the outcome being proposed? In general, though not always, the more people, the higher the initial threshold. Beware, though, of the "tyranny of the majority," especially in the context of a culture that is habituated to majoritarian rule. Sometimes, in the same circumstance, you would opt for a lower threshold precisely to give the minority a sense that their needs matter.

When there are two groups with two different preferences, it's more efficient to hear the reasons for the preferences of the smaller group first, simply because there are fewer of them and if there is a shift in either direction, you will never need to hear the reasons of the larger group.

- *Willingness to shift:* Are there some people who have a lot of willingness to shift? If so, the invitation to stretch issued to those who seem less likely to shift would be weaker, meaning that you would likely use a lower threshold. This is an instance of a direct application of the principle that fairness is not as important as what's possible. Conversely, if, for example, there is a high significance of the proposal for those who crafted it, you would likely raise the threshold to invite more stretching from those who may not have it as their preference.

In my experience I have found that transparency often supports establishing and maintaining trust in the group. In particular, any time you are making a choice about going with this or that proposal, name the needs you believe it addresses, and express clearly why you are choosing it. Given the high commitment to majority rule in the culture, this is especially key if you are choosing to put a minority position on the table. For example, you might say: "Although fewer people want to keep the way we now do production of the magazine, on the basis of what I've heard so far I sense that the needs for continuity and integrity are really important to them, and thus I would like to try to see how many people, hearing this, would be open to delay the changes until further connection has been made with the minority?"

- *Group purpose:* What is the purpose for which the group got together? If the group is in a production-oriented mindset, their tolerance for process is likely to be lower regardless of who the individuals are. This would be a time to raise the threshold. That said, if the issue at hand requires innovation, you would need to lower the threshold, since creativity arises from exploring objections.

- *Trust:* If you are confident that people trust that their needs matter, then they are more likely to speak up for themselves and cross a *higher* threshold in order to express an objection. If you are working with a group you don't know, or where you have a concern that people may be timid or polite and accept a strategy that doesn't work for them, *lower* the threshold.

- *Length of consequences:* If the decision would have only short-term consequences, you are likely to want to reduce the amount of discussion and therefore raise the threshold. Conversely, if the decision that the group is making has long-term consequences, say a five-year strategic plan, a strong buy-in is more important, as well as getting a decision or plan that will attend well to needs. In this case, you will likely want to make more space for objections.

Wherever you start, whatever threshold you choose initially, it's important that you have the willingness to vary it, and especially to raise it as needed. If you keep the threshold at the same level all the time, you will keep getting wonderful information that will make the product better and better, except there won't be any product... Many groups go through that process of trying to reach a perfect decision and reaching none.

It might help to remember that after a while groups develop something I call decision fatigue as they get further into the process. The more discussion, the more attempts to integrate more and more considerations, the less capacity people eventually have to engage meaningfully. This is another way of expressing why you might want to stop a discussion, even a seemingly fruitful one, in order to move closer to a final decision.

There's a story I remember hearing from a building contractor that helps me remember this bit of wisdom. As he was working with a family on a big remodeling project, there were more and more unexpected decisions that they had to make and then live with. In case you haven't been through a major remodeling project, it very often happens that many of these decisions appear huge and overwhelming in the moment and ultimately don't amount to much that will change the quality of life in the house. In this case, at some point, the contractor brought back swatches of carpet for them to choose the color. At that point, one of them threw the swatches to the floor and exclaimed: "Can't the carpet just be beige?! Can't you just make it beige?!" The risk with decision fatigue is that if you keep the discussion open at a low threshold level, a significant item will arise and the group will have no energy to deal with it, and therefore compromise in disgust instead of using its precious and limited willingness resources to find a creative solution to the things that are most significant.

Before ending this section, I want to emphasize that, although I hardly ever ask anything that would invite discussion, I actually love discussion and the exchange of ideas. It's all about relating my choices to purpose. Only a small proportion of groups come together for the purpose of discussion, and those are the only times when I would want to encourage open conversation. Most groups do not come together for discussion, and nonetheless that's what they do most of the time. This is your role as facilitator: Instead of letting words be dropped into a symbolic wastebasket, connect them with a purpose, so they can be digested, composted, and turned in a way that moves the discussion forward towards convergence on a decision.

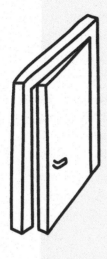

High threshold questions

- "How many people have too many concerns to give this proposal a try for six months?"
- "How many people would leave the group if this proposal were adopted?"
- "How many of you would find it challenging to participate in this project if we adopted this proposal?"
- "How many of you have issues of significant integrity with regards to this proposal?"
- "How many of you are absolutely unwilling to live with this?"
- "How many of you have so much objection to this proposal as it currently stands that you are willing for the group to not reach a decision?"
- "For how many of you would it be too much of a stretch to accept this proposal?"

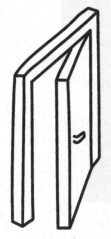

Medium threshold questions

- "How many of you see how this proposal can benefit the company and nonetheless are concerned about at least some aspects of it?"
- "How many of you have concerns about this proposal that might prevent you from accepting it?"
- "For how many of you would it be a stretch to accept this proposal?"

- "In this moment, how many of you have concerns about the proposal that are important for you to address?"

Low threshold questions

- "How many people have at least some aspect of the proposal that you're not super happy with?"
- "How many have a sense that you might accept the proposal and yet it's less than ideal for you?"
- "How many of you believe that your initial preference is better than having this proposal chosen?
- "How many people would have at least some disappointment if we adopted this?"
- "How many people have a different preference?"
- "How many people have concerns about this project?"
- "How many of you have at least some discomfort about this proposal?"
- "How many of you have some things you would ideally like us to discuss before agreeing to this proposal?"
- "How many of you have some tweaks that would make the proposal more acceptable to you?"
- "How many of you see a better way of addressing all the needs on the table than this proposal?"

Focus and height

So far I've only talked about the height of a threshold, which is very much directly an attempt to make it easier or harder for people to "cross" the threshold in order to express dissent. Shifting from "How many of you have some concerns?" to "How many of you have significant concerns?" raises the threshold by raising the intensity of concern anyone is asked to evaluate within themselves before raising their hand.

Another way of varying the threshold is by focusing it, giving a specific context for people's attention rather than a more generic question. Changing the focus may or may not raise the threshold in and of itself; it only focuses the group's attention on a more specific or less specific aspect of the decision and its impacts[2]. In all the examples above except one, the focus was broad. The only one where there was a more specific focus was the reference to "issues of significant integrity," which is a narrower focus than "concerns." In real life, whenever possible, I use a narrower focus than the more generic "concerns" because it provides clearer information faster. Overall, the purpose of threshold questions is to gain information about the degree and depth of dissent that exists in the group. Gaining that information with the least amount of waste has been one of my key goals in developing Convergent Facilitation.

Consider a decision about whether or not Janine will be invited to join a meeting. The following examples provide a mix of high and low thresholds with broad or narrow focus, showing in this way that they can vary independently of each other.

"Raise your hand if you have even a small concern that you

2 I am grateful to Paul Kahawatte for spotting this distinction.

or others in the group would find it harder to speak if Janine comes." – The threshold is low, and very narrow and focused on being able to speak. In this case, the focus is likely to assist people in finding a response, evaluating the proposal accurately against their intuitive sense of things with little effort.

"How many of you have a major concern about Janine joining the meeting today?" – The threshold is low and the focus is broad: *any* kind of concern.

"Raise your hand if you are concerned that having Janine come today would disrupt the meeting in a way that would interfere with us achieving our purpose today." – Here the focus, on achieving purpose, is fairly narrow, and the resulting threshold is fairly high.

Additional examples of thresholds for specific situations

I trust that by now you can see that the range of possible thresholds is beyond anyone's capacity to codify and memorize; there is no way to eliminate the need for creativity here, and no way around the essential requirement to experiment and learn. That said, there are some situations and some examples of thresholds that I want to include as fertilization for your own experimentation.

Uncoupling disagreement from omission. I have seen people oppose a proposed solution because it isn't complete enough, not because there's anything in it that they are specifically opposed to. A discussion can be unstuck in such moments by uncoupling the two. Here's what a threshold for this might look like: "Please raise your hand if you have a major disagreement about what's currently in this proposal. I am not asking if anything is missing; we can look at that and add other elements later. For now, I want to focus on whether we can agree to this proposal knowing that it doesn't cover everything."

Thresholds as a range. One of the ways that you can sometimes gain more information quickly is by proposing a range of possibilities for people to choose from. This is particularly helpful when you are working asynchronously or over distances. As one example, when I wanted to check the level of alignment around a certain statement I wanted to put out in BayNVC's name, I sent the proposed statement to all the stakeholders, and solicited their response in the form of choosing a number among the list below, and entering it in a spreadsheet that all could see.

7 = I love this and am excited for this to go out.

6 = I am grateful for the initiative and happy to support this going out even though I don't love it.

5 = I have some misgivings, and they are small; go ahead and send it.

4 = I have some significant misgivings that I would prefer to discuss, and I am willing for this to go out without further conversation if there are no resources to do so.

3 = If you want to send this, please talk with me first, as I have some concerns that prevent me from true willingness for this to go out, and I want to make changes.

2 = I might shift after some discussion and some changes, and I am doubtful that it will work for me to have anything like this sent in my name.

1 = I cannot support this in integrity, and ask that this initiative be stopped.

Without having any of the familiar interminable email dialogues that so many of us dread, I knew within three days that there was sufficient support for the statement to go out. And what if there had been misgivings? Then I would know right away that my options are either to withdraw the proposal, to go ahead with it and incur loss of trust with some people, or to engage with the dissent. I probably would have chosen the dialogue, or I would have withdrawn it; there's hardly anything that I am willing to do against active opposition that I haven't engaged with. Others who are less inclined to total collaboration might well have been willing to incur the cost and clean up the relationships later, if the initiative had been sufficiently important to them. The point is not about what we do with the information. The point is about being able to have it as fully and efficiently as this method allows. This is, in part, because when we name the entire range, we normalize the possibility of dissent and make it part of what's acceptable.

Bringing attention to where we are. Sometimes, especially as the time for decision-making is coming to an end, calling attention to where the group is as part of the threshold can support convergence. Here are two examples of that:

> *Facilitator:* "I want to remind us all that the value of making a decision is greater than the value of making a perfect decision. With this in mind, and knowing that we are approaching the end of our time together, please raise your hand if you think that you can easily improve in the areas where we still have some open issues."
> *Facilitator:* "Does anyone want to advocate for taking more time to make this decision?"

Breakthrough Insight: Engaging with Dissent as a Gift

You asked for dissent and you got some! What now? Your task now becomes seeing where the opening is. This is one of the moments to hold on strongly to the knowledge that everything that's being said, and how you respond to it, changes the sum total of willingness in the room. If you are new to facilitating collaboration, you might want to slow down the pace at this juncture, so that after each thing is said you take a moment to decide where to go next.

To begin with, focus on the person who expressed the dissent. Especially if they are the only one who is in enough disagreement to express it, they are likely in some vulnerability. Remembering this can help you acknowledge and thank them for expressing the dissent, and then find the ease and patience to start by hearing from them. Then, as in the criteria-gathering phase, and any time someone is expressing their position about anything, identify and reflect what's important to them in noncontroversial language. The field is now different from before this person spoke. Others may find new ideas, more openness, or more annoyance. Stay open to any of it, and follow your intuition to know where to go next.

For example, you may ask the group: "Now that you've heard this, is anyone else interested in changing the proposal we've been discussing?" Or you may notice that what you reflected is actually a new criterion, and the list needs to be extended. At this point, you may want to ask the group to come up with tweaks or alternatives. Or you may ask the person who expressed the dissent to think of a way of addressing their concern while attending to the needs that the original proposal attended to.

Sometimes it will happen that being heard so fully and patiently will be enough for the person dissenting, and now they will find more capacity to stretch and accept the proposal. People are usually much happier to stretch into willingness and let go of their preferred outcome if they see how it benefits the group as a whole and trust that their needs are held with care. You could also schedule a time in the near future to check in with them to see how the decision is playing out.

Sometimes, however, you find no willingness on the part of the person who expressed dissent. This is the moment to see if the rest of the group might be willing to stretch to meet this person's concern. This can happen either through asking *the person who is not willing to stretch* to come up with an alternate proposal that transcends the challenge, or by asking the rest of the group about stretching. For example: "Hearing how important this is to Erin, how many people are willing to accept Erin's proposed changes?"

Here's another example. Imagine that the group is working on a new seating arrangement for the department, and Bob raises his hand when you ask the group if there's anybody who cannot live with the new seating arrangement for six months. How might you respond?

If you want to invite Bob to stretch towards the group, you might say: "Thank you, Bob, for speaking up. That takes courage this far along in the process. Could you live with it for three months?" Bob might still say "no," at which point you might say: "In that case, I'd like to know if you have a suggestion for how to alter this proposal so that you could live with it and it would still attend to everything we've already identified, so it might also work for others."

If this doesn't work, or right from the start, you might ask Bob to tell you more about what makes the proposal so challenging for him to agree to, even for three months. Knowing this might give you more information to help you choose whether to ask Bob to stretch towards the group or to invite the group to stretch towards Bob.

Once again, there are no rules and no predefined outcome. This is an essential ingredient of collaborative facilitation: You keep moving towards where there is openness and willingness, until one of three things happens that, in the end, brings the group together:

a. The person or people dissenting relax and open their willingness to go with the proposal on the table;
b. the dissenters' energy shifts the previous majority and they are now ready to take the dissenting view on board;
c. the group as a whole creates something new – a third way – together, moving in another direction that takes everyone's needs into consideration.

Along the way, you may discover the magic I have encountered time and again, which is that as the group integrates the concerns of dissenters, the emerging proposal, with the amendments that keep being added, ends up improving the plan for everyone without losing anything.

Part of why is that this process continues to lean on the group's shared commitment to the whole. You are not the only one hearing the concerns. Everyone hears them, including those who liked the proposal. That affects everyone in the room. If you can continue to hold the practical and radical vision that this is not about who wins; that you are committed to bringing the entire group to a place where it works for everyone, then it will keep moving towards convergence.

Another reason why this works is that although people

want their way to begin with, everyone is happy to have a decision that feels robust even if it's not their preference. We all know how demoralizing it is to have no decision or to be forced into one, and this is part of what motivates people to trust you and stretch.

One of the things you will need to learn along the way is to let go of understanding everything to the last bit. As soon as someone is fine, there is no more reason to engage with them unless you don't trust what they say. There is really no need to delve into the why. You only need to explore the deeper layers when there are needs that are not satisfied for someone.

Another element that helps is to maintain utmost clarity that you are not looking for the best solution. The outcome that everyone converges towards may not even, in the end, be anyone's preference. It only needs to be workable *enough* for everyone. How much is "enough" is precisely what goes into choosing the threshold and then engaging with the dissent that emerges.

One of the ways you continue to nurture trust is by continuing to remain open to dissent all the way. Even if it looks like everybody is on board, you can continue to let people know that dissent is still encouraged. Your invitation will gradually reach even the people who are initially silent because of thinking this is a charade.

Drawing people out

There are people who take longer to sort through information and needs, and sometimes they feel embarrassed, as if it's too late to express anything after they missed the window. There are others who don't want to rock the boat, who may have a strong opinion but don't want to vocalize it.

If you have any reason to believe, whether because of

knowing anything about the group, or from your gut intuition, or based on your general experience in facilitation, that there are people who are not speaking, then it's vitally important for you to find a way to reach them. Being in a room of nice, polite people spells trouble for the potential for collaboration, and requires more work from you to get the truth out, truth that is indispensable for getting to the best possible decision.

How can you invite people to speak? For example: "I'm surprised that only one person has raised their hand... If you're not expressing what's on your mind, the decision will not be as robust. You will serve the group better by saying what's on your mind."

If you're not sure that people truly feel free, you might say something like: "I'm noticing that no one expressed an objection to what I'm proposing, and I'm actually feeling uneasy about it because I really want you to accept this proposal only if this is really something you can live with. I'd rather you raised an objection and we can work it out." Especially if this is a moment in which there is pressure to just produce a decision, wait, slow down, and ask again if necessary, until you are really sure. This way you convey to people that their needs matter.

As a last resort, this kind of situation is one of the exceptions to my concern about going around the room. People are more likely to express their opinions and concerns if everyone speaks. They may be withholding, still, and this is the limit of what you can do.

When willingness is not emerging
No matter how carefully you craft your threshold questions and work with dissent, you're bound, sooner or later, to reach this dreaded moment in which you set a really high threshold,

and somebody still raises their hand in dissent, after hours of discussion and adaptation of the proposal. What can you do then?

The starting point is to notice what is true, and let the group know. For example, you might say: "The reality is we can't right now make a decision that everybody can live with. That means either we lose some people or we take more time." Then you can engage with the group to decide which way to go. Although it may seem that agreeing to lose some people means the group is right back to majority rule, the process that you have gone through with the group is likely to result in a different experience. This is because the group *is acknowledging together that they couldn't* figure out a way to get everyone's needs attended to. It's a very difficult moment for a group, and it's still very different from simply overruling some people's needs.

Even in this difficult moment, there could still be openings. For example, if you sense that the one person who raised their hand in dissent is not sufficiently held by the group and feels alone, you can respond differently: "I know it's only one person who disagrees, and it may be tempting to accept it without their support. Still, I feel deeply concerned. If we move forward with a strategy that doesn't work for this person, it's a very high price right now for our group. Given this, I want to try to turn it around again and ask again the people who were not willing to go along with that other strategy from before, knowing how costly it would be for this person, might you now be open..." and then proceed as before. Saying it like this gives that person a sense that you are willing to go to bat for them, and, paradoxically, can move them towards the group just enough to be willing to embrace the previously fought strategy. Or it may bring the group closer to that person.

You have no way of knowing how such a moment will unfold. You are looking, as always, for the most opening to shift, and for the most togetherness in the group, even if it's togetherness around not reaching a decision. Your primary search is for willingness. That's what you are trying to maximize.

If no decision is emerging still, you can invite the group into the dilemma. The reality is that there is too much controversy for the amount of time you contracted for. Before turning to other options (see below), you can issue a final invitation: "Hearing that we are almost out of time, how many of you feel strongly enough about your position that you are willing to hold back the group and the decision in order to address your needs?" This is a high enough threshold that it runs the risk of people hearing it as an attempt at coercing them. Convey clearly that this is only a request for information. In particular, try to convey a welcoming intention towards those needs that people feel strongly about, and rigorously check that people don't stretch beyond willingness. If anyone stretches beyond willingness, then it de facto turns into coercion, which you want to avoid.

Another way of issuing this invitation may be: "We are running out of the 10 minutes that we have contracted for. It's not possible for everybody to have their preferred strategy and we want to consider all needs. With all this in mind, are you willing to stretch to accept this strategy even though it's not your preferred strategy?" This way you are reminding people again, as often as necessary for people to really get it, that preference and willingness are not the same.

One other way in which a decision can still be made is by naming that the almost-decision doesn't attend to certain needs, and invite the group to take on the task of attending to those needs in some other way, now or later. This way, the group continues to hold all of the needs even if they can't fit them all into the current proposal.

To summarize as well as add to your toolbox, here are your options when you reach an apparent impasse:

- If there is another proposal that hasn't been explored, you can pick it to work with. In this case, you would be going over the exact same steps with the new one.
- If the decision is truly critical to make, you might vary your threshold. A last-resort one might be: "How many have so much objection to the proposal as it currently stands that you are willing for the group not to reach a decision?"
- If the impasse is due to running out of the contracted time that you have with the group, and you believe that convergence can still happen, you can ask for an extension of time. This can be in the moment, to simply continue the process of engaging with dissent and integrating concerns, or it can be at another time, after people have had a chance to arrive at other proposals. This option also includes the possibility of inviting a small group of people with strong and diverse opinions to do another proposal-creation phase, where more attention can be placed on articulating needs and criteria in full and ensuring that others hear and take ownership of all the needs. If the group is small enough (3-5 people representing the diversity of views in the group), and they work out the details and come back to the group with a proposal on how to address all of the concerns, then that proposal might be accepted by the group.
- If nothing else seems like an option, you can get agreement from the group to other forms of decision. This is quite different from having these methods used without consent of the group. If the group agrees to a majority deciding, or to

having one person or a small group being entrusted to make the decision knowing all the needs and considerations that happened so far, then it is still a collaborative decision, even if at another level.

If none of the above is a path that the group can agree to, the remaining possibility is simply and mournfully to invite the group to hold the dilemma with you – that, given the resources available to the group and the level of contention, no decision is emerging. There could still be magic even then, because this level of mirroring and shared holding is generative and illusion free.

Engaging with Outliers

Core question: *What gifts do these persons bring to the group?*

In my early years of facilitating groups, if things got intense, I was worried that people in the group would judge me. What I noticed instead, repeatedly, is that people would often come up to me after the session and tell me that they learned the most from how I handled that one individual who was presenting the most challenges and intensity. Gradually, I came to realize that this person was probably not a new phenomenon for them; that they probably have known this person for a long time without knowing what to do, and now they suddenly see a new way of responding.

For purposes of this process, I define an outlier in a simple way: somebody who doesn't agree with the majority of the group a majority of the time.

I now believe that outliers hold the key to reaching wise decisions as efficiently as possible. Most often, outliers encounter impatience and lack of interest. When this is their experience, they will remain outliers, which means both that the wisdom they hold would be lost to the group, and that the energy will remain tight and focused on them without moving forward. Outliers remain outliers until they trust that what's important to them matters to the group. The process of getting there is what creates convergence in the group. Because of this, I now believe that what I sign up for when agreeing to facilitate a group is to love everyone in the group, even the people that most annoy me or others.

The gifts that outliers bring to a group can be significant if the challenge is handled with care and clarity. The key is *not to think that your job is to bring the outlier to where the group is.* Instead, if you remain focused on the task of creating convergence, you will gravitate towards some combination of having the group move towards the outlier and having the outlier move towards the group. You may not immediately know what the gift might be, which is why curiosity is one of your main assets in responding to outliers. If you can cultivate this in yourself, your body will align with your words, and the group will relax with you more easily as you respond to outliers.

If you have ever been an outlier, you will likely have an easier time recognizing that very often outliers are simply people who see, and are willing to articulate, things that others don't see or don't have the courage to speak about. Often outliers are perceived as troublemakers although more often than not they are actually motivated by serving the whole, and are defensive only because of years of being maligned and not recognized for what they bring.

Outliers often contribute ideas that other people haven't thought about. If listened to well, they can offer improvements or even breakthrough solutions. In that way, they also act as a lightning rod for testing the real support for proposals. In all these ways, outliers provide an opportunity for greater synergy as the group modifies the solution to integrate what the outlier says.

In an oversimplified way, you could think of outliers as the only ones you need to engage with deeply, because, as you probably know already if you've been facilitating groups, most people, most of the time, and as long as they are heard, will go along with whatever is decided. (Beware, though, of *expecting* them to go along, because then they won't!)

With this in mind, here are some tips and skills that will be helpful to you in attending to the challenges that outliers represent.

Maintaining dignity

Because outliers represent such a challenge to a group, it's essential for you to be relaxed and present when responding to an outlier. In this way you are shortening the distance both the outlier and the group will need to traverse to converge. For the outlier, who is often used to being dismissed, your warm and genuinely curious presence can, in and of itself, provide an immense relief. For the group, your demeanor serves as a reminder that your intention is to include everyone, including the outlier, and that it's possible to connect with and benefit from the outlier.

All of what I just said before notwithstanding, there are, still, times when all the outlier wants is to be heard sufficiently to be able to relax and continue with the process. This is because, after a period of time, sometimes even years, in which the outlier is being dismissed, it gets progressively more challenging to have trust, which is the main element that's needed for shifting. For example, sometimes something as simple as the following can be enough: "Thank you, Jane, for saying this. I get a sense this is a really deep value of yours and I'd like to make sure that someone remembers to bring it up at a staff meeting when it's the main topic. Is anyone willing to track this item?" Jane is honored and she also knows that what's important to her is not dropped just because it's not part of what we're doing now. Imagine how different Jane's experience would be if you responded with "Jane, I am sorry, this is off topic."

That said, this is not the typical scenario in my experience. More often than not, in the process of listening to the outlier, something else happens, and I can't tell you what it will be, because of the inherent mystery of being human. Sometimes it will be a new and important need that then gets added to the list; sometimes it will be an insight about some previously unidentified obstacle to making the decision that requires the group to do more research or engage with additional people for input; or it can be that someone else finds a new and improved solution to the dilemma while you listen to the outlier. And this list doesn't exhaust all the possibilities. I am only listing them so you can be prepared for the unexpected, and be ready to listen with your full presence.

Supporting the group
Even though outliers are so vitally important, they also often tax group energy. If you are even in the least bit challenged by an outlier, chances are good that the group is really struggling. This, too, requires attention and care.

When you sense that the group can no longer stretch to

include what the outlier says, you can do one of two things. One is to invite the group to stretch. This is an example of tending to the group's energy, similar to what I discussed there. You can address the entire group and say, for example: "I want to remind you that we're trying to hear all the concerns so we put energy into the process now rather than making a decision hastily and having problems later. So I invite us all to take a deep breath and hear Jane's concern." As soon as you say that, people are likely to have more inner willingness to hear the concerns that previously they may have had nothing but irritation about.

The other direction you might want to go in is to let the outlier know that you want to shift focus away from them. The key skill you would be using in this case is to be transparent about the transition – what you want to transition to and why you want to transition – and to verify that the person you are speaking with is willing to bring their participation to a temporary closure.

How do you decide which of the two to pursue? As often, there is no one right answer. If you are confident that the gift from the outlier has already been received, and trust yourself to navigate the potential discomfort of shifting away from them, you might want to try that path. Bear in mind that whichever direction you start with, if you are committed to a collaborative outcome about the process and not just about the final decision, then you can move to the other side if the attempt you started with is not yielding willingness. Things shift constantly in a group and in each of us, so checking something again after a couple of minutes can result in an entirely different outcome from before. The main key, as always, is that you look for where the opening is that allows for movement, and use that one.

Closure

Although I provided significant detail about how to attend to an impasse, in my own experience they have been the exception. The overwhelming majority of times when I have used this process – in its fullness or while applying the principles to immediate facilitation challenges – the group converged. In particular, the most complex and long term project I have worked on – the Minnesota Custody Dialogue Group – continued to converge despite significant hurdles which I explain in Chapter 7.

Although the goal of this process is convergence, its conclusion announces itself in the most indirect way possible: *By an absence of hands going up when you invite dissent.* The visual experience of this is minimal amount of energy, which is in stark contrast to the significance of the moment. As a result, this is a moment that's important for you to name and acknowledge explicitly; to let the group know that a decision has been reached and the process is complete.

Here's how you will usually arrive here:

- Decide what threshold of willingness/dissent to set
- Ask a question of the group that reflects that threshold
- If you get dissent, identify what's important
- Decide whether to raise the threshold or tweak the proposal
- If you tweak the proposal, check to see how many people believe the tweak makes the proposal better and how many believe it makes the proposal worse relative to the criteria/needs
- Check for willingness of the people in the group
- Check for willingness of dissenter(s)
- Decide where to ask for stretching, and repeat steps as necessary

Once you believe that the group has actually converged, take one more deep breath and invite dissent one last time: "My sense is that we're all in support of this proposal. For the final time, is there anything else anybody believes we need to look at before finalizing this decision?"

If no hands go up and you trust this, then this is the moment in which you know that a decision has been made. It's time to congratulate the group on making a decision. Especially if there was a lot of stretching and creative problem-solving that were needed, this is a major accomplishment, and naming it helps the group settle into what it has done together.

Time Constraints

As a sweeping generalization, the fewer resources a group has for the process, most especially the willingness to remain in dialogue even if it takes longer than planned and even if the process is uncomfortable, the more stretching will be needed to arrive at a decision, and hence, the less robust the commitment to the decision will be over time.

That said, as a facilitator, there is much that you can do to support the group in moving forward with the most togetherness possible. Paradoxically, you can begin to build more togetherness by acknowledging and naming that, in the existing circumstances, the group runs the risk of incurring "casualties" in terms of trust or goodwill in the process of reaching a decision.

With more time, you can relax significantly the responsibility you otherwise take on for guiding the group and providing leadership. You can then build more skill and facility within the group – asking more questions that will guide individuals to hear each other, to express themselves with clarity, to track needs, and to come up with proposals that address all needs identified. Under time constraints, however, much more depends on you to guide the group to a decision they can all embrace.

In other words, your awareness and skills as facilitator can be such an important asset to the group that shifting responsibility back to you may be crucial. Often enough, this will mean that you will be the one to make a proposal and revise proposals rather than waiting for the group to do it despite how empowering it is for a group, in general, to be responsible for solving its problems, which tends to leave it with more ownership and commitment.

Overall, what you can do under time constraints is a combination of more rigorous application of all the tools to support efficiency that we have already covered as well as stronger invitations to stretch. It's even more important under time constraints to minimize discussion, because of the extreme unlikelihood, especially under time constraints, that a discussion will reach resolution. You do this by continually reminding people to speak only what hasn't been said; by stepping in more often to identify the noncontroversial essence; and by asking show-of-hand questions to move the process forward more quickly.

Absent time constraints, you and the group would generally be able to tolerate more disagreement and invite more needs and criteria into the process of generating proposals. That tends to result in a more robust and sustainable decision, precisely because of not requiring a lot of stretching. This is a trap for you as facilitator, because as wonderful as that experience is, aiming for that outcome under time constraints runs the risk of having no decision at all, which tends to be demoralizing for a group. Because of this, one of the most important things you can do as a facilitator under time constraints, is to strengthen the invitation to stretch into willingness, so that a decision can be made at all.

Is There a Bias in This Process?

On the face of it, there is a peculiar bias built into this process: Basing decisions on people's willingness to stretch is skewed in the direction of the people with the least capacity to stretch. I bring it up both because I want you to be aware of it and consider, from time to time, whether you want to shift anything, and because I want you to have the capacity to address such critiques if they arise in the course of your own ongoing experiments with supporting collaboration.

Three considerations come to mind about this apparent limitation.

First, often enough the strength of the intensity around a preferred outcome is the result of not trusting that our needs matter. Over time, if a person experiences the group's willingness to lean in their direction, the tightness may relax and more willingness to shift can develop.

At the same time, if you work with a group over time, watch out for some people always being the ones to stretch into willingness. This in itself then may become a cost to the group's functioning. When you sense this may be happening, bring it back to the group. You may say: "I've seen that for the fifth time in the last two months Susan is agreeing to something that is not her preference because other people have expressed a strong preference. So at this moment I want to put more priority on Susan's needs being addressed, and I'm no longer as willing to accept her stretching. I want us to look at this so we can come up with something that will work without Susan having to stretch as much." Stay open, however, to the possibility that Susan herself may be quite comfortable with stretching.

Lastly, although it may seem "unfair" to have some people stretch more than others, overall this is what I want in my world anyway: Where the need is strongest, that's where I want to lean. I want to increase my capacity to accept and relax about people having strong opinions, needs, and wishes, or even just a strong attachment to their strategy of choice. It's part of my vision for a world that works for all.

Key Points to Remember

I come back here to the point I made in Chapter 1 about *the significance of scarcity, separation, and powerlessness* – the three pillars of our structures and consciousness. As a facilitator, I am well aware that these are the biggest obstacles to convergence. This is why I specifically want the experience of the decision-making process to be the exact opposite: multiplicity of options, connection, and freedom and power.

This intentionality is directly built into the process that I described in this chapter.

First, creating a shared list of needs and principles is a way of overcoming separation. Doing it, and doing it consciously, brings people in the group together. It literally gives the message that people are not separate from each other; that they are engaged *together* in this task. That creates magic because it allows people to let go of having to hold on to something that's important to them.

Second, by continually asking what strategies can attend to all the needs, this process generates an experience of abundance for people. Instead of the habitual either/or, people realize that they have more options than just the one that works for them and the one that works for someone else. They recognize, even if slowly and without conscious clarity, that they are creating new options together.

Third, by continually inviting dissent into the room, people learn that they are not powerless. They realize that they are part of a whole, and that their own voice matters. They begin to believe that they can shape the outcome instead of being forced into something that they have no say about. Although in theory people always have the power to choose, the risk of consequences makes true choice beyond the reach of most of us most of the time. As a facilitator in this process, you can reduce the risk of consequences by varying the threshold. In how you ask the questions, you literally increase people's sense of power to participate

This is one frame that you can hold for yourself, then. In any situation that you come into while facilitating that is not covered by what I shared with you, which is one way of saying almost all the time, you can ask yourself this simple and radical question: What can I do here, in the most conscious way that I know, to counter scarcity, separation, and powerlessness? If you do that, you are more likely to be moving towards fruitful magical collaboration.

As you may realize already from just reading this chapter, when facilitating a group, especially when there is high charge about reaching a decision, there's constantly something happening in the group that requires your attention so you can track and respond to it. Accordingly, when you begin experimenting with Convergent Facilitation, I want to offer you these few core ideas to help you navigate the process in a way that, indeed, maximizes connection, abundance, and power.

You can keep reminding people of the difference between their immediate energy for (or against) a proposed outcome, and what they can live with given the overall goals of the group, what they hear from others in the group, and the consequences over time. You can aim to remember, and remind others, that the key to opening up a stuck moment lies in connection with deeper needs instead of working only with strategies and positions. You can keep inviting everyone into collective ownership of all the needs necessary for an outcome that works for all. And you can remind yourself and them, again and again, that it's not about what's fair; it's only about what's possible.

Attending to Power Differences

CHAPTER SIX

BEFORE READING AND DIGESTING this chapter, I highly recommend that you get your feet wet. The previous two chapters cover all of the basics in great detail. Although power differences are prevalent in our culture, there are also many instances in which the basic skills will be enough for you to start experimenting. Gain some experience facilitating groups, lead a decision-making process, deal with some outliers, and see what you learn from doing. Once you integrate this learning, come back here and immerse yourself in the study of the complications that surface as you look directly at issues of power.

The main question that I address in this chapter is how *it is possible to create true collaboration in the presence of* power differences. I address this question first in terms of power differences within the group, such as positional power within an organization, or differences in social power (gender, race, class, and others).

Then I shift focus to look at questions of power related to your own role as a facilitator. What is your power as a facilitator, and what can you do to enlist that power in service of the group? What changes when in addition to being a facilitator, you are also a member of the group and might have your own preferred outcomes? What if, on top of that, you are also someone in a position of power in relation to the group? Lastly, how might you gain sufficient trust from a group when you are not the designated facilitator?

In approaching each of these topics, you will know you have reached a level of integration and confidence when you are in a state of flow, applying and adapting all the tools at your disposal to the specific challenges you are facing. Please consider the specific tips below as examples of how you work out which tools to apply rather than as prescriptions about how to respond.

Attending to Power Differences in the Room

To the extent that there are power differences within a room, which is essentially always, the potential for collaboration becomes more elusive. This is because true collaboration emerges from attending to controversy, challenge, and dissent – all of which require trust and freedom, two qualities that tend to be affected by the presence of power differences. Within such a context, you can view your task as being even more focused on supporting people to have the experience that their voice, needs, opinions, and contributions matter, and that they have the freedom to say no without risking overt or subtle retribution.

Many of the key tools at your disposal are ones that we have looked at already: transparency about what you see as going on, listening and reflecting the noncontroversial essence, and varying thresholds to invite more or less stretching from specific individuals based on the power distribution. How you can apply these tools and others I present below will vary depending on the kind of power difference that is present in the room.

Power and collaboration

In order to support clarity and effectiveness, let's establish a baseline of understanding about what power means. I define power as the capacity to mobilize resources to attend to needs. I have found this definition immensely useful in working with individuals, groups, and organizations, because it makes it immediately obvious that all of us need power in order to live at all. The challenge to collaboration that power differences present is the result of how we have structured access to resources within our social order, and of how we have been habituated to view power and use power.

Many of us have come to see power as residing in certain individuals, positions, or groups, and as being a zero-sum game: the belief that when someone has more power, someone else necessarily has less power. Sadly, this is true in the social arrangements we have collectively created in the last several thousand years, in which people use their own or their group's power *over* other people or groups in a way that limits those people's options or access to resources, and in particular delivers consequences to their behavior when those in power dislike it.

Examples are endless. People don't speak up because they are afraid of being fired. One person decides how much money everyone else makes. Most people of African descent in the US have significantly less access to educational opportunities and to wealth. Currently, there's no country in the entire world where a woman earns as much as a man for doing the same job.[1] People under the age of 18 cannot legally make most decisions for themselves. Everywhere you look, within a world structured as ours is, power differences shape people's behavior and affect their responses to what is happening.

The most common power differences are structural or social. In a structural power difference, such as between a boss and an employee or between a landlord and a tenant, it is the nature of the relationship that creates the power differences, and they do not exist as such outside the relationship. In a

1 From a World Economic Forum report which also found that the U.S. ranked 65th in wage equality among 142 countries. money.cnn.com/2014/10/27/news/economy/global-gender-pay-gap/

social power difference, such as those of race and class, the power difference emerges from legal, historical, and/or cultural conditions that affect the individuals in question and which persist beyond the conflictual relationship itself.

In either case, the person with less power is less likely to advocate for their needs. In the case of social power differences, the system as a whole does not favor people with less power advocating for their needs. In addition, cultural norms tend to favor the behaviors and needs of those in the dominant group, making it even less likely that the person with less power would advocate for their needs fully. To add to the complexity, the legal, historical, and cultural conditions that shape the social power landscape within society overall also affect who is likely to be boss (more likely white and male, for example) and who is likely to be an employee. Often enough, the person with less structural power also has less social-structural power, and thus has several barriers to overcome to have their needs count.

As a facilitator, the more you know about such dynamics – both overall and in the specific local and cultural context in which you function as a facilitator – the more you are able to serve any group that aims to make a collaborative decision. In part, this is because people with greater access to power, especially social power, are often not aware of the difference and even less so of the effect that their power has on others.

Structural/positional power
There are many types of relationship in which structural/positional power functions: the relationship between employer and employee, parent and child, landlord and tenant, and many others.

As an example, consider the effects of positional power

differences in the workplace. When people from different levels within an organization are present in the room, everyone's tendency is to assume that what the person with the most power wants will be the result. As the CEO of a company I consulted for said: Having power means you rarely hear no. Ever since hearing this statement, I have been even more attentive, in my own organization, to ensuring that everyone on staff feels free to express their no, especially to me as the only remaining co-founder of the organization as well as the one who generates the most revenue for the organization. Based on my own experiences in this arena, I have come to believe that a commitment to use power with others is not *sufficient on its own, because most of us have internalized the* power-over view of power and act accordingly regardless of what the person with more power does.

Here's an example from a live situation I was present at and about which I wrote an article in the *New York Times.*[2] This is an example of the power of changing the threshold. I was at a client site, and the CEO called his entire team of about 25 people into the room. He had just gotten a huge contract, bigger than the company had ever had, and was holding his hand in a gesture of being about to sign it. Then he said: "Is there anyone who's not ready for me to sign this contract?" I was totally unsurprised that no one said anything, even though I had reason to know that many were full of doubts about their capacity to deliver. What could I do, then? First I said: "I don't know if there is anyone who's not ready. What I do know is that the way you framed the question, it's unlikely anyone would feel free to say so." This was my way of telling the CEO

2 "Want Teamwork? Encourage Free Speech," nytimes.com/2014/04/13/jobs/want-teamwork-encourage-free-speech.html

that the threshold he picked was too high, and didn't leave room for enough dissent (see Chapter 5). I then offered him a different threshold: "Does anyone have any concerns they would like addressed before I sign the contract?" This lower threshold lets people know that he is actually interested in their concerns, and, indeed, resulted in five hands going up right away, and several others later, in the course of the discussion that ensued. The lowered threshold shifted the group into a collaborative exploration of the viability of the contract. As a result, some of the terms of the contract were changed before it was signed, reflecting an adaptation on the part of the CEO to what he was hearing. What's more, the salesperson for the account voluntarily reduced his commission by 30 percent to improve the profit margins, because he was so impressed by the collaborative spirit.[3] All of this emerged from just one change in a question! I am sharing this example in the hopes that it will give you the wisdom to use these differences when you are the one choosing the threshold, and the courage to propose such changes to the person in power.

In this case, part of the elegance was because the CEO – after many months of working with me – was receptive to my offer and the people stepped forward instantly as soon as the door opened. That is not always going to be the case. In many situations, you might need to engage both with the person in power and with those with less power in order to establish the basis of a productive collaboration. The starting point is the fundamental purpose of the meeting: Getting to a decision that everyone can wholeheartedly accept, even

---

3 This bit was not published in the original article, as the NYT editor was concerned it wouldn't be believed! My own experience is that such generosity, which flies in the face of our established view of human nature, is a common occurrence when true collaboration is invited.

if they need to stretch to get there. I remind people of this essential purpose as often as necessary to support the flow of open exchange that is vital for that outcome to emerge. I move back and forth between the different players, depending on where I sense an opening at any given moment.

For example, at a certain moment, if I sense there is reluctance in the room, I might start by acknowledging it. Sometimes just naming what is going on might release some of the fear. I might say, as part of opening the meeting: "I imagine there are some people who are reluctant to express their truth and I'll do everything I can to support them in finding a way to do that." Or I might explicitly invite people who may have a different opinion to contribute their thoughts: "We've heard a lot of support for the proposal, and I would like to hear from people who may not be as excited about it." I may remind people that having a decision that is not based on everything in the room is likely to backfire: "I am concerned in this moment, because if there is something that isn't spoken, it is unlikely to disappear. I hope someone will have the courage to speak your concerns, to reduce the chances that something will show up later, when we are no longer in the room together, and it might even undermine the decision we're in the process of making." All of these are, essentially, examples of lowering the threshold to make it easier for people to express their concerns and dissent. I keep lowering the threshold as far as I can: "Does anyone have even a really minor discomfort with any part of this proposal?" Humor helps to diffuse tension, too, and I like to use it when possible: "Does anyone wish someone else raised a concern?" People are likely to laugh, and, in the relief of that, someone might find a bit more courage to speak.

Given that the person in power is in the room, and everyone

knows there may be consequences to what they say, I weigh carefully what I am about to say before saying it: Is my intuition that what I say will increase or decrease the sense of freedom people have? While I have no way of knowing, I continually aim to learn more about how to subvert power dynamics.

If no one speaks, still, this might be a moment to engage the person with power and bring the dilemma to them. "So no one is voicing any opposition and if I were you, I'd be concerned at this point that you're getting consent from people that is not real." With the person in power, I focus on the cost of having a decision at too high a threshold.

Another strategy for overcoming a power dynamic in a room is to have people move into small groups to share their concerns. This gives them an opportunity to speak with far fewer consequences, and also to bring their concerns back from a group perspective which is less exposing of any one individual.

Just like with the CEO in the example above, I continually want to bring up any subtle way in which the choice of words or way of speaking discourages people from participating: "Given what you just said, I'm concerned because if I were one of the people in the group, I would have less trust that I could speak without being penalized. Are you open to another way of framing it?"

In situations of positional power difference, it's easier to see the challenge to those without power, and yet the person in power is also deeply challenged. If they are habituated to their power, and see it as their job to control the outcome, letting go of that can be intensely unsettling, even scary. Without control, the experience can easily be one of losing power – the ability to mobilize resources to attend to needs – altogether. In addition, people in power are often separate from everyone else in two significant ways. One is that they are often caught in a lonely place of having immense responsibility and a lot of competence, which reinforces the habit of making unilateral decisions. The other is that they are, perhaps, somewhat aware of others' fear and discomfort, and without real trust that their own needs, as the person in power, would matter and be considered if control is released.

Because of both of these, even though the frame is explicitly that of a solution that works for everyone, people in power often believe that they will need to give up what they know about what's important for the organization if they agree to a collaborative, inclusive process. I make a point of countering this implicit belief by saying, explicitly, that no solution will be adopted that doesn't work for them also; that if we're truly aiming to include all the needs, that means their own needs too. This is especially important in organizations with an explicit commitment to collaboration, where the person in power may feel compelled to go along with others against their better judgment, and create enormous stress for themselves when they are accountable for the consequences of a decision they didn't really support.

Sometimes one way of moving through a tense moment of such mistrust is to ask the person in power: "What might you guess are the concerns that others may have?" Then, once they are articulated, you can write them on the board, and, one after the other, ask: "Are there people who resonate with this concern?" If the person in power names concerns, it's easier for others to step into them. After a while, asking for additional concerns may not be as scary for people to respond to.

Naming concerns increases others' willingness to express their own. People's willingness to speak is not binary or static.

Often enough if there is one courageous soul willing to say something, and that person is received in a way that feels good to others, the room fills with more trust, and some others feel emboldened to speak too.

Remember that changing the power dynamics is a slow process for two significant reasons. One is the habits of the person in power, and the other is the habits of those with less power. If someone has been using their power over others for a while, it is likely to take time for them to learn new behaviors, to do the personal and spiritual work of shifting out of aiming to control outcomes, and to become truly open to hearing from others. Similarly, for those habituated to being penalized or dismissed, it will take some time to acquire trust. In part, this is because we are wired in such a way that it takes five or six positive encounters to counterbalance one negative encounter.[4] If the person in power doesn't get "perfect" right away, the shift in trust is easily undermined and needs a lot of care and tending to become established.

These changes will not happen in the room, in front of you, in any permanent way. Still, when you are aware of the difficulties that positional power differences entail, I hope the discussion above will equip you to handle them with grace and confidence.

Before ending this section, I want to stress that I only agree to take on facilitation engagements if I am able to trust that the people in power care about *something* other than just money and control. If I don't have this trust, I cannot usefully serve them, and thus also the group. What helps me, often, is to remember that the person in power operates in exactly

4 There is a range between different studies. Here is one summary description of the results: https://collectivehub.com/2017/05/how-many-good-experiences-finally-outweigh-a-bad-one/.

the same way as any other human being, using the same "algorithm" to make decisions as I do. In every moment, this algorithm calls all of us to notice the vision we have of how we want things to be; then to assess what's possible in the reality we face; and then to make a decision that pushes things in the way of the vision as much as possible. After the decision, we can then mourn the gap between the two and reflect on how we can approximate more and more alignment with our values and vision next time.

Over the years, I have been able to remove the assumption of evil in my dealings with people, regardless of what they do. I no longer write off people when I see them do stuff I don't like. I lean into the only other alternative I know: to have a coherent, empathic understanding of the choices the person in front of me is making. I want to be able to tell the story in a way that they would tell it to themselves. This enables me to include them in the human tapestry, a precondition for facilitating a group this person is part of.

Seeing things in this way helps me have more tenderness towards people in power. I can see their human innocence more and more, even when I am actively horrified by their choices. Then I can focus on easing their fears and supporting them in seeing more possibilities and openings. With that, I can reground myself in the reality that *as a facilitator*, it's never my role to reform the institution. What I can do is facilitate the group the person in power is part of to make collaborative decisions about what they have the authority to make decisions on. Paradoxically, this can induce a gradual change in the institution over time as more and more decisions are made collaboratively.[5]

---

5 To be clear: I am not in any way implying that I would never do anything to create

Although I have written this entire section about a workplace power difference, the same logic applies to other circumstances where there are structural power differences that leave someone with the possibility of using their power over others: parents and their children, teachers and their students, and many other similar situations.

Social power and privilege

Regardless of the specific positions that exist within a group, even if everyone is in theory equal, everyone brings with them dynamics of power and privilege from outside the context. Almost all societies in the world, these days, have social divisions that carry power differences. There are structural dimensions to such power differences, with aggregate levels of often stark differences in access to resources. Those are based in part on historical legacy, and in part on continued policies at many levels that perpetuate these differences.

One of the manifestations of social divisions, which is informed by structural power differences and extends beyond them, is that social divisions also affect individual, interpersonal, and group level behavior. As one small example, whenever I facilitate or train mixed-gender groups, pretty reliably the men in the group speak first and far more often than the women. Much of the time, they are not aware of it. They simply are habituated to feel more comfortable speaking in a group.[6] Of

transformation in an organization. Indeed, I have worked with organizations as a consultant leading massive change efforts. I have coached many leaders in shifting into more and more collaborative approaches to leadership. And I have worked with many activists and others committed to changing our entire systemic structure within which our current organizations function. What I wrote here is only a statement about the role of the facilitator.

6 I am talking about men and women in this example, because this is the dimension I have observed and noted over the years. Because my own awareness of the dimension of multiple gender identities is recent, I have no specific data about course, this is not true of all men or all women. I, for example, never had any trouble speaking in a group from a young age and all the way through life. It's not individual variation that I am focusing on; I am talking here about a social phenomenon of the kind I want to be alert to as a facilitator.

The more you know about the way social power operates in the context in which you facilitate, the more you can do to increase the likelihood that the needs, perspectives, opinions, and preferences of people with less social power will still be part of the outcome. While there isn't anything you can do, as a facilitator, to affect the structural dimension of social life, you can intervene and affect the outcome on the level at which *it operates within the* group you are facilitating.

If you know, for example, that members of certain groups – such as racial and ethnic minorities, people with lower socioeconomic status, or people with disabilities, among others – are likely to be ignored when they speak, you can change it by overcompensating so as to remove barriers to full participation.

The reason for overcompensating is precisely the fundamental commitment to a solution that works for everyone. If social power dynamics tend to operate to minimize and discard the voices and concerns of certain groups, then, as a facilitator, it's vitally important to find ways to make the commitment a reality rather than just a declaration. This looks quite different depending on your own position within society.

If you are yourself a member of a privileged group along any social division, then it is absolutely critical for you to learn about such dynamics so that you can decipher what usually

different behaviors in groups as they relate to people's experience of their own gender when the male-female classification doesn't fit them.

remains hidden in a room to those with privilege.[7] Your own position of privilege almost invariably means that without specific attention and self-education, the dynamics of such privilege will be invisible to you, and you will not have the full range of capabilities to support the group in reaching a collaborative decision when social power divisions are present.

Conversely, if you are a member of a group with less privilege, those people who, like you, are underprivileged may trust you more than if you were of a privileged group, while those of a privileged status may find it a bit more challenging to trust that you will still be open to them and able to attend to their needs. While the permutations may be varied and complex, so long as you keep your sight focused on attending to all the needs present and cultivate your willingness to overcompensate, you are likely over time to find your own ways to create environments in which social power differences are less and less likely to pose insurmountable barriers to collaboration.

One way of overcompensating is to give your full attention to what happens when certain people speak, and act to encourage the widest possible participation. If no one picks up on what's said by someone from a less powerful social group, you might want to step into the discussion and say something

---

7 In the dimension of racial inequality in the United States, there is a veritable information explosion on the internet about the systemic nature of white privilege. A classic starting point is Peggy McIntosh's "Unpacking the Invisible Knapsack" which you can find as a video here: https://www.youtube.com/watch?v=DRnoddGTMTY or as an article by googling the name. Also a classic is Tim Wise's "White Like Me", both a video https://www.youtube.com/watch?v=T6SL-iCp-Y4 and a book. Here are two additional pieces: http://www.tolerance.org/magazine/number-46-spring-2014/feature/peggy-mcintosh-beyond-knapsack; http://www.agjohnson.us/glad/what-is-a-system-of-privilege/. You might also consider looking up SURJ – Showing up for Racial Justice for ideas and resources: http://www.showingupforracialjustice.org/resources.

like: "Hang on a second. Before you go on, I want to make sure that we capture what Jenny said. Jenny, do you want to make sure that what the group does with the grant is aligned with the purpose for which it was written?" Conversely, if someone speaks more often than others and you sense that there is a power dimension to that, you can support others by saying something like: "Jonathan, before you go on, I would like to make sure that anyone who disagrees with you has an opportunity to say so. Could you wait a moment while I check with others to see if they have any concerns about what you've been saying this morning?"

Here, as with positional power, if there is anyone in the group you have any reason to believe doesn't feel free to speak, you might ask them directly to express their opinion before a decision is made. You might say something like: "Hanna, I haven't heard much from you today, and as a result I am not sure that you are truly on board. Are you up for saying something about how you see the direction the group is going?" Bear in mind, though, that in some cultures speaking up is frowned upon, and be prepared, instead, to ask a yes/no question such as: "Hanna, I haven't heard much from you today, and I want to check in with you. Is there anything that concerns you about the discussion so far?"

Another, trickier way to overcompensate might be important if you believe that some people might not even feel free to express divergent opinions if someone from a more powerful group has already spoken. In this case you might want to establish an order of speaking that prioritizes the people who usually are less likely to speak. This practice goes against the norms of "business as usual" in most places, and can be challenging, both for you and for people in the group, whether privileged or not. For example, I have on occasion asked to hear first from people of color before hearing from white people in a room that was almost all white. There was evident discomfort for some of the white people, and I was in acceptance of it knowing how much invisible discomfort there is for the people of color most of the time just by virtue of being in an almost all white group. Sadly, given the history and continued persistence of power dynamics in society and within groups, and the number of people who have been traumatized by the realities of power differences, this strategy, though designed to support the less powerful, can also call attention to them in ways that could also feel uncomfortable. Nothing you do is going to work for everyone. Facilitating in the context of power differences requires both courage and a lot of knowledge and experience.

Intensity, privilege, and facilitation

One of the repeating patterns that happen in mixed-race groups, for example, is a sequence in which a person of color, say, raises an issue they have regarding the lack of awareness of a certain white person in the group. Then, before the facilitator has had a chance to hear the person raising the issue, the white person in question has a reaction, often a strong one.[8] Quite often the attention then moves to the white person, sometimes even with the active or tacit support of the facilitator. The white person's upset gets heard in full instead of the white person being gently and fiercely invited to respond with kindness and vulnerability to the person of color despite their reaction. Even more painful is the fact

---

8 Although I have some concerns about the term "white fragility" as a term, the descriptions that come with this term can illustrate the underlying mechanisms that create this in the first place: http://goodmenproject.com/featured-content/white-fragility-why-its-so-hard-to-talk-to-white-people-about-racism-twlm/.

that so often the group's attention never goes back to the person of color who spoke up, an experience that reinforces centuries of oppression.

In thinking about these kinds of situations, it became clear to me that two reasons combine to make this sequence so common. One is that part of the social dynamics of power is that the comfort of those in the dominant group is invisibly prioritized, starting with the way society is set up, and including the way we are all trained to experience different people's expressions of upset. Whether the facilitator is white or a person of color, it is very likely that unconsciously the needs of the white person in distress would be prioritized. If the *facilitator is also white, a white person's expression of upset* may be less challenging for them to respond to than the original expression of the person of color who is calling a white person to task on their words or actions. If the facilitator is a person of color, they may well feel internal tension regarding how the group may see them. If they choose to support the person of color in being heard, they would likely do it while absorbing the risk of being seen as a militant or angry person of color. This may very well lead the facilitator to also choose to soothe the upset white person, while even then they incur an extra risk of being seen – by themselves or by others – as colluding with a power system that marginalizes or ignores the concerns of people of color.

The other reason why the white person is likely to receive attention is a general facilitation pattern: It's easy for a facilitator to follow intensity and to put attention where intensity is most visible to them.

This means that if you would like to transcend patterns that reinforce the separation between races and the implicit prioritizing of the needs of one race in relation to another, it will require you to grow capacity in two areas.

The first is to find out, with as much honesty as you can muster, how genuinely open you are to all, both white people and people of color. This goes in both directions. One is the one I mentioned above: Facilitators of all races, for different reasons, may well defer to white people in the situation above, because of societal patterns of prioritizing the needs and experiences of white people. The other is that any social-justice-oriented facilitator can fall into the trap of judging the white person and "siding" with the person of color. Still, given societal patterns, the most significant inner examination is for white facilitators to continue to reach for more and more openness to the experience of people of color. I am speaking here of openness beyond abstract thinking and care; I am talking about openness that tears the heart sufficiently to be willing to take uncomfortable action to support the shift that will truly make everyone's needs matter.

The other area that will likely require attention from you is working on being able to choose to divert attention away from intensity and towards purpose. This is a core facilitation competency, which takes great focus and skill, particularly to do it with care for all, and all the more challenging in a context of power differences and societal patterns.

Once you have worked your way through these stumbling blocks, you can begin to be flexible and respond to each moment fully, not just from within your fear about what might happen. If you see a white person responding with an upset expression to being called to task on their previous actions, you probably will want to start by asking that person to wait until you're done receiving the message from the person of color. Often enough a small act of acknowledging humanity may be all it takes for the white person to accept waiting, as it's often about dignity and being seen, not about the specific contents.

What if the white person is not finding the willingness to wait while you switch back to the person of color? This is a uniquely tricky moment, because so many layers are simultaneously present in the group. One of them is that there are, in this moment, two people with an emotional charge, and it's always delicate to navigate even in the absence of any power differences. The general principle that would apply would be the same as in mediation: Whoever has more capacity to listen is the one that will be asked to listen first.

As hard as that is, it becomes exponentially more complex in the context of power differences. In addition to each person's *individual* life story, specific wounds, and trauma, there is also the power context which rearranges everything into a *social* story in which, typically, the white person mixes up their personal "goodness" with the hurt of the person of color, and loses their capacity to hear, while the person of color is devastated by the experience, yet again, of not having any room to express their experience without the floor being taken away from them and focused on someone else. Then there are all the other people in the group, with their varied and unknown levels of awareness of the dynamics at play. And there is the relationship between the group and the facilitator, where everyone is tense and internally looking to the facilitator to "fix" the situation.

Overall, in such situations, my goal as a facilitator would be to get the white person to be able to overcome the intensity of feeling, to let go of attachment to being seen, and to be able to open their heart fully to the experience of the person of color. Sometimes, in order to get there, it may take a bit of back and forth with the white person, during which time the person of color would be exposed to an experience that is painfully common for them and likely invisible for many of the white people. As a facilitator, I want to do all I can to minimize the risk of this.

There are no magic pills for this kind of situation. There is only the loving, committed willingness on the part of the facilitator to consider, moment by moment, which is most likely to attend to as many needs as possible for as many people as possible. It's possible that, if the white person cannot, on the human level, shift their attention back to the person of color, the person of color might find true willingness to open to the process until the attention can shift back to them. How to know true willingness from internally forced willingness is not a small task. Or it may be necessary to protect the person of color from the exposure – either by asking the white person to step outside with support until they are able to come back and listen, or by dividing the group based on how they are responding to the situation, or sometimes directly into racial caucuses to attend to the breakdown and come back as a group later. However that plays out, I see it as vitally important to come back to the original item that was brought up initially by the person of color. This, in itself, is a small subversion of the common dynamic.

Relational power

In addition to the above types of power, another form of power also often exists which I like to call relational power, because this power emerges within a relationship. This is the kind of power that is given to a person for a variety of complex reasons, ranging from natural authority because of knowledge, capacity, or willingness to take responsibility for making things happen, to the kind of status accorded to people because they happen to have traits (such as beauty or being "cool") that are valued. This form of power is particularly tricky for two reasons. One is that often enough the person who has it neither asks for it nor wants it, and it can be challenging to recognize and own as a result. The other is that by virtue of being *relational* power, the person who has it has very little say in it being there or not, as it's *given* by others. Nevertheless, I include it here because it's ubiquitous and thus not attending to it, alongside other forms of power, is likely to interfere with a truly collaborative decision. Much of the discussion of structural power below would apply to relational power as well.

Strategies to Attend to Power for the Three Phases

To sum up, power differences within the group add a layer of complexity and are almost always present. In each of the phases, those with less power are less likely to be part of the process unless you bring conscious attention and take deliberate action. Here's how the challenges show up in each phase and some general guidelines for how you can support full collaboration.

Because power differences are so critical, they are one of the six factors that the facilitator tracks in all phases to help the group reach its collaborative decision.

Phase 1: Ensuring a full criteria list

When people lack power, they are less likely to speak in the group and bring their perspective.

What you can do, if you are aware of power differences – within the group, or even in relation to you – is to remove barriers to speaking. If the group is small enough, risk redundancy by inviting every person to say what's important to them so that everything important is included. In larger groups, you might invite people explicitly. This entire chapter contains a number of examples of how you can do that, starting with this one: If after you've asked if there is anything else no one speaks, you could look around the room, pause to make eye contact with anyone you want to hear from, and say to the whole group: "I am still waiting because this is an important moment. It's vital to the process that we have all the criteria. This is not a time to be shy or defer to others. Even if you're unsure, please speak now."

Phase 2: Supporting the creativity necessary for the outcome

People with less power, especially those whose life experience leaves them without power and say in society, are less likely to participate fully in all the aspects of proposal creation: It's safer to leave it to others, especially when life has been an ongoing experience of not being taken seriously. Without actively changing the power dynamics, the group will be deprived of crucial ideas that can only arise from those without power, who most often hold a different perspective that affects what potential solutions could look like.

What you can do if you notice such dynamics in the group is one or more of the following:

a. For part of the time, break the group into pairs, where it's easier to speak and harder to disappear. Once a person has come in contact with their own ideas in full in this way, they are more likely to share them with the group later. Note that even the process of dividing into pairs may be challenging, so consider which combination of people choosing their partners and you assigning them to pairs in a way that attends to power differentials you want to use.

b. Amplify what you hear from people with less power when they do participate. Engage with them fully. State how you see what they've said contributes to the process.

c. Ask lots of questions designed to elicit ideas, and direct them at different people all the time rather than only those who are actively carrying the conversation.

d. Engage with those in power, as described earlier, to create an explicit larger opening for creative ideas from all.

Phase 3: Surfacing dissent

When people don't trust that their opinion matters, they are less likely to speak it. When they are afraid of negative consequences, they are less likely to express dissent. Since the point of Convergent Facilitation is an outcome that works for all rather than a quick "yes" from everyone that isn't a true agreement, the success of the whole process depends on your ability to surface and handle dissent.

Accordingly, you will want to find ways to lower the Threshold of Dissent for those who may not otherwise acknowledge discomfort with proposals. For example: "Here's the proposal that Jenny has created. I would love it if you could poke some holes in it, because that will give us more confidence, in the end, that the decision will be sound and include everyone's input."

You could even devise a dual threshold: "I would like to hear from the field workers, and only from the field workers, if you have even a fleeting thought that there may be issues with implementing this proposal; I want to give more weight to your concerns because you will be the ones carrying out the plan if we accept it. For everyone else, I only want to hear if you have serious concerns."

Using Power as a Facilitator

In addition to power differences within the group, another dimension of power differences has to do with the power you have by virtue of being a designated facilitator. To be able to give the group your utmost, learning about that dimension is also a significant part of preparing to facilitate a collaborative process.

When you are the facilitator, especially an outside facilitator, usually people have some willingness to trust you initially because you are the person in authority. What this means, essentially, is that when you speak more weight is given to what you say than when others speak, all other things being equal. This power may change in the course of time, depending on your choices of how you use it, which can increase or decrease the trust that people have in your skill and in your care for their needs.

Being in clear choice about your use of power is an important aspect of your facilitation, because your power is a resource you can use for the benefit of the group. The most significant aspect of your power is that as a facilitator you are making choices every moment about what happens next – Will you be speaking or will you ask others to speak? When is a process finished? What threshold will you use? These are all decisions *you* make about how *you* use your power to guide people through a decision-making process. At any point in time, one of the decisions you make is the degree to which you involve the group in making decisions about the process, especially in moments of transition from something that is happening to something else. Consider this diagram, which shows use of power as a spectrum.

Abdication of Power	Power With	Power Over
Only Others	*Everyone*	*Only me*
(The Group)	(Facilitator and Group)	(The Facilitator)

Who is making the decision?

Initiating transitions

At every moment of potential transition, it's part of your role as the facilitator to choose whether to continue or shift focus, and whether to make a unilateral decision about it or to involve the group in deciding what comes next through *asking questions* of the group.

Transitions are key moments in facilitation (as well as in mediation). Overall, once the group gets to the finish line, if you handle transitions with care and full choice, people are more likely to have a sense that they mattered the whole time.

The fundamental information that informs your choice about whether to continue or to transition, is the information that you are tracking: purpose, time, people, criteria/needs, and open loops (see Chapter 5), along with an ongoing assessment of how the power relations within the group are playing out.

The possibilities for what to do when you notice something that you want to respond to are wide-ranging, including a variety of actions, such as:

- Interrupt
- Ask someone to wait to speak
- Not address an issue that's come up
- Address something that's not on the agenda
- Move to the next item on the agenda

Like everything else about facilitation, the first part is internal: You notice something that prompts you to want to make a transition; you figure out what you want to do about it; and you decide whether you want to make a unilateral decision or involve the individual or the group in the decision.

How do you know which way to go? There is no simple or "right" answer. There are no rules you can apply to know for sure. There are only some factors you can consider that will help you with experimenting and developing your own intuitive style and understanding. There are also no "wrong" choices. If you choose in a way that doesn't support the group, you will soon find out, and you can course correct. Note that the more relaxed you are about mistakes, the easier it is to gain the trust of the group for changing direction.

Some of the factors you might want to consider in making this decision include:

- How many people are likely to have a strong reaction to the decision
- The magnitude and duration of the effect of the decision on an individual or on everyone in the group
- The energy level of the group
- How much you trust people in the group to speak up for their needs
- How confident you are that you are making a contribution.

The more likely it is for a strong reaction to occur; the larger and/or longer the magnitude of the effect; the higher the level of energy in the group; the less I trust that people will speak up; and the less confident I am in the decision – the less likely I am to make the decision unilaterally. I am most likely to make a unilateral decision about process when I am confident that people will be fine with it; that the significance of the decision is minor; that the energy of the group is low; that people will speak up if they are not happy with the outcome; and that my decision is actually serving the group's purpose.

Even when you are making the decision unilaterally, if there is a shift in energy flow or focus, or if you are changing an agreed agenda or process, transparency will most often support you in retaining the trust of the group (see Chapter 2). In particular, let people know what has happened that's leading you to make a transition and what you are planning to do next, or what you want the group to do next. Most importantly, make it clear what your decision is and why you're making it, speaking as explicitly as possible about how this transition serves the group's purpose. There is usually more willingness from a group to support your choice when people know why you're doing something.

Here's an example of what you might say at a given moment: "My own energy level is low and I imagine that may be true for others also. Let's take a 10-minute break. I trust that this break will help us come back refreshed as we figure out the timeline for the project."

When you do want to involve the group, the main difference is that you add a request at the end – the same kind of request you might use in leading the group in a decision about content. You are asking individuals or the group for the information that will help you figure out if the transition you are proposing will, indeed, serve.

Here's an example of what might happen when, during a decision-making process, you notice one individual has been speaking for 10 minutes and you don't think people are listening to him:

"Bob, I know you have more to say. I'm concerned about staying with you because I don't sense that people are engaged with what you are saying. I want to hear from other people now and come back to you later to see if you have anything to add. This is because I want everyone paying attention because it's EVERYONE'S engagement and ideas that are going to create a proposal that works for everybody. Are you okay with me shifting to other people now even though you are not done?" As always, Bob may say "no," at which point you have a basket of tools for responding.

You may have noticed that the language I am using here is quite different from what often happens in groups. Often enough I've been in a room when a facilitator says something like: "We're going to take a break," while here I am advocating speaking from within you, saying, instead: "I'd like us to take a break." There are two reasons for this choice of mine. One is, simply, that I believe it's cleaner and more honest: It acknowledges that I'm making the choice, not "we." The second is a corollary: In this acknowledgment, I leave more room for someone to say if they aren't on board with what I would like without having to oppose anything I say.

As you consider whether or not to involve the group, note, also, that if you involve the group "too often," two things can happen. One is loss of energy, however small, that can happen when you ask a group for input on things that they don't really need to decide, which is the bulk of process decisions. This is one of the main reasons why you are there: to make process decisions they don't need to decide so that they can focus on content.

The other risk is that people might lose confidence in you. If you are like most facilitators, you probably have more patience for process than the group. Often enough, the group will welcome your making a unilateral decision about process so they can just focus on the content. At the same time, most people don't like to be told what to do. What is usually most supportive of a group is a combination of decisiveness and complete openness to shift.

One final and important point about your own power: If you are a member of a group with social privilege relative to some or all people in the group you are facilitating, everything I say above regarding tending to your power with care is magnified and you will need even more care and attention to encourage everyone's participation. Conversely and sadly, if you have less privilege relative to some or all people in the group you are facilitating, at least some of them may not trust your capacity, which makes your navigation of power far more complex. Even if you are the designated facilitator, you are facilitating from the social sidelines, so to speak. This can be extraordinarily challenging because it is likely to remain unspoken, and the inner turmoil attendant on having to gain people's trust by "proving yourself" instead of automatically by virtue of your role can be quite intense. Although I haven't myself been in this situation, I have been in two types of related situations that give me some sense of what might be at stake and how this navigation can happen.

One is a situation in which my facilitation is not completely welcome for reasons that have nothing to do with my social group. The other is the myriad situations, especially earlier in my life when I was working in programming in the 1970s and 1980s, when far fewer women were doing so, and I walked into meeting after meeting in which I knew right away that my technical expertise was not taken seriously.

These experiences lead me to offer two basic tips. One is to be even more transparent about transitions and other facilitation decisions, so that people have the opportunity to understand and semi-participate in your decisions, thereby gaining trust that their needs are held. In choosing transparency, however, watch out for the trap of trying to gain the group's approval, especially if you are feeling insecure. The purpose of the transparency is to increase partnership, not to get them to like you! The other is about doing enough inner work to have the willingness to sense mistrust and continue to show up with sufficient self-trust to support others in relaxing with you over time.

Facilitating When You Are Part of the Group

One of the times in which your power as a facilitator may complicate the process of reaching a collaborative outcome is when you yourself are a member of the group you are facilitating and have your own preferred outcome about the issues the group is attempting to decide about. Given that your voice as a facilitator carries more weight, you might end up swaying the group in your favor without even trying to do it. Once the special conditions of you being the facilitator are gone, people might suddenly become aware that they agreed to something they might not otherwise have agreed to.

The solution? If you guessed "lower the threshold whenever possible," then you are probably integrating the lessons of this book. The existence of a power difference makes it harder for people to express dissent. The combination of having a preference plus having power in relation to the group (by virtue of being a facilitator) is what creates that challenge, and making it easier for people to express dissent is one key way of compensating for that difference.

What's more, having a preferred outcome makes it harder

for you to be multi-partial and advocate for everyone. This is one of the instances in which being an effective facilitator requires some inner work. Specifically, you would benefit immensely from working to release any attachment you have to your particular outcome.[9] It means training yourself to remember that you get to participate in the same way that others do: Your own needs are also part of the process and you will need to include them. This requires facility in discerning the noncontroversial essence underneath your own positions and separating it from any outcome you are favoring. Once you can do that, you then include each one of yours along with everyone else's. Essentially, your aim is to include your needs in the eventual outcome, no more and no less than anyone else's needs. This means you participate in the evaluation of proposals relative to the criteria (see Chapter 5), and also in expressing dissent when you are not aligned with a particular proposal.

When you also have formal power

No matter how much you lower the threshold, when you have formal power, people might just not find any capacity to speak up and express dissent. What, then, can you do? What I aim to do is to pump energy into people's potential willingness by speaking from an intention to partner with them about holding the complexity. This means being transparent about the dilemma you are holding. You might say something like: "Here's the dilemma we have: I'm your manager and I also have an opinion in the matter. I can see how it would be difficult to express an opinion different than mine. Since I would like

---

9 One way of working on this is by applying the principles in my article "Wanting Fully without Attachment," *Tikkun*, Jan-Feb 2010.

us to have the strongest decision possible that would truly work for all of us, I want to hear all your concerns." Every reminder to people that they matter increases the chances that they will speak up. I've, indeed, heard from people that such expressions help them feel more at ease expressing themselves.

Your focus, here as always, would be what would be best for the entire group and the purpose for which you came together. It is not the same as your own preferred outcome. The more interested you are personally in the decision, the lower the threshold needs to be to correct the bias in your individual position. Scout out for disagreement if at all possible.

If you are also the one to craft the new proposal or if you have participated in crafting it, and especially if you have any attachment to outcome, you can support the group by making it visible how you are changing your original proposal to address new needs named in the process. People are unlikely to notice on their own that you are including their needs unless you make it explicit. For example, Deena (fictitious name), a business owner committed to collaboration, wanted to introduce a new process for getting things done in her company. She was concerned that one of the employees would be anxious about her proposal because this employee needed to know what to do in a clear sequence to give her a certain kind of order. If Deena integrates this need, she might then say: "This is the original change I wanted to make, and now, hearing that you need order, I am adjusting it in this way ... which I believe will give you more of the order that you want. Do you sense that this tweak addresses your need sufficiently for you to be able to live with it?" Again, one core reason for doing this is because it sends a message to that employee that her needs indeed matter to you. Well beyond facilitating any particular decision, this kind of message is likely to transform the overall relationship with the employee for that very reason.

While aiming to invite dissent and expression of divergent opinions, watch out for the tendency to diminish and abdicate your power in the process. Expressing clearly what is happening and why – one of the core tasks of facilitation – is not the same as oppressing or dominating others. Your leadership in your role as facilitator, your very willingness to inhabit that power, is essential for the group to be able to function. The task is to hold your power and weight with tenderness and care, as service to the whole, rather than to aim to undo the power to make yourself more comfortable and connected to others.

Facilitating from the sidelines

One final configuration I want to explore before ending this chapter about power is when you are a participant in the group without being the designated facilitator or leader of the group. I remember the day when I learned viscerally about the effect of being a participant rather than a leader in a group and therefore having no entrustment from the group (i.e. not being trusted by it). Because I so often facilitate or lead groups, I had "forgotten" about that experience. Until I was in a group, maybe 10 years ago, where I used the exact type of words I would use as a facilitator – in that case it was about wanting there to be a time limit for each person who spoke in a group of 35. I articulated what I wanted and why I wanted it, and asked to see a show of hands of who also wanted it. The reaction, instead, was a wave of people saying some version of "just let the next person speak." I didn't just understand something new about facilitating from the sidelines... I actively *felt* it in my body: Facilitating without the entrustment of a group – what I call facilitating from the sidelines – is an art form that requires a higher level of skill to make up for the absence of the implicit entrustment that people generally give to someone in a position of leadership.

Once I got it, it was easy to understand why this would be the case. In the absence of structural power to provide a reason for others to listen, the only power available to you when attempting to navigate a group to collaborative decision-making is the connection that you can forge with others. In the absence of a structure that supports it, the path to such connection is more complex.

If you do want to facilitate a decision-making process from the sidelines, here are some additional tips that might be helpful:

- **Contract for time:** Ask the group for an amount of time the group is willing to give you to try to reach a decision, as if you are "contracting" with the group for temporary leadership. People are often anxious about having an open-ended process for making a decision. Contracting for, say, five minutes and then re-checking with the group really helps calm a lot of people.

  If the group says yes, that establishes the entrustment. Without it, people are less likely to respond to your requests as you present them, and the group can more easily dissolve into discussion, advice, and dissent. How much time to ask for? Enough that you have some confidence you can "deliver" some results, and not more than your sense of what the group can tolerate. If you are not confident in using Convergent Facilitation, ask for more time upfront, so you don't exceed it unconsciously. Whatever amount of time you ask for, make sure you have a timekeeper that will support you in finishing within the amount of time you have contracted for. Practice before you use

Convergent Facilitation live, because it's unlikely that a group will grant you more than 10 minutes unless you are the official facilitator, and even then their willingness to continue engaging in the way you propose will diminish rapidly over the allotted time. I once led a group through a complex decision in 10 minutes, but in order to do that I repeatedly had to remind people that they had given me their agreement and asked them to wait with their objections to the process until after the 10 minutes were up. By then they all saw that a decision had actually been made.

Here's how it could sound: "I'd like to ask for 10 minutes of your time to see if we can reach a decision about this. I am confident that within 10 minutes we could either reach a decision or learn that we need more mutual understanding and time to create a decision that everyone can live with. Does anyone object to using 10 minutes in this way?"

If the group does not grant you the contract, you are unlikely to get a decision in any amount of time. But you may want to try again after a few more minutes have passed. The longer a discussion continues without decision, the more willing the group might be to grant you the contract.

- **Transform emotional upsets:** If you are asking to facilitate from the sidelines because you are not happy with existing facilitation, work through whatever emotional upset you have on your own before speaking up. You cannot facilitate a situation if you are internally upset. This is not an easy stretch for most, and yet it's essential: You can only approach the group and the existing facilitator effectively if you manage to reach a place of acceptance about what has happened, even if it includes the experience of not being heard by the facilitator, which is particularly hard to transcend.

- **Embrace holding the whole:** From the sidelines, as at any time when you want to facilitate a group, move from the position of holding your needs to the position of holding the whole, which is the foundation of leadership. Whatever you want to say or talk about, do it from the point of view of the group. For example, if, indeed, you are not being heard by the facilitator, and you've managed to overcome your upset, you might say something like: "I'd like to pause for a second to check something with the group, because I'm having a hard time trusting that I am being heard, and I want everyone to be heard." You can't facilitate from the sidelines if you are focused on yourself.
- **Support the designated facilitator:** Position yourself as an ally to the facilitator instead of someone trying to challenge the facilitator. Ask yourself what you can do to support the facilitator in reaching the goal of a collaborative decision and trusting that this is what they truly want, even in moments when it's hard to trust. As an example, you might say something like: "I've been watching what's been happening in the group, and I would like to say something. I believe your purpose in this moment, as you are facilitating this group, is _____. Is that right?" If your guess is accurate, then the facilitator might experience at least a bit of being understood, which then leaves room for you to say something like: "I have a suggestion for how to move towards that purpose. Are you open to me sharing it with you and the group?" If you didn't guess accurately, or you did and the facilitator nonetheless is not open to suggestions, your path to facilitating from the sidelines is much reduced, and you likely will need to consider other paths, such as connecting with the facilitator at a break.

Summary: Supporting Collaboration Across Power Differences

Although I have explored a number of permutations within this chapter, they all boil down to one core insight: In order to maintain a high level of collaboration and efficiency, you will want to be aware of all kinds of power differences that may affect the decision you are trying to facilitate, so that you can counterbalance the power differences and people's attendant fears sufficiently to encourage the full flow of information, feedback, and dissent within the room.

Your main tools for this task are no longer new. One is an acute awareness of how to play with thresholds to increase (or decrease) the level of dissent that will enter the discussion. A second is an even higher degree than usual of transparency as a way to humanize yourself and increase trust. The third is anything that supports the individuals in the group to know that they matter, which also includes continuing to reflect and glean additional considerations if a new noncontroversial essence emerges. The last, key to this entire approach, is affirming and reaffirming the commitment to and faith in the possibility of a solution that works for all.

Case Study: Contested Child Custody Legislation

CHAPTER SEVEN

WHEN I WAS INTRODUCED TO JUDGE BRUCE PETERSON from Minneapolis, Minnesota, and asked to talk with him about potentially supporting a group of complex stakeholders, nothing would have led me to imagine that less than three years later the process that was started that day would yield an elaborate piece of new legislation in the area of child custody that would involve revamping the very criteria used by the family court system to decide custody cases. Even less would I have imagined that, after more than ten years of ongoing mistrust and debate, the final legislation would pass unanimously in the House and 61:3 in the Senate, to be followed by a commitment to additional, non-legislative measures in recognition of the culture-changing aspect of the work of the group.

At the time, Convergent Facilitation was even closer to its birth than it is now, this and many other far smaller projects later. I had not facilitated any public deliberation events, and most of my facilitation had been while leading workshops. I had already been teaching Convergent Facilitation since 2008, and had collected a few experiences – some my own and some of students – that confirmed my complete conviction that miracles are commonplace when collaborative decision-making is structured to maximize willingness and efficiency. That was enough for me to say "yes" to the invitation, knowing that I would learn, discover, and invent the tools necessary to reach a solution acceptable to all.

Because of the richness of such a long and complex project, there are already several pieces written about it: a case study, a blog piece about one aspect of it, and two articles.[1]

1 The case study is at efficientcollaboration.org/results/. Articles: "A Blueprint for Collaborative Lawmaking" by Miki Kashtan, *Interdisciplinary Journal for Partnership Studies* (*IJPS*) Vol. 3 (2016) Iss. 1; "Bringing Nonviolence to the State

I am reproducing here only the bare bones of the timeline, leaving the rest of this chapter for a focus on facilitation and the more "technical" aspects of the project which have not yet been written about.

Timeline: From Mistrust to a Shared Future

I am providing the following timeline so that those who wish to orient themselves could do so. None of the descriptions and analyses of process that follow require understanding the timeline or the issues facing the group.

May 2012: Governor Mark Dayton vetoes proposed child custody legislation, calling on opposing groups to work together.

November 2012: Judge Bruce Peterson convenes a dialogue group facilitated by me.

January 2013–May 2014: The group produces a set of 26 shared principles. Subcommittees operationalize the principles, leading to unanimous passage of preliminary legislation.

June 2014–May 2015: The group dramatically revises **Best Interests of the Child** laws and finds a solution to its core conflict over when and how to keep both parents in their children's lives. A second legislative package passes unanimously in the House and 61:3 in the Senate.

June 2015 onward: Former opponents continue working together to educate lawyers and judges, ensuring their legislation is implemented in line with their intentions.

Legislature," *Nonviolence*, Vol. 1 (Summer 2016); "Family law: Re-focusing on the needs of the child" by Rep. Carolyn Laine, at Twin Cities Pioneer Press, October 14, 2015. Blog post: "Strengthening Collaboration through Encouraging Dissent."

The sections below follow this chronology from the perspective of shedding light on how I used Convergent Facilitation principles and practices during this project. Each section title includes the date or range of dates that it covers.

Getting People to the Table (LATE FALL 2012)

Often enough, your work as a facilitator starts long before you and the people are in the room. There are three main reasons for this. One is that there is so much mistrust or lack of faith in the process that people aren't even sure they want to be in the same room together, and careful facilitation is needed for them to agree to attend an event. A second is that people may come into a room without experiencing free choice about being there. Without working with people ahead of time, it's hard to then discern how much freedom to express dissent there is in the room or how true the commitment might be to a solution that works for all. Both of these are essential driving forces of Convergent Facilitation, and work ahead of time may be crucial in establishing the necessary trust and commitments even when people *appear* willing to be in the room together. Lastly, work ahead of time, when possible, provides you with invaluable information about the situation, offering even the possibility of arriving already with a partially digested criteria list.

In the case of the Minnesota child custody project, all of the above were present: Many people weren't willing to be in the room because of lack of trust; others expressed willingness without speaking their grave concerns; and I didn't have sufficient background information about the challenge facing the group.

The struggle in Minnesota over proposed changes to child

custody legislation had previously gone on for years without any success in establishing true dialogue. As a result, people didn't trust others' intentions about their positions, often seeing each other as having "an agenda," not having any confidence that others would be open to their own positions and needs, and having almost no faith that any positive outcome could come about through a collaborative process.

I found it important to recognize that only the last form of mistrust had to be handled *before* we were in the room together. In the conversations that led to the agreement, I focused my attention on mistrust in the process more than on mistrust of each other, because I anticipated we would be able to attend to that form of mistrust once we were together.

Attending to skepticism

When I came on the scene, the stakeholders in the child custody debate had already been engaged for over ten years in a traditional, hence by definition adversarial, legislative process. Although the governor of Minnesota insisted on a collaborative process instead of accepting a bill passed by the legislature, they remained suspicious.

The key moment in which the skepticism shifted was when I was able to demonstrate the critical aspect of trust building that Convergent Facilitation provides: finding the noncontroversial essence behind opposing positions. (This is the story I alluded to in the Introduction.) Here's one way I described the moment in a blog post (slightly amended):

> Ben (all names are fictitious), one of those present on a conference call in November 2012, said something like: "Let's just face it... There's a philosophical difference here, and there's no point in dialogue. Some of us think

that a presumption of joint custody is just not a wise thing to do, and that's all there is to it." Ben was representing a group of lawyers, and this was his way of letting me know that he wasn't going to support the attempt to bring everyone together to seek a collaborative solution to the acrimonious debate about child custody legislation that was raging in Minnesota at the time.

Recognizing this as a moment of immense potential, an unexpected gift to the process, I proceeded as follows:

I started out by asking Ben what exactly made it unwise to have a presumption of joint custody. I asked, because I didn't know, and it was too broad for me to try guessing. His words in response were something like: "You can make too many mistakes this way, because you end up looking at all families in the same way." That was enough information for me to take a guess next. "Let me see if I got it," I said. "Is the gist of it that you want to ensure that each family is handled according to its specific circumstances?" That was, indeed, it. Then I took a gutsy move, on the phone, without seeing anyone's faces. "I bet anything that Jenny would wholeheartedly endorse this principle even though she is in disagreement with you," I said, hoping and having faith that this would be the case. Jenny was representing the opposing view. "Yes, of course I do," she said, "but..." I stopped her before the fragile accomplishment would dematerialize. "Hang on, Jenny," I said, and then addressed the whole group again, pointing out the unexpected agreement between warring parties, and explaining to them that this – the finding of agreements on principles in the midst of disagreements on positions – was what we would do on the day we came together. That would also be when we would hear from Jenny about her "but," and look for another point of agreement under the disagreement.

Even though we were on a conference call, without seeing each other's faces and with noise on the line, I could literally *feel* the energy shift when we got to that point. No more needed to be said, and we moved directly to the scheduling of the specific dates.

In the face of disagreements, the habit of backing out of collaboration into a win/lose orientation is deeply ingrained. Because of this, I wasn't expecting that initial willingness to carry us to the end. Indeed, over the life of the project doubts arose repeatedly about the capacity of the process to get us to a finish line acceptable to all. I always saw it as an integral part of my role as facilitator to infuse faith into the process. Gradually, over time, some of my faith became integrated into at least some individuals within the group, starting even with the first day (see below). Still, you as a facilitator are much more likely to retain the faith than participants in the process, and I see it as uniquely important for you to be able to reflect that faith in so many words to groups you facilitate.

The complexity of representation

Because Convergent Facilitation is still so new, many situations confront me with new elements that I had not thought of before. The one that took me completely by surprise in the child custody project was the fact that so many of the people who were going to be in the room were representatives of larger constituencies.

Initially, I was making a case for people being in the room as themselves. This turned out to be a mistake. Instead, what eventually made it work was acknowledging that people were representatives, and articulating, repeatedly, that no decision we came up with as a group would go into effect until ratified by all constituencies.

In practice, once people came to the room, and especially over time, they de facto *did* act fully as themselves and not as representatives of anyone else. The mistake was not in anticipating that; it was in asking for it before trust was established.

I learned several important lessons about working with representation that I believe you can apply to your own situations in which some stakeholders represent larger constituencies. First, as I already said before, a full and relaxed acknowledgment of the complexity is indispensable before being able to work effectively with representatives. This is because they tend to feel a sense of responsibility to toe a line that interferes with allowing themselves to be affected by what they hear, and with stretching to embrace a solution that may not be ideal based on the inner transformation that happens on account of the commitment to a solution that works for everyone.

Because representation is so sensitive, and because individuals may shift personally on an issue while their constituency has not shifted, confidentiality became imperative in this project. Throughout the life of the project, questions about what would be shared and how were some of the more challenging to address. This is, in part, because confidentiality is protective and can reinforce entrenchment and distance, while transparency tends to increase trust and lead to more openness, and yet for many representatives, without confidentiality they most literally would not have been able to participate fully. At every step of the way we navigated as much transparency as possible, often resulting in stretching in both directions. Some people shared far less than they wanted to share with their constituency and with the media. Others, at the same time, stretched outside their own comfort zone by agreeing to share things earlier and more fully than they sensed was wise. Only once did this tension flare up into active conflict, at which point older mistrust resurfaced, much to my surprise, and required careful facilitation to help people hear each other again and trust that the challenging event was done without intent to harm.

Because of all these challenges, representation makes it all the more imperative that people truly embrace a solution rather than give in. The reason is that if they are not fully on board, they will have an exceedingly hard time being true ambassadors of the proposed solution. Their own conviction and willingness to share the solution with their constituency as a positive thing makes or breaks the process. If they come to their constituency as subtle victims, the constituency is more likely to generate significant concerns, since the constituents themselves were not in the room, and thus didn't really go through any process; they are just presented with the results. As facilitator, bringing people back to how they present things to their constituency is a significant factor in the success of large-scale decision-making processes of this kind.

The issue of representation remained with us throughout the life of the project. Over time, I developed guidelines for how to work with constituencies to increase the chances of success and minimize the risk of intense challenge coming back from the constituency, especially when the proposed solution delicately integrates multiple needs for groups that are unlikely partners to begin with. Here is the introductory paragraph of the document I finally created for everyone:

> **The Challenge:** Whatever you want to call it, we all know that we've experienced magic in the many, many months of working together. None of the words below capture it – they only point to what we did to create it. At the same time, we could not and never will be able to have everyone in the room because of the number of people involved. Your task, then, is to find a way to transmit this magic to people who've never been in the room with you, with all of us, so they can have some sense of how and why *you* got to where you are. Your task is made more challenging because people may see you as having gone too far and you will need to engage with them in a way that supports them in trusting that you continue to hold their needs, which are also yours, as seriously as ever. You can do this by listening and informing, staying away from defending or apologizing.

By naming the challenge and acknowledging the special experience that people in the room have been through, this introduction provides motivation for taking on the role of ambassador which keeps the representative an integral part of the group working together even when they are with their own constituency. In this way, they can invite the constituency in rather than leaving in order to join their constituency.

Beyond this overall orientation, here are the core principles the group was invited to use in their work with their constituencies. The original document is more detailed. Essentially, this document – and any that you may tailor from it for your particular facilitation circumstances – provides representatives with enough understanding about the process that they can almost be "proxy" facilitators. Note that the "you" in these items refers to the representatives that receive these guidelines, not to you, the facilitator of the process.

1. *Basic agreement with constituents.* Establish an agreement of trust, whereby you commit to represent the constituents' interests, needs, and perspectives while engaging with others in the process, and they commit to mostly abide by your decision given they are not actually in the room.

2. *Collaborative process.* Keep constituents clear and informed about the process of collaboration used in the group rather than only reporting on outcome. Understanding the process increases the chances of trust in the outcome, because it helps them see that *everyone* commits to the same things; that *everyone's* needs and perspectives are owned by all; and that *everyone*, sooner or later, will find themselves stretching.

   a. *Underlying approach.* Simply put, the collaborative process I used in this project aims to identify and address as many of the stakeholders' needs as possible by identifying those needs at a level that is deep enough to be noncontroversial and specific enough that they can provide constraints on the outcome.

   b. *Decision-making process.* The group operates on the principle of aiming for decisions and solutions that are acceptable to all, such that the needs and concerns of all of the participating stakeholder groups are included in the final outcome. (The original document specified, in addition, the conditions for assessing that the proposal, indeed, works for all.)

c. *Win/Win problem solving.* By focusing on everyone's *needs* in a deeper way, the process keeps moving towards more and more convergence and goodwill. The entire group accepts shared ownership and responsibilities for *all* the needs, aiming to attend to addressing as many of them as possible, and always ensuring that whatever progress is made includes everyone.

d. *Principle of willingness.* Rather than voting or any other method that requires people to agree at some point, in this process each person only agrees to what they are willing to agree to. Willingness is different from preference, and it is also understood that in order to reach a collaborative solution everyone's preferred solutions are unlikely to be the outcome accepted by all. Instead, each representative continually considers what they are able to stretch into accepting with complete willingness. Just as much as willingness is different from preference, willingness is also different from compromise, because it is wholehearted, and comes from understanding and embracing care for everyone's needs, while also trusting that others will care for their needs.

e. *Keeping constituents informed.* Err on the side of too much rather than too little information. Constituents will demonstrate more willingness if they feel involved in the process and trust that they are taken seriously and are able to influence the outcome.

f. *Ease of giving input.* Provide your constituents with many avenues to give you input. This might include in-person meetings, a comment feature on your website, one on one meetings, etc. The more open you are and appear, the more likely people are to trust the process.

g. *Realistic expectations.* Let constituents know that the nature of a collaborative process is that in order to reach an agreement all participants and constituents need to focus on their most important needs, because it is quite unlikely that everything they want in exactly the way they want it will be part of the eventual solution. Remind them of the obstacles (time, expense, reputation, past failures, impasse) to other ways of working with the disagreements (legislative advocacy, fighting, impasse), and explain how a collaborative process creates a new foundation that supports everyone.

h. *Support for challenges.* If you sense that your constituency will have a great deal of trouble accepting a direction that the group looks likely to take, discuss your concerns with the full group and the facilitation team so that preventive measures – such as a meeting with your constituents – can be taken.

i. *Hearing constituents' concerns fully.* When constituents voice a concern, stay focused on hearing their concerns in full rather than rushing to tell them it will all be okay. Listen to them fully, give them a sense that their concerns and needs matter by asking questions that invite further sharing and by reflecting back the essence of what they have said. Try to identify what need underlies their concern and reflect that back too. Only after they have been fully heard is the time to speak to or address that need. Remember that your main focus here is to hear and understand their concerns, and that, in itself, may be enough for them to trust that you have been holding that concern with them during the multi-constituency process.

j. *Advocating for the process.* See yourself as an ambassador of the group to your constituents. Help constituents to bridge gaps in understanding, seek creative resolution of differences, and show support for agreements reached within the group. Explain to them what has happened, how you and others may have shifted through mutual understanding, and why you trust the process and its outcome. If you don't, then seek support from the facilitation team before approaching your constituents. How *you* present proposals to them makes all the difference in terms of how likely they are to accept them.

During the life of this project, there were three major occasions for seeking feedback from constituents. First, right at the beginning, when the group created the list of principles that would serve as the foundation for the rest of the work. During the first day, in January 2013, the group arrived at 25 principles, which members then presented to those they represented. The main result of this round was a 26th principle, added to allow some groups to accept several others by creating sufficient balance for them. In addition, a few of the other principles were reworded slightly. This round of engaging with constituents was the least dramatic of the project, and the integration resulted in bringing people together more strongly. It still took three months to complete.

Members of the group went back to their constituents

a second time during the first round of legislative changes. That was a particularly challenging time, as there had been no precedent yet for the kind of stretching-to-stay-together-and-find-a-solution-that-works-for-everyone that the group was working with. There was quite a bit of pushback from constituents at this time, and significant engagement with some constituencies. As you will see below, trust was built through a difficult process of recognizing the limits of how far the whole group could walk *together*, so that no group would be left behind. It was also the first time that small coalitions were formed for the purpose of advocating for the proposed solution, with people going to different groups to present what had been accomplished.

The third time that people went back to those they represented was with the final bill. I find it a deep testament to the strength of the process that the much larger and more far-reaching changes of that last leg of the project required less engagement with constituents and fewer changes to the proposed legislation than the previous round which consisted only of minor revisions. At the same time, although we reached the finish line together, some members of the group continue to be disappointed that the proposed changes didn't go far enough. Part of the complexity of this is that this assessment is not shared by all, not even those who share the overall perspective of those who remain disappointed. Ultimately, the question of whether or not the project truly solved the problem that gave rise to it can only be answered through case law as lawyers, judges, custody evaluators, and others in the State of Minnesota grapple with the ramifications of the changes.[2]

2 The most difficult piece to assess is the revision to the Best Interests of the Child

Building Trust (JANUARY 2013)

Given how difficult it was to bring people together, I knew that issues of trust would arise once we were together, and I planned accordingly. My design for the day included a variety of activities that tend to increase trust. I am including them here as illustration of some of the ways that trust can emerge in a group process, not as prescriptions or even a general template.

Uncharged connection

In a low-trust environment, people tend to reduce each other into two-dimensional narratives, identifying people too narrowly with their positions on issues, and thus struggling to see their full humanity. One of the ways to subvert this tendency is to include, early on, an activity that takes the focus off the topic of the day, and, instead, brings attention to the common humanity that people share.

My specific activity to achieve this purpose was inviting people to mingle, find someone they don't commonly engage with, talk with each other until they have found three things they have in common which are not visible (to avoid focusing on having glasses or other items that don't require actually getting to know each other), and then sit next to someone they just met.

Raising expectations

In a low-trust environment, people tend to have very low expectations about what can happen. I imagine we do this to protect ourselves from disappointment, and that this

Factors which were entirely rewritten with the intention to refocus the attention of the court from "Who is the best parent?" to "What is the best arrangement for the child and the family?"

narrowing of expectations tends to reinforce distance and mistrust. As a result, in this group as in many others, I started the day by asking people to include in their introductions, in addition to their name, affiliation, and relationship to the topic, their thoughts about what would be a "wildly successful" outcome for the day. By having everyone share and hear others' highest hopes, the scope of possibilities widened, and a more positive atmosphere began to permeate the room. In their sharing, many people specifically named hope for trust and opening to hear each other.

I did something similar at the close of the day, also something I regularly do: I asked each person to identify something positive and meaningful that happened to them during the day. Once again, this raises the bar on the experience and bonds people with the positive energy. Overall, what people named was increased trust, learning about each other's perspectives more deeply, and a desire for continuing to work together.

Creating agreements

When a group comes in "ready" and trusting, I rarely take the time to establish explicit agreements. My experience tells me that most of the time a committed group can handle what arises with the support of a facilitator who provides the implicit agreement about how to function. Besides, creating group agreements rarely results in behavior changes, and often results in agreements being used as "weapons" when there is charge and someone appears not to keep them.

I still decided to focus on group agreements because I intuited that it would be a first accomplishment for the group, and would help people relax. Here are the agreements we arrived at that first morning:

- We would aim to hear fully from everyone, and start with those who needed to leave early. This was to attend to the commitment to arriving at an outcome that would include everyone.
- Anyone who found themselves upset or highly uncomfortable with something that was happening would speak up and express their upset rather than leaving the room or responding angrily.
- We would maintain complete confidentiality with regards to what any individual said, and would share with others only general statements about what happened, what we learned, and the product that was created without attributing anything to who said it.

Perspective taking

We engaged in an activity in small groups of four people each whereby each person expressed themselves on the issue from four different perspectives in a rotating assignment: A proponent of the legislation that was vetoed by the governor, an opponent, someone who is unfamiliar with the issues, and a child. This was one part of the day that people were particularly impressed with and learned from. For some, in particular, the experience of occupying the position of the child was informative.

Perspective taking supports trust by humanizing multiple positions: As each participant takes a position that's opposed to their own, for example, they can *feel* the possibility of someone having that position even if they disagree with it.

When Plans Fall Apart (January 2013)

I came into the first in-person day knowing that a few people were going to leave early. I had no idea that the entire day would be marked by people leaving as early as 11 a.m., and that others would still be joining in the afternoon, after we were already deep into collecting criteria and principles, albeit without ever explicitly naming to the group that this is what we were doing.

The plan I had instantly fell apart. I had hoped to take a few more gradual steps of building up to the moment of inviting people to speak to what was important to them about the solution. I had hoped to give people a chance to commune with themselves or with others to gain clarity about what that was; what was truly important for them. None of this could happen. Instead, much of the day turned into a mad rush to manage to hear from each person who was leaving. Literally so, in that as a person would get up to leave I would ask them to stay long enough to give us whatever they had to say about the big custody legislation puzzle we were there to attend to, so that, at the very least, I wouldn't lose vital information that only that person, and then that person, and then that person, would bring forth.

For most of that time, I didn't realize that I was, de facto, beginning the process of identifying the noncontroversial essence for each of what was shared, and thus already constructing the list without ever introducing what the list was or what we were going to do with it. I could barely keep up with the comings and goings.

In addition to just capturing what was important to each person, I also was keen on giving each person who spoke an experience of being heard and of mattering – a vital building block for trust and willingness. I engaged with each person that expressed themselves to identify the core principles that were important to them in terms of what any solution would have to attend to for it to work for the person who spoke. It was this distilled version that I added to the list.

Reaching a shared list

At some point, I had an epiphany that led me to realize what was happening: The very process of hearing, reflecting, distilling, checking with the person, and putting it on the board *was* the criteria gathering. It was then time to let the group know what was going on. When no more people were scheduled to leave before the end, I slowed the process down, and invited everyone in the room to look and see what else needed to be added to the list for it to be comprehensive enough and represent their concerns sufficiently. There would have been no way, at that time of day, to hear each person's voice. As always when facilitating, I wanted to capture all the needs, not necessarily all the voices. I kept moving visually around the room checking to see where people were, inviting people to step forward as needed, and, with each person who spoke, doing the same thing I had been doing already before: listening for the noncontroversial essence, and adding it to the list.

Once no more items needed to be added, everyone was invited to review the list during a break to identify which items were either unclear or raised concerns for them. Then we reviewed the items together one after the other to clarify the language and, in some cases, modify it so that everyone could agree to it. Everyone present was urged to speak up as needed, since this list was highly significant as a first step towards the possibility of a collaborative and creative breakthrough solution for the impasse.

Because of the thoroughness of the process, and because of my facility with identifying things at the level that is both noncontroversial and specific enough, an overwhelming majority of the 25 items on the final list were accepted with little to no controversy. This is the moment that most counters the polarity in a group decision-making process. People were genuinely surprised, as they quite often are, to discover how much commonality there was. This, again, supports trust in forming and growing for many.

A few items did raise significant concerns and necessitated careful dialogue and facilitation to arrive at a principle that could, indeed, be acceptable to all present, enough that they could take it back to the constituency while advocating for what we did. Some few items were removed based either on redundancy or because they were process items and not related to specific content of the legislative solution. Nothing was removed that was important to anyone present. Instead, we either added something else, or modified the language so that everyone could accept it.

One example of how we worked out differences may illustrate the power of what we did. The most challenging item was the principle of "judicial discretion within parameters," as this touched on one of the sore spots for many players in the longstanding debate.[3] Initially, the list item only stated "judicial discretion." Some suggested taking out this item altogether, given that judicial discretion exists for any application of the law. This created discomfort for some who were concerned about the potential that taking out this item would be interpreted to mean that judicial discretion

---

3 One party was claiming that judges needed to be told what to do, or else they would continue to favor mothers over fathers.

would be eliminated. Conversely, others were concerned that leaving it without any qualification would be interpreted to mean support for unbridled judicial discretion. Then the additional language of "within parameters" was added. This still left some people uncomfortable. The final willingness on the part of all to accept this language despite some lingering discomfort was articulated as an invitation by one participant to everyone to stretch so that there *could* be a solution. This was the first of dozens of moments in which people from within the group made critically important suggestions that moved the process forward, or embraced the process in ways that inspired others. In this instance, the participant urged everyone to note and take in that coming together means everyone moves toward some common ground from being on a polarized end.

Towards the end, as the list solidified, everyone present was urged to present the list to their constituency in the same spirit by inviting them to rise to the same standard we established during the day: working for the whole and stretching to make things work for others in addition to themselves.

Confronting mistrust

At one point in the day, one participant "threw a bomb" into the room by giving voice to his utter mistrust in the intentions of those who identified with the opposite position of his. I instantly knew to recognize this as a moment of growing trust. Why? Because expressing mistrust fully is an act that carries some vulnerability with it and doesn't tend to happen under conditions of total mistrust. I attended to the moment by asking if there was anyone with an opposite perspective who could reflect back what they heard from the person who expressed his mistrust. This was me trusting the process: Even though

I didn't know the individuals, I leaned on my conviction that any group contains people who can rise to the occasion. As it turned out, two people came forward, and the man who expressed the mistrust was stunned to experience the relief of being heard. From then on, throughout the many moons that we all worked together, he was a champion of the process.

Moments like this cannot be orchestrated, only utilized when they arise. The key is to be willing to throw away any plan in order to notice the opportunity and open to it. It's not only the person heard whose trust increases. Others, by seeing the power of the transformation, get a visceral sense that their own expressions of mistrust, concerns, or anything else could also be heard. In this way, the entire group moves forward towards more convergence any time one person is heard.

How Constraints Can Lead to Creativity (SPRING AND SUMMER 2013)

In the early days of the project, everyone was hopeful about getting my work funded. Several participants managed to get small funds from their constituents, and a few grant proposals were submitted. We were entering Phase 2 of Convergent Facilitation – proposal creation. Optimistic about funding, I adopted a design calling for the establishment of multiple, parallel, small groups that I would facilitate. Their task would be to take the 26 principles that the large group had agreed on, and develop specific proposals from them. Their timeline was the summer of 2013.

Hardly any funding ever materialized for the project, certainly not enough to ever make it possible for me to focus fully on this project, since it was essential for me to do other work to sustain the small operation that supported my work.[4] I soon recognized that there simply would be no way for me to do all the facilitation of the small groups, which would have amounted to several meetings a week.[5]

Necessity is the mother of invention, says the old proverb, an insight that became apparent in this project. The breakthrough for handling the funding dilemma was to pass on part of the work I would be doing to others. Instead of facilitating the small groups, a few key members of the group stepped forward to be conveners of the small groups. Together, they assigned individuals to the groups, and I shifted my focus from facilitating the small groups to offering facilitation coaching and support to the conveners. This turned out to be a powerful and creative step. First, they were much more equipped than I was to set up the groups, and the result was a remarkable degree of bringing people together across divergent polarized positions. Second, and even more significantly, each group focused on where there was an opening within it, thereby coming up with four entirely different approaches to their

---

4 Towards that summer, some donations arrived through constituencies and through my own fundraising efforts. Some months later, a grant arrived from a newly created Minnesota State Office for Collaboration and Dispute Resolution that was, in part, supported by the child custody project in that one of the legislators involved in the project became a supporter of the bill to establish this office once he saw what was possible that first day in January 2013. Mariah Levison, who runs that office, became a major supporter of the project offering tracking, some degree of project management, occasional co-facilitation, and behind-the-scenes participation in attending to conflicts and issues in the group. It's hard to imagine how the project would have reached the finish line without her support and active participation, since her work was paid for as part of her job, while if I were to do the things she did there would be no funding or budget for it, and thus I would be unlikely to be able to set aside those extra hours. Mariah also supported me, along with one of the group members, as co-holder of the entire project at the level of design and the intangible attention to the whole.
5 I was based in Oakland, California, so it would have been a major expenditure of time and money to go frequently to Minnesota.

tasks which resulted in significant steps for the project. I am quite confident that were I to have facilitated the small groups, they would have focused too narrowly on the literal meaning of coming up with a proposal, and we would have missed out on the opportunities that arose. Each of the groups brought together some former arch-enemies and served the purpose of building more trust and mutual understanding. In addition, they created the following four outcomes:

- A significant analysis of the gap between the existing system and the 26 principles. I suspect that this analysis supported many people in the group in continuing to find meaning in the process and willingness to participate.
- A vision and framework which went beyond the initial principles and united the group in the possibility of bridging the divide. This was the only product that was ever "formally" evaluated against the original 26 principles and was accepted unanimously by the group. At a later stage, when we worked on revising the Best Interests of the Child Factors legislation, this vision and framework supplied substantial bits of the revised legislation.
- A list of elements that all members of one small group could all agree on. For a while, it didn't seem like much. Then, just before the next in-person meeting to evaluate and work with the results of the small group work, this group came up with an initial legislative package proposed by one member to that small group. This could not have come about except through the ongoing interaction between former adversaries that transformed one of them into a major advocate for collaborative solutions and processes, well beyond this project.

- Details of proposed legislation in an area that hadn't previously been seen as part of the project – child support. This legislation didn't get reviewed until the second round of legislative changes a year later, and then was accepted with few changes by the group. The reason for this being tied into custody and parenting arrangements was that the then-existing legislation was such that for one parent to agree to even small changes in parenting time percentages could mean losing significant amounts of child support. By reducing that incentive to fight against more equal parenting time arrangements, this group sought to support the focus on what's truly the best for the child rather than creating a battlefield between the parents.

To get there, I met with the conveners every few weeks and did whatever handholding was necessary. When one or other of the groups reached an impasse, I stepped in to do spot-facilitating of the small group itself, which happened twice through the entire intensive process of several months. The conveners became the embodiment of holding out for a solution or path that everyone can embrace, stepping beyond advocating for their own positions only. Each time we got together, they asked questions and I supported them in learning more and more how to facilitate.

This was the phase during which I first became aware that even though I wasn't formally training people, or working with them on shifting their consciousness, the experience of focusing on converging on solutions and paths that worked for everyone changed them. One of the conveners, for example, a family lawyer, said at one point that she could see her entire approach changing; that she had never been much for process or collaboration, and now she saw the new possibilities that opened up through using this kind of process. Another person with extensive experience in legislation concluded the third in-person meeting saying he wished to see our model extend to other legislative issues and all the way to the federal government.

Here are some of the lessons that emerged from the work with conveners, lessons which can be applied both to your own facilitation as well as to instances when you might need to work with small groups in the same way I did:

- By focusing on genuine interest in learning about why someone does things the way they do it is easier to reach common ground than by aiming to change their mind. This certainly seemed to apply to people who were particularly opinionated or talkative, where habit would suggest trying to control and contain rather than engage with them more deeply.
- Speed interferes with creativity and generosity, both of which are indispensable for any path forward that everyone can embrace. Slowing down in the moment speeds up the larger arc of a collaborative process.
- Relationships are key to any attempt to bridge differences, because they humanize people to each other and generate willingness to shift in support of each other.

In the Face of Disagreements (SPRING 2014)

I have often said to people and groups when working with major challenges and disagreements: We will only go as far as we can go together. This became painfully apparent at one point in the process, after the initial legislative package was endorsed by the group in October 2013 and brought to constituent groups.

Several constituencies endorsed the package without any changes. Some others raised a few significant points and proposed tweaks which the group then accepted. One constituency, however, was adamantly opposed to one aspect of the proposed legislative package and also had substantial changes to other parts. In the end, the specific provision they were opposed to did not get included: That's what the commitment to only decide what is acceptable to all means. This was a tough moment in the trajectory of the project, and, still, in some ways it solidified even more the depth of the commitment to collaboration. Here's how this happened.

The power of active participation

The constituency that opposed part of the package had not had adequate representation in the process. For scheduling or priority reasons, no one from this group was present in most of the meetings, especially not in the in-person meetings where most of the extraordinary shifts happened. Thus, there was no one in that constituency who could advocate for a result they were part of reaching, because that never happened. On the practical plane, I don't know what we could have done differently, since scheduling these two-day meetings was always really difficult. On the learning plane, I cannot emphasize enough how vitally important it is to include stakeholders who are in a position to block the results of a process. The more stakeholders can experience the quality of the process, the more likely it is that they, too, can experience shifts emerging from being heard and hearing others. This didn't happen for this one constituency. Indeed, they eventually left the project altogether. Even while they were part of the project, because of significant absences from key meetings, they never fully embraced the orientation of a solution that works for everyone, and remained, largely, advocates for their own positions only. Not embracing the needs of everyone, they persisted in seeing the issues as not particularly relevant to their overall legislative focus, and thus continued to maintain an attitude of just trying to block changes that they saw as detrimental to their population.

Working with the outlying positions

Given that Convergent Facilitation works, most effectively, by integrating concerns, perspectives, and needs of the more extreme elements within a group, much of my own efforts went into navigating the continued differences between two specific groups which took most of my attention.

In a process such as this one, which extends over many months and includes representatives of multiple stakeholder groups, this invariably means taking some of the work offline, and working only with the people on the edges. It's almost always the case that when those on the edges are able to work out thorny issues, the larger group will wholeheartedly accept the solution. Both Mariah and I had many conversations with only a small subset of the group to work out specifics, and this was one of the ways that the process moved forward.

When one of those groups left the process, I continued to reach out to them myself, and to advocate for them during large group meetings given they were not there. For me, advocating for those not present is consistent with the role of being multi-partial: If no one else is holding the torch for certain needs, as facilitator I see it as my own role. This was not an easy task, because although I was advocating for their needs, not their positions (I didn't actually "agree" with anyone's positions within the group), some group members managed in certain moments to get confused and think that I was "on their side."

Pouring resources into major roadblocks

In the process of working through the differences, I ended up making an emergency last-minute trip to Minnesota to meet with a subset of the people who were able to be there. Although that meeting didn't result in a willingness to accept the entire package, and we ended up removing one provision from the proposed bill, it still moved the group forward in its evolving understanding of what would be needed to reach a solution that would work for everyone. Indeed, the second package that was developed a year later, although much more comprehensive and with wide-ranging changes, and although without the participation of the group that left, still managed to get through without that group's opposition. Since many in the group feared that this constituency would block the passage of the bill, this was a major success.

Why is it that an apparently "failed" meeting managed to move the group forward? Of course there is no way to *know*, and, still, I believe that a few factors combined to make this happen.

- The level of commitment to only do what works for everyone deepened the developing shift from advocating for specific positions to the shared commitment to work on a joint problem. At the same time, even though we didn't manage to find a solution, the attempt showed everyone the difference between compromise and integration as we were looking for solutions that would honor lots of issues.
- The depth of inquiry and persistence in identifying deeper needs resulted in a surprising discovery of there being so much common ground despite many disagreements, even between the constituencies that were most at odds with each other.

- The fact that so many people managed to come to the meeting and participated in the attempt to work out the solution in itself increased trust that this truly mattered to everyone.
- Even though a specific solution to the impasse didn't emerge, new agreements did emerge that supported trust and willingness. For example, one of the topics discussed during the emergency meeting was the reality of how much unavoidable suffering there is given how difficult so many of the situations are. During this discussion, the group agreed that it is better for the parents to take on the burden of suffering than the children.
- All in all, the group got to experience more deeply what it means to aim for something that everyone can accept, not necessarily wholehearted endorsement from everyone. On the one hand, it means that everyone is asked to stretch as far as they can go, which happened a lot during the process before and after this meeting, so people knew what it meant. On the other hand, no one is pushed to embrace something that is truly unacceptable for them. When we removed the contentious provision, although many were disappointed, all could appreciate that a commitment to making things work for everyone sometimes means letting go of things that don't work for everyone.

Beyond either/or

More and more, I have come to believe that whenever a problem is presented as a choice between two opposing positions, the possibility of collaboration diminishes. Either/or solutions lend themselves to power struggles and to a win/lose approach. Human experience and needs are almost always more complex than that, and if we are serious about integration, we will need to leave behind either/or solutions.

The Minnesota child custody project was no exception. It started out with a narrow definition of the problem: Will there or will there not be a presumption of equal shared parenting and joint physical custody? There could have been no solution in this way. In order for all to come together, the either/or frame of the solution shifted to a more generative frame. This was not a pronouncement as much as it emerged organically.

For example, as one small group began comparing the existing family law system to the 26 principles, and another focused on creating a vision and a framework, it began to be clear that reaching any solution would require a broader frame. *The group started seeing that a cultural change was needed*, not only a statutory one. In addition, even within the narrower focus on legislative change, a wider frame was required. This is how it came to be that the proposed legislation, in the end, included areas that no one initially thought would be attended to, most especially one of the core pieces of family law: the Best Interests of the Child factors.

Another example, which remains unfinished work, was the realization that, in regard to many of the issues that concern "opposing" stakeholders on the issue of presumption[6] – the very issue around which the battle went on for so many years – certain stakeholders from both sides would actually benefit from better assessment of the presence of domestic violence. Better assessment tools – an area that is woefully underdeveloped in the US court systems overall – would both reduce the incidence of custody arrangements that result in compromising the safety of children *and* reduce the likelihood

---

6 Legal presumptions about what parenting arrangements would be the default in the absence of information that would shift the arrangements.

of parents being barred from being with their children because of unfounded concerns about domestic violence.

We Are No Longer Sides (Summer 2014)

Once the first legislative package was passed, which was unanimous, the sense of possibility expanded, and the group was ready to engage with the core issues it was facing from the start. Perhaps more would have happened in the first legislative session if I had been able to facilitate more actively, or perhaps not; there is really no way to know that. What remains clear to me is that however small the initial package may have seemed to some people, it was a watershed event, and it built confidence in the group.

At the end of the meeting in October 2013, after reviewing the work of the various groups and adopting the legislative package, the group also made a long list of remaining issues. It was now time to attend to them.

Once again, we created small groups, though we approached it differently. In the first legislative round we had parallel groups all working on creating proposals for action based on the 26 principles. Now, each small group worked on different issues. Why the difference? First, because there was so much work to do, and if all the groups worked on the same issues, they wouldn't manage to complete them. Second, because there was now enough trust within the group that people didn't feel compelled to be involved in everything (although some people still tried to be in all the groups).

With the help of Mariah Levison, we created a charter for the rest of the work of the group. This document included the purpose, the makeup and subject matter of the small groups, and all agreements about how the various groups would function. It was especially important to name a shared purpose, as it served as recognition that a problem existed in the system as it was, something that initially was contested by some members. In hindsight, if I had to change anything, this would be one of the areas I would focus on: to define and agree on an inspiring shared purpose right from the start.

This document was another way of continuing to attend to the lack of funding that meant I couldn't be available to facilitate small group work. Since the conveners were unavailable for meetings with me, the scaffolding was provided by written agreements. Given how much the groups took on, and the number of ongoing issues about internal and external communication, we scheduled a number of large group conference calls that sustained us through this challenging period of intense work and persistent concerns.

As we were setting up the small groups, someone asked to make sure that all the sides would be represented in all the groups. That was when the reality of how much progress the group had made became apparent to me. One of the legislators involved in the project responded by saying: "We are no longer sides. I don't want to be identified with a side. We are a group of people working together to solve a problem." The move to collective ownership had been completed.

This doesn't mean that all the mistrust evaporated, or that everything was smooth sailing from then on. It only meant that the group, and certainly most people within it, took on more responsibility. People were looking out for each other more, for example. More than once, members of the group, in this phase, said that a proposed solution would work for them, and yet they were concerned it might not work for someone else who was previously seen as an opponent.

Another issue that arose at this phase was that as the group broadened the scope of its work, it was clear that additional people would be needed because of their expertise, and yet it was challenging to imagine how to fold people into the level of trust and shared responsibility that was already the baseline by then. Indeed, a small group formed just to attend to orientation for new members.

All in all, the hallmark of this phase was making dramatic shifts that previously were deemed impossible because of having a stronger foundation and a shared commitment to attend to the deeper issues. This was the biggest example of the move beyond either/or: In order to attend to the fundamental concerns, it was necessary to make changes at the foundational level. This is why the Best Interests of the Child factors had to be rewritten. It was no accident that doing it was also the part of this phase that almost fell apart and where I ended up stepping in most directly.

The Hard Work of Reaching Decisions (FALL 2014)

Because of the intensity and scope of what was being addressed in this phase, we scheduled two in-person meetings, six weeks apart, before and after engaging with constituencies. Both of them were about finding ways to convert proposals to actual decisions. In the first meeting, we had 17 different pieces of legislation to look at, ranging from very minor tweaks in some to a complete overhaul in others.

My facilitation considerations in this phase were primarily about managing the level of energy in the group, and about assessing how much stretching was possible relative to how important certain pieces were. In a couple of instances I ended up recommending to the group to drop proposed changes altogether precisely because the level of concern about the changes was high while no one saw those changes as particularly critical to completing the task. This is what decision-making is made up of: an ongoing, careful dance that brings together the strength of wanting a decision and the strength of any opposition to the proposed decision. In all those instances there were some who did want the proposed changes, and yet they were able to let go of having them, since they could see that the amount of work it would take to find ways of attending to the concerns was beyond the level of energy present in the group. I was surprised and heartened by seeing how much care for the whole people held that allowed us to move through such decisions with so much ease.

For each of the proposed changes, I chose very simple thresholds to help us assess how much work would be necessary to reach agreement. On a flip chart, I wrote the whole set of proposed legislative changes, and counted one of four responses:

- Accept
- Minor, friendly tweaks
- Manageable revisions
- Significant dispute

To help navigate the complexity and breadth of what we were looking at during those two meetings, I then considered in what order to attend to the 17 proposals. For this, I juggled three variables: how important the piece of legislation was for the process to complete; how extensive the proposed legislative change was; and how strong the level of opposition was to the proposed change. I also wanted to sustain the level of energy for the group. We ended up alternating between easy wins and more complex tasks, though the easy wins were soon finished, while major tasks continued for most of the two two-day meetings.

As a facilitator, this was intensive work of the highest order, entailing ongoing assessment of where more stretch was possible and where letting go would be more important as well as tending to the energy of group and individuals at all times while tracking everything that was happening and attending to open loops.

Throughout the meetings, I continued to uphold and reiterate the following principles in support of the group's ability to work with the challenges:

- Moving forward only with what the group can agree to while aiming for solutions that everybody can be invested in
- Returning to where there is commonality, highlighting every moment of it to support faith
- Displaying utter trust that any breakdown could lead to breakthroughs because of the depth of the quality of respect, trust, and mutual understanding that the group was in, and, specifically, having faith that the solutions would come from the group, not necessarily from me or even from specific "leaders" within the group. A good third of the group were instrumental at one point or another in coming up with wording or suggestions that broke through a logjam
- Leaning on the insight that collaboration is more efficient when suspicion is sidestepped and participants engage with others before making a new proposal or a rebuttal, as a way to shift the "debate and convince" energy into "collaborate, understand, and generate" approach

- Inviting, at this late phase, anyone who is not happy with a proposal to be the one to offer a way to address others' concerns while advocating for their own position
- Insisting, time and again, that people accept changes even if they seem unnecessary to them if someone else wants them and there is no harm in having them. Indeed, several significant changes were included in the legislative package because of this principle.
- Noting that we were looking for agreement on particular measures, not change in opinion about what is best, and not necessarily consensus on what's the best path forward; only agreement that what was moving forward was acceptable.

By the middle of December 2014, we had the draft legislative package done. While there was still much work to be done during the intensive lobbying period, and while some members of the group still believe that not enough was accomplished, the group made the historic move that subsequently resulted in a near unanimous passage of the package.

Final Words

When I accepted the invitation to engage with this group, I could not have imagined the full range of roles and functions I would be playing, nor how much support would be needed. To support any reader who may at one point or another be in a similar position, I am offering here some more reflections on my approach, on the variety of roles I took on beyond the immediate focus on supporting collaborative decision-making in a group, and on the vital role of support.

Mixing directive and emergent approaches

Overall, Convergent Facilitation tends to be a directive form of facilitation in order to support convergence. It's the facilitator who usually extracts the noncontroversial essence rather than leaving the words of participants. It's the facilitator who chooses the threshold for decision making, even though it's each participant who checks to see if the proposal is acceptable at that threshold. It's the facilitator who engages with outliers to create shifts within them or within the group.

At the same time, in an extended project with as much content specificity as this one, I also believe it's essential to trust the group to be the one to come up with solutions. Although I got my hands "dirty" many times, including, at one point, providing a draft legislation to support one small group to move beyond an impasse, just about all the creative breakthroughs came from the group itself, and I needed to be relaxed and trusting enough in moments of great tension to communicate that trust to the group. It worked.

Moral authority

It is important to note here that this group never had any formal authority. Although the project was partially supported, both financially and practically, by the Minnesota State Office for Collaboration and Dispute Resolution, it was never an official project of the state. The group had no authority to make any decisions. It was, ultimately, a civil society group, a collection of individual citizens, a multi-stakeholder group that came together, in their respective roles, to come up with a *proposal,* not a decision.

Why, then, did the legislature so overwhelmingly adopt their proposal? The answer lies beyond the scope of what normative, dominant views of social science and human nature espouse. It wasn't because of any self-interest that was served, for anyone. The amount of work that people poured into this project, and its ultimate success exist, primarily, in the moral realm. People did the work because they believed in what they were doing, and were committed to their shared goal beyond what I would reasonably have expected. I was moved to tears, often.

Once they came up with a product that they all agreed to, it carried an immense moral authority that was not lost on anyone. That such a diverse group came together; that such fierce rivals agreed on a new bill; and, most specifically, that the result was *unanimous*, played a key role in legislators accepting it. As I look into the future of humanity, this is what I could bank on: groups of people in massive disagreements coming together to solve apparently intractable problems and, through the act of coming together, becoming a moral authority that carries others with them.

Nor am I surprised, because this is only the most dramatic experience I've had, and not a unique one. I have seen, time and again, generosity and willingness that are beyond what the current ways of being say is possible. The very same *exact* process can work both for CEOs and for the activists who may want to dismantle corporate power.

Faith and love

Although I have spoken about faith already throughout this book and even in this chapter, I want to speak again about how vitally important it is both to have faith and to articulate it to the group. We live in times when collaboration is dismissed, when most of us are habituated to have little faith and to repolarize even when we accept the necessity of working through disagreements. As the facilitator of a group, and this group in particular, I regularly offer positive reflections. I note in particular moments of commonality, instances of increased understanding of others, of hearts opening, of new frames emerging, of successes, even small ones, and of purpose and vision.

Similarly, I make an active point to let everyone know that they matter to me. This project was truly tough, with a lot of ups and downs, and some major disappointments alongside the extraordinary breakthroughs. I sometimes engaged with people in ways that created discomfort for them as a way to try to bring about stretching towards convergence. Still, even in those moments, I continually conveyed to people that I would do all in my power to support them in having their needs attended to. In the end, even those who are not as happy with the outcome as I hoped they would be are still admiring the process we went through, and know it's the most we could do while keeping everyone together.

Convergent Facilitation is a labor of love and an exacting discipline of the mind. It has the potential to support unprecedented transformation even in intractable conflicts because it brings together the heart quality of immense and uncompromising care with the meticulous attention to efficient use of resources so as to move the process forward towards a truly workable solution. It is my greatest hope that this chapter, and this book as a whole, provides you with sufficient motivation and information to support your own experiments. Developing processes for collaboration is, in and of itself, a collaborative process, and it will take many of us experimenting, learning, and sharing the results to get to where the tide turns and collaboration in decision-making becomes the norm.

Acknowledgments

THE MOST SIGNIFICANT GRATITUDE goes to all the groups I have facilitated: participants in hundreds of classes, coaching calls, workshops, and retreats; communities making decisions about their future; teams within organizations facing a variety of challenges; and multi-stakeholder groups that came together despite mistrust to attend to issues affecting all of them. Despite facilitating groups for many years, I am still learning each time from people's responses, the feedback they give, and the path they take to reaching their various purposes.

I also want to thank, in more specificity, the people who have studied and applied Convergent Facilitation, now numbering a few hundred people. Their questions and insights have deepened my own understanding and pushed my thinking forward in ways I might not have found on my own. Through them, I've had access to many more groups and processes than I would ever have managed to have direct contact with, and learned from the experiences of groups I would never have connected with.

None of this book, or anything that I do, would ever come into being without meeting, and then learning from Marshall Rosenberg. Although I have created my own materials, developed my own thinking, and branched into territories he didn't directly visit, everything I know is informed by the books I read, events I attended, and conversations I had with him. The image of standing on the shoulders of giants seems apt here.

Lifelong conversations with my sisters Arnina and Inbal are intertwined with everything that I am. That Inbal died in 2014 is a perpetual loss of thinking partner, friend, and co-facilitator. We specifically had many discussions when I was still developing Convergent Facilitation. Arnina and I continue to learn together in many areas.

Lisa Rothman moved Convergent Facilitation from a rambling, associative version to a coherent, logical process, with clear skills associated with each phase, and with focus on each aspect of it. I don't believe I would have the opportunity to teach so many people, nor to write this book, without her steady, joyful, and honest support. Lisa remained involved with the book all the way through, offering encouragement, advice, tweaking of content, and last-minute edits of the many little bits that suddenly needed to be added.

Roxy Manning was an "early adopter" as well as the designer of the handout that we give away in workshops. She also read and commented on earlier versions of the chapter on power differences, making it all the better for doing that.

A few close colleagues have engaged in many conversations with me over the years, asked pointed questions, shared examples that required me to think more deeply, and brought Convergent Facilitation to contexts that served to expand my own vista. I want to name, in particular, Mars Gafforio, Paul Kahawatte, Uma Lo, and Verene Nicolas, all of whom have also co-taught with me, both Convergent Facilitation and other related content. Paul has also contributed specific ideas, and ways of communicating them, to Convergent Facilitation and the final version of this book.

Anna Barnett wrote the case study on which the last chapter was based, as well as pointed out to me how essential faith and love were to the process, which before then I had been unconsciously not speaking about.

Ariane Korth, Uma Lo, and Paul Kahawatte did a massive job of combing through many transcriptions from multiple workshops I led about facilitation and about Convergent

Facilitation. Chapter 3 is the result of their collective capacity to turn notes into a coherent topic list I could work with and complete into a chapter.

Jean Meier was effusively enthusiastic about this project and kept pushing me to not give up when I couldn't find a publisher. Her support kept me going in times of doubt. Jean also read the manuscript and offered creative and complex suggestions for revisions and restructuring. I believe the book is significantly more accessible and clear because of her contribution. She also assisted me in putting together a proposal for the publisher who eventually didn't accept it, a process that, in itself, sharpened my thinking and led to tweaks in the book.

Dave Belden did the editing work on the manuscript, bringing to it his usual depth of engagement, exquisite mix of lightness of touch and seriousness of output, and willingness to both challenge me and accept my ultimate choices. He then embarked on a second run-through after Jean's comments arrived.

A manuscript doesn't become a book by itself, and I want to name the people who made this happen. Carissa Honeywell did the proofreading and showed me that this, too, can be done with love. Jean McElhaney stepped in at the last minute to do additional proofreading under immense stress, and came through for all of our benefit. Nicias Sejas designed this book from scratch, and I am wowed by her capacity to enhance the content with visuals with such beauty despite us never meeting before. Pierre Gos volunteered to do the indexing and approached this thankless task with great enthusiasm and dedication. Emma Quayle picked up the complex task of moving it from manuscript to a self-published book without any prior knowledge in the area and held it until Roberta

Werdinger came on board and brought it to the finish line with grace and competence. That the book is now in your hands is purely because Emma managed to make it a priority when no one else did.

Lastly, I want to thank Rebecca Sutton and Emma Quayle, both friends and advisors, for ongoing steady support of me the human being through many upheavals and challenges in my life and in the world. Their friendship, collaboration, and gentleness kept me going and brought me to the finish line.

References

JEANNETTE ARMSTRONG, "Let Us Begin With Courage." *Center for Ecoliteracy* http://www.ecoliteracy.org/essays/let-us-begin-courage, accessed Jan 6, 2015

DAVID BERCELI, *Shake It Off Naturally: Reduce Stress, Anxiety, and Tension with TRE.* CreateSpace Independent Publishing Platform, 2015.

ERIC BOWERS, *Meet Me in Hard-To-Love Places.* Eric Bowers Publishing, 2016.

CHILD CUSTODY DIALOGUE GROUP, "Transforming polarized politics in the Minnesota state legislature: A Convergent Facilitation case study." *Center for Efficient Collaboration,* August 2015. http://efficientcollaboration.org/minnesota-case-study accessed 26 May, 2020.

GARY CRAIG, *EFT Manual.* Energy Psychology Press, 2008.

BRIDGET DE MAINE, "How Many Good Experiences Finally Outweigh a Bad One?" *Collective Hub,* https://collectivehub.com/2017/05/how-many-good-experiences-finally-outweigh-a-bad-one/, accessed July 22, 2020.

ROBIN DIANGELO, *White Fragility: Why It's So Hard for White People to Talk About Racism.* Boston: Beacon Press, 2018.

ALLAN G. JOHNSON, "What is a 'system of privilege'?" http://www.agjohnson.us/glad/what-is-a-system-of-privilege/, accessed May 26, 2020.

MIKI KASHTAN, "The Gift of Self: The Art of Transparent Facilitation," in Sandy Schuman (ed.), *The IAF Handbook of Group Facilitation: Best Practices from the Leading Organization in Facilitation.* San Francisco, CA: Jossey-Bass, 2005.

MIKI KASHTAN, "Wanting Fully without Attachment." *Tikkun* (2010) 25 (1): 39-42.

MIKI KASHTAN, "Want Teamwork? Encourage Free Speech." *New York Times*, April 12, 2014. nytimes.com/2014/04/13/jobs/want-teamwork-encourage-free-speech.html, accessed May, 2020.

MIKI KASHTAN, "A Blueprint for Collaborative Lawmaking." *Interdisciplinary Journal for Partnership Studies* (2016), 3 (1).

MIKI KASHTAN, "Bringing Nonviolence to the State Legislature." *Nonviolence*, Vol. 1 (Summer 2016).

IVANA KOTTASOVA, "US is 65th in World on Gender Pay Gap." *CNN Business* money.cnn.com/2014/10/27/news/economy/global-gender-pay-gap/, accessed October 28, 2014.

CAROLYN LAINE, "Family law: Re-focusing on the needs of the child." *Twin Cities Pioneer Press*, October 14, 2015. https://www.twincities.com/2015/10/14/carolyn-laine-family-law-re-focusing-on-the-needs-of-the-child/ accessed 26 May, 2020.

PETER LEVINE, *Waking the Tiger.* Berkeley, CA: North Atlantic Books, 1997.

DAWNA MARKOVA, *Wide Open: On Living with Purpose and Passion.* Miami, FL: Conari Press, 2008.

PEGGY MCINTOSH, "White Privilege: Unpacking the Invisible Knapsack," in Anna May Filor (ed.) *Multiculturalism* (Educational Resources Informational Center, 1992). https://files.eric.ed.gov/fulltext/ED355141.pdf?utm#page=43, accessed May 22, 2020.

MARY PARKER FOLLETT, *Dynamic Administration: The Collected Papers of Mary Parker Follett.* Eastford, CT: Martino Fine Books, 2003.

SARAH PEYTON, *Your Resonant Self: Guided Meditations and Exercises to Engage Your Brain's Capacity for Healing.* New York: W.W. Norton & Co., 2017.

MARSHALL ROSENBERG, *Nonviolent Communication: A Language of Life.* Encinitas, CA: Puddle Dancer Press, 2003.

CARNE ROSS, *The Leaderless Revolution.* New York: Simon & Schuster, 2012.

SHOWING UP FOR RACIAL JUSTICE: POLITICAL EDUCATION, Toolkits, and other Resources. http://www.showingupforracialjustice.org/resources, accessed May 26, 2020.

ADRIENNE VAN DER VALK, "Peggy McIntosh: Beyond the Knapsack." *Tolerance Magazine,* Issue 46, (Spring 2014). http://www.tolerance.org/magazine/number-46-spring-2014/feature/peggy-mcintosh-beyond-knapsack, accessed May 26, 2020.

DAVID WEINSTOCK, *NeuroKinetic Therapy.* London: New Atlantic Books, 2010.

DAVID WEINSTOCK, *Becoming What You Need: Practices for Embodying Nonviolent Communication.* Independently published, 2017.

TIM WISE, *White Like Me.* New York: Soft Skull Press, 2011.

Basic
Meeting Flow
APPENDIX

a. Purpose
1. Provide a framework to support efficiency, clarity, and collaboration towards shared purpose
2. Offer tips for people new to facilitation

Note: This meeting flow is for any kind of meeting, and most of the topics within it were not covered in this workshop, which focuses only on the decision-making process.

b. Blank Agenda:
1. Opening
   a. Review of purpose
   b. Round of celebrating what's working
   c. Review of agenda and adding any new items
   d. Identifying a note taker if it's not a regular role of someone in the group
   e. Prioritize agenda items

2. Specific agenda items
   a.
   b.

3. Closing
   a. Review all decisions and action steps
   b. Choose facilitator
   c. Feedback and appreciation .

c. Detailed Explanation of Structure

# 1. Opening	Set the tone, align around purpose, bring focus, clarity, and presence
### Review of purpose *What would be accomplished by having this meeting and this agenda?*	Reminds people of why they are there, and inspires them to contribute directly to the purpose
### Round of celebrating what's working *What's something that's happened for each person since the last meeting that is a positive step, project, event related to the work of the group or organization*	Allows people to connect with an authentic positive experience and feel motivated to participate
### Review of agenda and adding any new items *Read agenda out loud and invite anyone present to add anything that's important*	Note: ideally, the agenda is distributed ahead of time and everyone has a chance to add; it still happens that last minute items are added anyway
### Identifying a note taker if it's not a regular role of someone in the group *Unless it's part of someone's job responsibilities, making it voluntary is essential for goodwill*	Provides continuity and accountability for the group
### Prioritizing agenda items *If there are more agenda items than can be covered, consciously choose which one to start with, which is second, etc. This can be done by asking everyone to select what is most important for them, or by having the functional leader or the facilitator choose, or by any other method that everyone knows will be used*	Allows the group to choose consciously and to reduce the frustration of not getting to high priority items because of not tracking them

2. Attending to agenda items

Decide whether to time-limit the item or take it to at least partial resolution

Allows for focused energy and conscious choice about use of group resources

---

Relating to purpose

How does this item connect to the purpose - for this meeting, for this team, or for the organization

Increased focus

Discussion as needed

What's wanted about it, and from whom, in order to bring it to closure

Preserves group energy by focusing on closure rather than discussion without outcomes

Full round of opinions as needed

For complex or new issues, or where there is controversy or power relations that are challenging, have a round where everyone expresses their thoughts, ideas, and what most matters to them. If there are multiple levels of leadership, hear first from those in lower levels

Allow wisdom, freedom, and collaboration; counter fear of power

---

Bringing each item to full closure:

Identify what's possible to do with the item for this meeting and make that explicit

Increase hope and commitment through clarity

Decision or agreement

Item can be complete through decision or agreement about how to handle it, or by removing it from the agenda

Action step(s)

Note who is taking the action (can be anything, including a smaller group that will meet to discuss and present)

Retain or put back on agenda

Note the date by which you want to come back to the item to review

---

3. Closing

Create alignment, capture the energy and the wisdom, learn

Reviewing all decisions and action steps
Align everyone with the same understanding about what was decided and what each person agreed to take on between this meeting and the next one

Creates shared holding of responsibility and clarity about closing loops

Choosing facilitator
Unless the group has a regular facilitator, choose someone explicitly for the next time

Supports cohesion and group function from meeting to meeting

Feedback and appreciation
Round of what each person appreciates that happened at the meeting

Prepare the ground for learning and transition

Full Table of Contents

Chapter 4. Facilitation Principles for Efficient Collaboration

Breakthrough Insight:

Index

D

decision, final 111, 163, 168-169, 197, 216

dissent 8-9, 14, 28-30, 79, 105, 181, 184, 188-192, 194, 200, 203-209, 211, 217-218, 222, 226, 230-231, 247, 254-255, 257-258, 261, 264-265
  engaging with 30, 189-190, 204, 211
  inviting 9, 14, 29, 184, 191, 222

E

efficiency 13, 24, 32, 43, 87-88, 109, 112, 117, 128, 131, 135, 138, 146, 173, 182, 190, 192, 219, 261, 263, 313

either/or solutions 292-293

energy 7, 13, 28-29, 66-68, 72-73, 78-79, 82, 84-86, 89, 97- 98, 100, 109, 112, 121, 124, 129-130, 134-135, 144, 151, 158, 189, 191-192, 197, 206, 213, 215-217, 223, 250-252, 255, 268, 278, 296-298, 309, 315-316

evaluations 46, 49, 57-58

experience 7, 10-11, 18-20, 26-27, 39-40, 43-47, 49-54, 57, 59-61, 81-82, 93, 95, 98-99, 106, 109, 113, 116, 125-126, 128, 131-132, 134, 137, 139, 142-143, 145-146, 152, 160, 163, 164-165, 167, 171, 174, 176, 195, 208-209, 213, 215, 217, 219-221, 225-226, 229-230, 232, 234, 237, 240-243, 246, 253, 257, 259, 260, 263, 271, 278-280, 284, 287-289, 292, 301, 305, 314

F

fairness 83, 115, 162, 195

fatigue, decision 168, 196-197

feedback 55-59, 76, 84, 87, 89, 91, 93-94, 132, 185, 261, 275, 305, 313, 316

Follett, Mary Parker 108-109, 122, 123

frame 27, 78-79, 83, 90, 96, 145, 162, 222, 229, 233, 293, 302

freedom 38, 51, 66, 100, 125-126, 221, 226, 232, 265, 315

G

generosity 24, 99, 127, 230, 288, 301

group
  agreements 144, 278
  energy 84, 86, 89, 129, 191, 215, 315 *see energy*
  privileged 237-238

group's purpose 47, 78-80, 91-92, 98-99, 106, 179, 251

I

impartiality 46 *see neutrality*

impasse 211, 217, 274, 281, 287, 292, 300

inner clarity 65, 82

integration 48, 108, 122-123 225, 275, 291, 293

interruption 98, 100

intuition 8, 14, 56, 67-70, 84, 90, 93, 102, 106, 155, 161, 188, 190, 193, 204, 208, 232

L

leadership, mistrust of 37

About the Author

MIKI KASHTAN IS A PRACTICAL VISIONARY PURSUING A WORLD THAT WORKS FOR ALL, based on principles and practices rooted in feminist nonviolence. Miki is a founding member of the Nonviolent Global Liberation community (NGLcommunity.org), a co-founder of Bay Area Nonviolent Communication (BayNVC.org) a certified trainer with the Center for Nonviolent Communication, and has taught, consulted, and engaged with projects globally. This is her fourth book after *Spinning Threads of Radical Aliveness: Transcending the Legacy of Separation in Our Individual Lives*, *The Little Book of Courageous Living*, and *Reweaving Our Human Fabric: Working Together to Create a Nonviolent Future*. Miki also has hundreds of posts on *The Fearless Heart*. Her articles have appeared in *The New York Times*, *Tikkun*, *Waging Nonviolence*, *Peace and Conflict*, *Shareable*, and elsewhere. An Israeli native with significant roots in Mexico and New York City, she lived in Berkeley and Oakland, California, for three decades before choosing to vagabond in search of learning about liberation and community. She holds a Ph.D. in Sociology from UC Berkeley.

If you would like to support Miki's projects and her goal of moving more of her work into a gift economy mode, please donate to her Circle of Support.

Next Steps

INSPIRED BY WHAT YOU'VE READ? Want to deepen your practice with support?
I warmly invite you to visit our website:

www.convergentfacilitation.org.

There you will find a variety of resources including:

- Coaching Calls led by experienced Convergent Facilitators
- A web app that helps people involved in Convergent Facilitation processes easily collect criteria, raise and address concerns about them, and quickly evaluate proposals. With this app, facilitators can create an online page for groups of any size to collaborate in making a decision. You can create an account and use it in your organization or community on a gift economy basis.
- Ideas and stories about what other people are doing with Convergent Facilitation, which has so far been applied in areas ranging from movements for social change, corporations, and multi-stakeholder groups shaping public policy to intentional communities, philanthropic groups and cross organization collaboration in the non-profit sector.

You can also join Collaborative Decision Makers Unite, our Facebook Group, where you can ask questions and get answers.

Welcome to the Convergent
Facilitation Learning Community!

Also by
Miki Kashtan

Nonfiction

Reweaving Our Human Fabric:
Working Together to Create a Nonviolent Future

Spinning Threads of Radical Aliveness:
Transcending the Legacy of Separation in Our Individual
Lives

The Little Book of Courageous Living

Fiction
Without Flinching

To order, and to learn more about Miki's work, visit
https://thefearlessheart.org/store/